Rudolf Bultmann's Theology:
A Critical Interpretation

Rudolf Bultmann's Theology:
A Critical Interpretation

by
Robert Campbell Roberts

LONDON
SPCK

To

A.V.R. and E.E.R.

Portions of Chapter 10 appeared in a slightly
different form in *Scottish Journal of Theology*,
#2, 1976.

First published in Great Britain 1977
SPCK
Holy Trinity Church
Marylebone Road
London NW1 4DU
ISBN 0 281 02981 4

Preface

It was in David Kelsey's excellent seminar on Bultmann's theology that I got my first concentrated exposure to this man's thought and began to conceive the thesis developed here. Paul Minear's sharp criticisms of an early draft were fruitful. Hans Frei read several of the chapters at stages of the essay's development and made very useful suggestions; but more than that, anyone acquainted with his thought will no doubt espy certain reflections of it in these pages. To long hours of philosophical and theological discussion with Richard Olmsted could be traced many of the specific conclusions here achieved. And, if the study evinces any wisdom or analytical acuity, it is hard to imagine it apart from those happy years at the feet and under the fatherly influence of Paul Holmer.

Contents

Abbreviations

The following is a list of abbreviations used in the citation of Bultmann's works:

Essays:	*Essays Philosophical and Theological*
EF:	*Existence and Faith: Shorter Writings of Rudolf Bultmann*
FC:	*Form Criticism: Two Essays on New Testament Research*
FU:	*Faith and Understanding*
GJC:	*The Gospel of John: A Commentary*
GV, I, II, III, IV:	*Glauben und Verstehen*
HE:	*History and Eschatology: The Presence of Eternity*
HST:	*History of the Synoptic Tradition*
JCM:	*Jesus Christ and Mythology*
JW:	*Jesus and the Word*
KM:	*Kerygma and Myth: A Theological Debate*
MC:	*Myth and Christianity: An Inquiry into the Possibility of Religion Without Myth*
ONM:	*The Old and New Man in the Letters of Paul*
PCCS:	*Primitive Christianity in its Contemporary Setting*
TNT, I, II:	*Theology of the New Testament*
TWAB:	*This World and the Beyond*

Introduction

In a time when theological teachers and students busily spend their hours assessing every twinge and shudder of the spirit of the age, or even of the decade or the year, it is positively encouraging to contemplate the work of Rudolf Bultmann, who, as far as I can tell, has not changed his mind on any issue of importance since the early 1920's. The popular picture of Bultmann, propagated mostly by his more strident critics, is that of a man who, abandoning the eternal truths of Christian faith, listens recklessly and obsequiously to the fickle voices of the modern age. But Bultmann has not ambled through his career sniffing every pole and fire hydrant of modernity for an object upon which to bestow his theological blessings. He would think the picture of theologians twisting for every blip on the sociological radar screen, or of divinity faculties ever poised to sprinkle the latest good cause with droplets of churchly profundity, symptomatic of an odd misunderstanding of Christianity. The trumpeters of social change have failed to send Bultmann scampering back to his study to inquire after God's gender or the color of Jesus' skin.

No, he is a serious, scientific theologian and scholar, who has long and consistently preoccupied himself with solving a single problem which is of far more than passing importance: How can we come to understand the New Testament in such a way that we grasp for ourselves the benefits of the Christian life? And even his debt to modern science in the analysis of this problem is not of the sort which would require one always to have his ear to the ground. As he sees it, the motive for taking seriously the modern scientific world-view is the acknowledgment that science has merely clarified what was *always* the only right access to a certain side of reality.

The believer's faith is the focal point for Bultmann, and both his theological and his philosophical thought are committed to the service of making this faith possible for men. But this faith comes only on the basis of something we find in the New Testament, a set of writings not easy to understand. In this we can hardly disagree with him: if we believe, as he does, that the Christian life is a treasure beyond price which demands that we understand the New Testament whatever the difficulties, then we too are faced with the problem to which he has devoted his energies for more than fifty years. It is for this reason, above all, that Bultmann's work is important to us. In the following pages I shall subject his thoughts on this matter to the refining fire of conceptual analysis, attempting both to discern the deeper (and often hidden) logic of his thought as a whole, and to subject particular assertions, formulations, and solutions to critical scrutiny. The results of this process will not always recommend Bultmann to us as a thinker. But the seriousness of his problem will not escape us, and we will be indebted to him for what we learn from reflection on his proposals.

He is also important to us for another reason. He is like a paradigm for much of modern theology. To understand him is to understand much that the theological winds have carried to us from the direction of Germany. Not only the younger theologians who have made many of their little footprints directly in the cavernous ones of their pioneer, but even Paul Tillich, who in many ways is so different from Bultmann, will often be touched indirectly by our conceptual explorations. And Bultmann provides us the added advantage that he is a fairly clear writer, whereas three quarters of the work of analyzing some of his more recent followers would have to be devoted to the preliminary task of deciding what they are *saying*.

The New Testament research to which Bultmann fell heir was held firmly in the grip of Enlightenment ideas about knowledge and certainty and what can happen in the world. The methods and results which alone would be accepted as appropriate to scientific historical inquiry into the New Testament documents were determined by a Kant-like separation of the objective and personal worlds, the one world determined by inexorable causal laws the working of which was discernible through objective observation, the other the world of morality, religion, values, human freedom and responsibility. To this kind of science Bultmann had an uncompromising ethical commitment. His theological accomplishment would have to be bounded by what has recently been termed "the morality of historical knowledge."

The two issues of New Testament research which decisively set the problem for his theological work were christology and eschatology. Given the Enlightenment assumptions about objectivity and scientific knowledge, then if, as Bultmann says, "the statements of the New Testament about Christ [are understood] as statements about a world phenomenon," it should not have been difficult to predict that "the historical investigation of New Testament christology was its destruction."[1] The seeming result of this scientific work was thus to show that christology was mythology. In response to this theologically perplexing result some liberal protestant theologians (e.g., A. von Harnack, M. Reischle, J. Weiss, W. Heitmüller) attempted to by-pass the mythological christology and to build directly on the piety and influential personality of the historical Jesus. But it soon became clear that these liberal pictures of Jesus, though not mythological, were no more grounded in historical reality than the biblical. Thus it seemed a firm scientific conclusion that the christological picture of Jesus presented in the New Testament and accepted in more or less realistic terms in protestant orthodoxy was mythological, and that the alternatives offered by a simple-minded branch of liberalism were equally a product of human imagination. Christology itself, the center of Christian theology, seemed to be discredited.

Liberalism had read the New Testament through the lenses of a "pantheism of history,"[2] so that for it the religious significance of historical situations and occurrences lay in whatever eternal truths they revealed or religious insights they evoked from the "believer." But in Bultmann's formative years this way of read-

---

[1] *FU*, p. 263.
[2] *Ibid.*, p. 32.

ing the New Testament was overturned by the critical insight that from beginning to end it was preoccupied with *eschatology*. It was not concerned with eternal truths and religious insights (even if these were to be derived from Jesus) so much as it was about the end of time, the end which was beginning to break forth in the ministry of Jesus, and which was to be fully consummated in the near future. The liberal interpretation, whether or not it had anything to do with Christianity, had had the advantage of usefulness on Sunday morning. But what was one to do with a document whose main content was a belief in the end of the world, a belief which had obviously proven false? Thus again critical scientific scholarship seemed to have reduced the New Testament to the status of a relic, of interest only to the historian of religion.[3] For someone interested in preaching the Christian gospel and preserving Christian faith among men, this situation might have looked desperate. Yet it was precisely in this context that Bultmann desired to remain a Christian churchman, preacher, and theologian.

It was Heidegger's philosophy which allowed Bultmann to read the New Testament in such a way as to see that its true meaning was quite independent of "neutral" scientific scholarship. Once a person has seen that "the world which faith wills to grasp is absolutely unattainable by means of scientific research,"[4] he learns to welcome the radical negative results of that research, which free him from a false conception of the significance of history for faith.

All historical phenomena which are subject to this kind of historical investigation are only relative entities, *entities which exist only within an immense inter-related complex*. Nothing which stands within this inter-relationship can claim absolute value.

---

[3] This was of course only the pedestrian negative side of the matter. The German talent for seeing beneath the surface of a text was early at work, and it was this which enabled the young Barth and others to greet the discovery of eschatology not with grim resignation but with theological exuberance. For them it was an expression, in ancient dress, of that shattering remoteness of God which experiences in the First World War had already begun driving them to conceive. New Testament eschatology was to be welcomed as representing God's disruption of all human cultural self-assurance and the conservative religiosity it encourages.

[4] *FU*, p. 31.

Even the historical Jesus is a phenomenon among other phenomena, not an absolute entity.[5]

The philosophy of Heidegger allowed Bultmann to perceive the radical difference between Christ the object of faith and "Christ after the flesh"—a distinction Bultmann believes not to be a Heideggerian imposition, but one fundamental to the New Testament itself. Thus when asked how he "rescues" himself from the situation created by historical radicalism, he replies,

> I have never yet felt uncomfortable with my critical radicalism; on the contrary, I have been entirely comfortable. But I often have the impression that my conservative New Testament colleagues feel very uncomfortable, for I see them perpetually engaged in salvage operations. I calmly let the fire burn, for I see that what is consumed is only the fanciful portraits of Life-of-Jesus theology [and, he might also add, the metaphysical-mythological portraits of orthodox christology], and that means nothing other than 'Christ after the flesh'.[6]

This new understanding of "Christ after the flesh," stimulated by Heidegger, is very different from that of those "conservative colleagues." For now Bultmann thinks radically: the Jesus who can become an object of historico-critical research is *ipso facto* merely "after the flesh" and irrelevant to faith. Historical investigation, by its nature, can penetrate only to "world phenomena," but the truth is that such are not all the real subject matter of the New Testament. What the New Testament is talking about is a wholly different order of reality, and it was above all the distinction between these orders of reality which Heidegger enabled Bultmann to see. Whether he is being a little coy in averring that he has "never yet felt uncomfortable" with radical criticism, whether with a little more self-scrutiny he might acknowledge that it was a relief to be able to find Heidegger's view of human life in the New Testament, is a question we need not adjudicate. The fact is that the more or less Heideggerian understanding of existence allowed him to put together a radical skepticism about the history of Jesus with something like Christian faith. Whether

---

[5] *FU*, p. 31.
[6] *Ibid.*, p. 132.

or not his interpretation of Heidegger's ideas is *historically* a response to the "situation created by radical criticism," we can at least say that logically this kind of historical work and Heidegger mesh together so well that either might have been a response to the other; indeed, either might have been a means of rescuing the other.

Heidegger's thought also suggested a solution to the problem of New Testament eschatology. The "end of the world" which was the true meaning of biblical eschatology was thus no more a "world phenomenon" than biblical christology. Although the New Testament writers expressed their eschatology in more or less realistic apocalyptic vision, and in more or less actually expected hopes, its true meaning was not the end of the *objective* (scientifically observable) world, but the end of the existential world, the end of *my* world as an existing being. By his notion of authenticity as freedom towards death (conceived as the transcendent limit of my limited existence—my "end") Heidegger suggested a new way of understanding the biblical eschatology such that it was in principle not discreditable by observations about how history has continued. The real meaning of the New Testament writers' eschatological statements was the decision to live in this world as though it was no longer—to grasp their own life as having (paradoxically) ended.

A reader new to Bultmann who reads widely in this diversified authorship may be tempted to think there are in reality three Bultmanns. He will perhaps be impressed with a broad and beautiful consistency in the whole, and yet there will remain difficulties: Bultmann the philosophical theologian seems too clear and simple for Bultmann the exegete, and both seem too radical for Bultmann the preacher. The philosophical writings give the impression of an *a priori* thinker *par excellence,* a thinker highly systematic who grounds all his work in the most over-arching principles, and whose thought thus possesses in the large view an extraordinary simplicity and unity. Reading the exegetical works our neophyte may be dismayed by the complexity, subtlety, and mass of detail which this learned and skilful exegete can call into play—a complexity and modulation which may often seem counter to that pristine clarity and simplicity evident in philosophical passages. He may find himself exclaiming about this or that passage, "Can Bultmann really *mean* this? If what he said in such and such an essay is really his view, how can he also say this?" If in one essay he tells us that the word of God is neither information about God's grace nor a report or record about Jesus Christ,[7] and in another that the word of God is "a sober, factual account of a human life, of Jesus of Nazareth, possessing saving efficacy for man,"[8] then our reader may begin to crave a hermeneutical principle by which to understand these words. If in his exegesis of Paul, Bultmann seems to assume that Paul's ethical exhortations involve concrete and authoritative descriptions of the life of faith, while in a more philosophical essay he tells us that "the Christian life is not regulated by fixed prescriptions,"[9] then our reader may look around for a way of putting these ideas together. Again, if he turns to Bultmann's more sermonic passages, his difficulty may be compounded: here the author seems not only to ignore many of the critical issues raised in his more technical exegesis; he seems to use the language of Christian faith in ways expressly forbidden in his more theoretical moments. If in a poetic-sermonic passage he calls God a "power" and attributes to him action described with active verbs ("makes," "allows," "casts," "sets," "calls," "gives"),[10] while in another place he denies that God is a being,[11] then we have to "interpret" the saying from one or the other of these sources.

Obviously, when a man of Bultmann's stature seems to us to be inconsistent, our first responsibility is to consider whether we have *understood* him. Only after much interpretive effort will we be warranted in a hesitant little suggestion that he is inconsistent with himself. What cannot be denied, however, is that some kind of interpretive activity is required. But this means that the critical reader is faced with a question of weighting: what part of Bultmann's authorship is he going to take most literally? Which part is he going to make regulative for the rest of his thinking about Bultmann?

In principle it would be possible to interpret the whole by taking the sermonic moments as a point of departure, treating what he says there as the most straightforward kind of discourse, and adjusting one's reading of everything else by reference to that.

---

[7] *Journal of Religion*, 1952, p. 85.
[8] *KM*, p. 44.
[9] *HE*, p. 46.
[10] *Essays*, p. 5.
[11] *FU*, p. 45.

But this would be to reverse the natural order of academic things, assuming that he is speaking least directly where he is speaking most technically. So this would be an implausible hermeneutical procedure. It is likely that he makes the more direct and precise statements in his technical literature, and that the sermonic is best read in light of that. Shall we then make the exegetical or the philosophical work the more weighty? Again, it is certainly possible in principle to read everything in light of his exegesis.[12] But usually the surest way to discover what a man's own views are is to go straight to the point in his writings where he talks "on his own." The difficulty with using a man's exegesis as a source of insight about what he himself thinks is that it is often hard to tell where he leaves off telling us what, for example, St. Paul says, and starts saying what he himself wants to say. In theological exegesis both things are necessarily going on: as theological work it aims to derive insights which the exegete himself considers objectively valid; but as exegesis it purports to accomplish this precisely through telling us what, for example, Paul's thoughts were. And unless one is a raving fundamentalist, one acknowledges that these two things are not always the same. Therefore it would seem intrinsically overcomplicated and uncertain to execute an interpretation which took as its point of departure Bultmann's exegesis. We will do better to start with those essays and passages (which of course are also to be found in the exegetical works, here and there) in which Bultmann speaks on his own and is less bound to filter his views through Paul or John.

The present study is an attempt to interpret the whole of Bultmann's theological work taking as central some ideas most clearly expressed in his less exegetical essays. This procedure is justified in part by his repeated, and for the most part unqualified, acknowledgment of his debt to the work of Martin Heidegger. However, the ultimate warrant of an interpretation is not something which can be argued for, but something which must be shown forth in the interpretation itself: does it do justice to the

---

[12] A broad but very judicious critique of Bultmann's exegesis from the perspective of a technical biblical scholar, and one I think congruent with the present more philosophical study, is Nils A. Dahl's review of the *TNT*, in his *The Crucified Messiah* (Minneapolis: Augsburg Publishing House, 1975).

man's work? Does it explain things about his work which alternative interpretations do not? And obviously the only way to ask whether my interpretation is thus warranted is to test it in its details by reading it.

Although the point of departure of the present study is the "Heideggerian" side of Bultmann, it does not address the question of whether he is actually true to that philosopher's views. It is interested only in a critical analysis of Bultmann's own ideas, and so can prescind from the question of where he got them. Therefore, references to Heidegger are here only a convenient and perhaps rather imprecise way of labelling some tendencies in Bultmann's thought.

So what follows is not quite an "introduction" to Bultmann's theology. Though it certainly attempts to grasp his theology as a whole, by seeing its underlying principles as well as by treating all the specific major topics within it, the purpose of this essay is not so much to give a "feel" for his thought and its general perspective as it is to *understand* it. There are some excellent introductions available now, in particular those by Schmithals[13] and Malet,[14] and for the reader interested in getting an impression of the sweep and external character of Bultmann's reflection, these will serve much better than the present essay. But if what I am going to argue is correct, then it would be difficult for an introduction, which must necessarily follow the surface contours of a man's thought, to be as clear as this essay attempts to be. Whereas an introduction might be concerned to expound Bultmann in such a way as to preserve certain ambiguities which centrally characterize his thought (the book by Malet does this exceptionally well) my exposition will aim at penetrating and sorting out such ambiguities. I shall argue that in Bultmann's case the surface contours of his thought are sometimes quite misleading, and that to become clear about what he is saying requires a different sort of treatment—a critical interpretation. This is a kind of reading which Bultmann has expressly approved, namely one which, as he says, "distinguishes what is said

[13] Walter Schmithals, *An Introduction to the Theology of Rudolf Bultmann,* tr. John Bowden (Minneapolis: Augsburg Publishing House, 1968).

[14] André Malet, *The Thought of Rudolf Bultmann,* tr. Richard Strachan (Garden City: Doubleday and Company, 1971).

from what is meant and measures the former by the latter."[15]
Following this dictum, perhaps I will be able to do for Bultmann
the service he has done the Apostle Paul: to understand him
better than he understood himself.[16]

---

[15] *The Beginnings of Dialectical Theology,* ed. J. M. Robinson
(Richmond: John Knox Press, 1968), p. 241; but this felicitous translation of the phrase is Schubert Ogden's, *EF,* p. 14.
[16] Cf. *FU,* pp. 92ff.

Part I

Foundations

1

Freedom from the World

No one with an ear for the beauty of an idea's empire can have read far in the works of Bultmann without the impression of listening to something profound. The profundity of that literature lies not so much in any particular passage, but rather in the larger sweep and coherence of his thought. We are captivated not so much by undeniably true propositions, as by a vision which acquires through its consistency and the wideness of its application a compelling power over our minds. Though we can perhaps not easily say what holds it all together, we cannot avoid the impression that this work is an extraordinary unity, exhibiting the touch of a master German thinker who knows how to hold his every thought in place by the power of a single idea.[1] Our intellects are allured and delighted by the way each product of his thought and scholarship, every article and sermon and book, arises out of this single ground. By comparison with the cohesion and economy of this man's thought, the theology and scholarship of others strikes one as patchy and occasional.

---

[1] Dahl, speaking of the *TNT* in *The Crucified Messiah* (p. 98), says, "The inner consistency of this presentation is impressive; it is almost uncanny. It seems to rest on a kind of pre-established harmony of critical biblical study, Reformation faith, and modern existential philosophy. A defect at one point might easily make the whole impressive structure totter."

What is this principle which binds the work of Bultmann into one and captivates our minds? What is its specific character, and how does it effect this unity? These are the questions I will begin to answer in this chapter.

It will become clear that the fundamental idea shaping Bultmann's thought is a dichotomy of a peculiar sort, in which the reality of the human self is opposed to that of the 'world.' The insight into the disjunctive relation between these realities is not modern, says Bultmann, but has roots 2000 years old:

> Whereas to ancient man the world had been home—in the Old Testament as God's creation, to classic Greece as the cosmos pervaded by the deity—the *utter difference of human existence from all worldly existence* was recognized for the first time in Gnosticism and Christianity, and thus the world became foreign soil to the human self.[2]

However, Bultmann has thought through this utter difference in a more radical way than even primitive Christianity did. Because the New Testament does not clearly distinguish between human and cosmic reality, one who decisively grasps the gulf between them will perceive in the text a peculiar contradiction which runs through it from beginning to end, a contradiction which necessitates a critical interpretation of its "mythology":

> But the principal demand for the criticism of mythology comes from a curious contradiction which runs right through the New Testament. Sometimes we are told that human life is determined by cosmic forces, at others we are challenged to a decision. Side by side with the Pauline indicative stands the Pauline imperative. In short, man is sometimes regarded as a cosmic being, sometimes as an independent 'I' for whom decision is a matter of life or death.[3]

The dichotomy which leads Bultmann to see it as a contradiction that the New Testament pictures man both as a cosmic being and as a maker of decisions is usually designated by the words *world/existence*. For the sake of convenience, and since this terminology predominates in his pages, I shall adopt it in what

---

[2] *TNT*, I, p. 165.
[3] *KM*, pp. 11f.

follows, though in his writings the dichotomy assumes many forms and many names. Sometimes it is expressed as the division between "nature" and "history,"[4] or between "state" and "deed,"[5] between "possession" and "event,"[6] between "factual knowledge" and "historic self-understanding" or between "seeing" and "hearing,"[7] between the "objective environment" and "humanity,"[8] between "events of nature" and "truly historical processes,"[9] between "merely perceptual knowledge" and "something that can only be experienced and laid hold of by actually living,"[10] between a "statement of fact" and a "confession of faith,"[11] between "objective observation" and "encounter,"[12] between "the 'being to hand' (*Vorhandensein*) of worldly phenomena" and "human being as existing,"[13] between "nature" and "decision,"[14] between "the Ecclesia as an historical phenomenon" and "the Ecclesia as the eschatological Congregation guided by the 'Spirit's sway,"[15] between "cosmic process" and "revelation,"[16] between "the continuity of world history" and "the continuity of the Word of God upon which the sinner can rely,"[17] and so on. To put it succinctly, Bultmann divides reality into two mutually exclusive kinds: on the one side there is the authentically and specifically human kind of reality, which has its true being only in "decisions," which he also calls "acts." A human being has his true reality so exhaustively in his acts that Bultmann can say "only in act are we ourselves."[18] Another way he puts this point is to say that a human being *is* not any-

---

[4] *JW*, p. 4, and *EF*, pp. 64f.
[5] *JW*, p. 99.
[6] *GV*, III, p. 117.
[7] *FU*, p. 187.
[8] *PCCS*, p. 202.
[9] *EF*, p. 232.
[10] *Ibid.*, p. 63.
[11] *KM*, p. 207.
[12] *Ibid.*, p. 200.
[13] *Ibid.*, p. 194.
[14] *Ibid.*, p. 121.
[15] *TNT*, II, p. 96.
[16] *GJC*, p. 64.
[17] In Bultmann's reply to Thomas Oden's criticisms, printed in the latter's *Radical Obedience* (Philadelphia: The Westminster Press, 1964), p. 146.
[18] *FU*, p. 62.

thing; rather he is a "potentiality to be"—that is, his authentic being is purely to be a maker of decisions.

But since 'existence' as *potentiality* to be, as being-only-in-acts of decision, is radically different from everything which has its being merely by being *actual,* then any mixing of these two kinds of being will be a threat to 'existence.' Indeed, it will be the very demise of authentic existence. What is at issue in this dichotomy, then, is not merely a metaphysical insight, a way of dividing up reality. What is at issue is human *freedom.* As long as a man understands himself as continuous with the world, his true self remains in bondage; worse than merely unrealized, its very being is contradicted. To be at home in the world is to deny one's nature as existence. Contrasting Christianity with human- ism, which sees the essence of man as mind controlling and shap- ing the cosmos into a home for himself, Bultmann says,

> In the eyes of the Christian faith the world is the extraneous ele- ment, which even the dominion of mind cannot turn into a home. . . . For—the Christian faith feels obliged to say this— man's real life is not his mind, but an inner self which is at an even profounder level. . . . Man does not simply become aware of God in striving for the true, the good and the beautiful, but only when he can free himself from the world and soar up to the eternal as his home.[19]

But what is this "extraneous element" which threatens man's "real life"? What does Bultmann mean by "world"? And what is its contrary, this "inner self which is at an even profounder level"?

In an article from late in his career he stated the matter clearly:

> Now *reality* can be understood in two senses. Usually one un- derstands by reality the *reality of the world presented in objecti- fying sight,* the world within which man is to be found, in which he orients himself by placing himself over against it, the co- herence of which he both counts on and calculates, in order to master it and thereby to secure his life. . . . Like all phenomena of the world which surrounds him man can also subject him- self, insofar as he is to be found in the world, to objectifying

---

[19] *Essays,* p. 153.

sight. He sets himself over against himself, and makes himself an object. Thereby he reduces his authentic, specific reality to the reality of the world. So it is in an "explaining" kind of psychology (in distinction from an "understanding" psychology, cf. Dilthey) and in sociology.

He goes on to say that the science of history in the sense of a positivist historicism attempts also to treat human history in this objectifying manner, but that this is in the last analysis impossible because here

> the distance of a neutral seeing from the object seen is impossible. . . . [But] in the modern understanding of history *reality* is understood in another way than in that of objectifying sight, namely as the *reality of historically existing man*. The being of man is fundamentally different from the being of nature which can be perceived in objectifying sight. Today we are accustomed to designate the specifically human kind of being as *existence*.[20]

Several aspects of 'world' come out here. In the first place it is the environment "within which man is to be found," almost conceived as a container or recepticle which "surrounds him." As such, it is the physical world, or as Bultmann calls it, "nature." It is also something which man is "over against," something different from man himself. It is something which has a regularity enabling man to "count on" it, and since he can calculate about it and manipulate it, he can "master" it, bring it under his control, and thereby "secure his life" in it.

But it is not simply nature which we normally think of as being different from or over against man.[21] For we learn that man can himself be reduced to 'world,' something which happens when he makes himself an object. This occurs in certain kinds of psychology, sociology, and history. Indeed, as we will

---

[20] *GV*, IV, pp. 128f.

[21] The reader should not take my criticism of the existence/world dichotomy to be a rejection of the everyday distinction between persons and nature. This is a distinction fundamental to the prosecution of human life: we have no inclination to treat stones and trees as persons, and when we talk to our dogs and cats, and attribute to them intentions and expectations, plans and anxieties, we realize that our behavior has a comical aspect. The person/nature distinction is different from the existence/world dichotomy, and this difference should become quite clear in what follows.

soon see, 'world' is not by any means limited to physical nature, but includes anything which is susceptible of being made into an object, since an object must always be something actual rather than potential, as existence is, and will therefore threaten genuine existence. The snake offers the actuality of the object to existence, and if he takes a bite he falls forthwith from the radical insecurity of his true being into that other, alien, non-potential kind of reality. The reason the above-mentioned sciences are doomed from the beginning to fail to touch the authentic reality of man is that they are "objectifying." In attempting to study man, they fail by trying to turn into an object something which in principle cannot be made into one. Existence may seem to be objectifiable (i.e., describable in propositions), but this is only an illusion, for the account always ends up reducing existence to something other than itself.

But, of course, man can be understood in *some* sense, and so, corresponding to the existence/world dichotomy, we have an epistemic one, the dichotomy between "factual knowledge" and "historic self-understanding":

> In all such factual knowledge or knowledge of principles the world is presumed to have the character of something objective, passive, accessible to simple observation. That is, the world is conceived in conformity with the Greek understanding of being. . . . In such a conception of the world as an objective entity, man himself is regarded as an object (as a fragment of the cosmos); his self-understanding is achieved along with the understanding of the world (and vice versa). . . . [But] the existence of man does not have the character of an objective entity but is a *historic* existence; where it is recognized that man in his history can *become* a new person and *consequently* can also newly *understand* himself; where, therefore, it is recognized that the being of man is a potentiality to be. That potentiality to be is always at risk; its possibilities are grasped each time by man in resolve, in decision. An understanding of these possibilities of man's existence here and now would obviously be a new understanding each time, since a historical situation[22] with its character of pos-

---

[22] Bultmann's talk here about the possibility-character of a "historical situation" may make it look as though the authentic choice is the choice of this or that concrete historical possibility. But which historical possibility is actualized in decision is quite beside the point. What is really "at risk" is not whether the decision made is the "right" one, but

sibility is not understood if it is conceived as a 'case' illustrating a general law. The historical situation cannot possibly be 'seen' in the Greek sense as an objective fact; it can only be heard as a summons.[23]

The understanding a person has of the world is of a completely different sort from that which he has of himself, if he understands himself authentically. Knowledge of the world can be a purely passive beholding from a distance, because what is beheld has the character of actuality, and is thus inert and passive. Man can behold or not behold, at his leisure; that is in his control. But knowledge of existence can never be casual and distanced and controlled in this way. Existence is a potentiality to be, and as such *is* only when it is *not* this or that actualization of potentiality. It *is* only in its becoming, that is, in its decision-to-be. As Bultmann says,

> existence is on each several occasion *event* in the decisions of the moment. It is not to hand, but something which happens on each several occasion.[24]

As soon as it becomes *something* it ceases to be what it is, namely existence or being-able-to-become. But it is also clear that existence would not be what it is without self-understanding. For 'decision' is surely a consciousness-concept: trees and sleeping men don't make decisions. But if existence involves understanding of itself, this understanding can only be in the moment of decision, since as we have seen, existence is only in the decision. This means that the understanding of existence is not, like its worldly counterpart, a knowledge which can be distanced, passive, and at the discretion of the observer. Since the authentic self exists only in the moment of decision, the knowledge of that self can be only in that moment. Knowledge of objects can persist through time; but knowledge of existence is only in the mo-

---

whether or not, in whatever choice one makes, one makes *the* choice suggested by the fact that man is a "potentiality to be": the choice of choosing one's *own* proper being, that is, the choice of choosing to be potentiality to be. Concrete historical situations are only *occasions* for this meta-decision involving the choice of one's *self*.

[23] *FU*, p. 187.
[24] *GV*, III, p. 117.

ment. Anything the knowledge of which could be "possessed" through time would have to be worldly.

Bultmann also designates this worldly kind of knowledge as "knowledge of principles," or understanding which comes from seeing a particular case as an illustration of a general law. It is worldly not only because it is possible to have it outside the moment of grasping one's own being as completely open potentiality, but also because it is, like knowledge of worldly objects, a kind of knowledge upon which a person could depend for his security. It is something a person could collect and store away against hard times, thereby trying to close off some possibilities the future may offer. But such knowledge is counter-existential, since to exist is to affirm oneself as open to *every* possibility and therefore radically insecure.

If man's true being is conceived as possibility, and thus in opposition to everything which is actual, it is clear that two of the three dimensions of *time* will fall under the category 'world.' The only dimension not characterized by actuality is the future, and it is for this reason that authentic existence is described as "openness to the future." To be open to the future is to be open to one's self, thought of as radical potentiality. By way of contrast, whatever has happened in the past, or whatever is actual in the present, is worldly and a threat to this openness. Using Christian vocabulary to express this view of reality, Bultmann can say,

> The world indeed is simply the sphere which men have made into a power over themselves by whatever they have done in the past. To live on the basis of the world, that is, of the past, is what is called sin. To live on the basis of the future is called living in dependence on God.[25]

To understand myself with reference to what I have done in the past, or by reference to past events of history, "is called sin." The reason is of course that the past is fixed and actual—that is, no longer characterizable as possibility.[26] Thus the same thing can be said of the present. To understand myself as what I actu-

---

[25] *Essays*, p. 81.
[26] Bultmann does, however, believe there is a way of reading history as "possibility." Events of the past can be looked at not as things that happened (though of course they may also have happened), but as picturing

ally am now is to understand myself in continuity with the world and to miss myself as existence. Authentic man is only possibility, and therefore only future. Man is perpetually ahead of himself; to exist is to have one's life only in the "beyond." So Bultmann can say, "what we never are here and now, precisely that is our true being."[27] Thus to understand oneself in terms of one's actual capacities, emotions, dispositions, habits, or character traits (that is, to conceive oneself as personality in the sense of a definite and actual and distinguishable "someone") is to understand oneself in continuity with the world. The true self cannot be identified by any "quality . the soul."

These opening comments on Bultmann's dichotomy are terribly sketchy, but they have served to cast up some of the main features of the idea which lies at the foundation of his thought: 'existence' is potentiality to be, and therefore in its authenticity must cast off the securities of the actual, the 'world'. Thus one of the fundamental features of world will be that it is what man is able to *control* in such a way as to find his security. A second obvious feature of the concept is that 'world' encompasses physical nature. We have also seen that knowledge which can be possessed is thought to be a source of security and therefore a danger to man's true being as possibility. So a third aspect of world will be what he calls "general truths": descriptive propositions and fixed ethical principles. We have seen that the self can also be conceived in a worldly manner, when it is understood either in terms of its past, or in terms of the present in the sense of objectively observable and describable dispositions, character traits, or capacities—"qualities of the soul." So a fourth aspect of the concept 'world' will be the past, and a fifth will be the present as personality. Let us turn to a more detailed discussion of these five aspects of Bultmann's concept of 'world', one by one.

I. 'World' as the controllable

The concept of controllability is fundamental to Bultmann's

---

ways of behaving and understanding ourselves in the present moment. But it is important to notice that as serving this existential function, it is totally indifferent whether they did in fact happen, whether the historical account is *accurate,* etc. That is, to read history as possibility is to prescind from its pastness (its actuality), and to see it as pictures.
[27] *EF,* p. 281.

concept of world, and, though we may sometimes think its application a little strained, is capable of explaining most of the other features almost directly. We can control physical nature and thus force it to serve the purpose of our security. "General truths" such as descriptive propositions and ethical principles are "at the disposal" of our minds, if not of our hands, and by calling them to mind we can nestle into certain kinds of security. The past, though we cannot change it, is within our control at least to the extent that we can, through reading and memory, call it at will to mind, and can scrutinize and criticize it. We can also live in it, treating it like "home," by taking our pleasure in bygone times, or by carving out a secure little niche for ourselves as historical scholars. Qualities of the soul, though they cannot be predicted and controlled with complete success, are at least the *sort* of thing that can be achieved at will through education, culture, and moral nurture. Thus, by using the concept of control in this rather loose way, it is possible to bring together the main aspects of Bultmann's concept of world under a single category.

But for Bultmann, world stands in a dichotomous relation to existence; so it must be that what can be controlled, or the process of control, is inconsistent with existence. Why must it be so? In our everyday thinking about what it is to be human, we see no contradiction between being a natural creature who eats, sleeps, and reproduces in much the same manner as other "animals," and being a *person*. Nor does it seem to us contradictory that our "selves" should be describable in language which is at our disposal, or even constituted by our conformity or lack thereof to statable ethical principles. Similarly, our selves seem to be partly constituted by what we have done in the past, as well as by the socially remembered events which shape the context of our present life together, so that our awareness of our identity seems dependent on a memory which is at least partly at our disposal. Also, it does not seem contradictory to us to educate our children and ourselves, with a view to becoming this or that kind of person. Indeed, it is because we feel that the person we nurture is the person we get, that this kind of "control" is felt to be so important morally and religiously.

Why then is controllability a master feature of what Bultmann calls 'world', and contradictory to 'existence'? His answer is that in each of the four above cases we have failed to see what the true *essence* of man is. In thinking about human beings in such an ordinary manner we have not yet pushed deep enough to see the true being of man.

> We believe that we understand the being of man more truly when we designate it as *historical*. And we understand by the historical nature of man's being that his being is a *potentiality to be*. That is to say, the being of man is removed from his own control, it is risked continually in the concrete situations of life and goes through decisions in which man does not choose *something for himself*, but chooses *himself* as his *possibility*.[28]

So the reason that the true being of man is "removed from his control" is that "his being is a potentiality to be." When he chooses according to his authentic nature he chooses not this or that something which he could actually effect ("something for himself"), but rather chooses to be a chooser ("chooses himself as his possibility"). He chooses something which he could never effect, something which lies always and essentially in the "beyond": he chooses potentiality itself. Man in his true being always escapes actually coming into being; insofar as he becomes anything more than possibility, he has become inauthentic, has slipped into the kind of being called "world." To have chosen himself in the manner of choosing something for himself (to have decided to "become" a doctor or a Presbyterian, or to "be" good in accordance with some particular conception of goodness, etc.) is precisely not to have chosen *himself* because it is to have opted for something other than *potentiality;* it is to have chosen to be *actuality*, world, the controllable.

The desire to understand oneself in the terms of those elements of reality over which one can have control must also be seen as a desire for security. But since security is foreign to the authentic nature of man, the desire for it is always the inclination to fall away from true freedom into worldly being.

> True freedom, however much it is freedom in subjection, is not a freedom involving security, but a freedom which is always gained only in responsibility and decision and becomes an event, at any given time . . . and so it is a freedom in insecurity.[29]

[28] *FU*, p. 149.
[29] *Essays*, p. 314.

To be secure in one's existence, to have gained a mastery of it, is to have become worldly; it is to have denied one's authentic being as radical potentiality. But it seems odd that Bultmann should identify responsibility with insecurity. We may be inclined to say that before a person can be responsible he has to have a certain amount of security, a modicum of self-mastery and confidence. But to think in this manner is again, as Bultmann will tell us, to forget what it is to be a human being. Here we are thinking of responsibility as a disposition to behave in certain patterned ways, like the "responsible" clerk who takes care of the customers and keeps his receipts in order, or the "responsible" mother who is solicitous about her children's welfare and efficient in guarding it. But these are not cases of *true* responsibility, of the kind characterizing man in his authenticity; for these, as dispositions and character traits, are mere actualities. Being responsible must rather be thought of as a person's holding himself (or better, in every new moment renewing himself) as the *potentiality* for this or that possibility. One can see how responsibility in the ordinary sense involves security and being in control of oneself; responsibility is in that case itself a worldly disposition. But to be responsible in a way congruent with man's authentic nature is not to make this or that decision, or even this or that kind of decision, but in *the* decision of the moment to be open for decision as such. As soon as one *carries out* a decision in the actual world, this actualizing of the possibility constitutes a danger to his true being as potentiality. It has become world, and must be renounced. But since possibilities are always concrete possibilities in a historical situation, truly responsible existence stands forever poised on the razor's edge, dividing itself as potentiality from the actualities which are always the worldly by-products of its decisions. In deciding, it always has to be directed toward these possibilities as possible actualities, but as truly responsible it must be directed toward each not as this or that concrete possibility to be followed up, but as possibilities *as such,* so that it is held *always* in the moment of decision, never in the actual, and is thus constantly withdrawing from the security of accomplishment.

This seems to be the thrust of Bultmann's oft-invoked distinction (indeed, it is another permutation of his dichotomy) between 'act' and 'work':

Indeed, the less faith is a 'work', the more it is an act; and it will now perhaps be clear in what the difference consists: in the case of the 'work' I remain the man I am; I place it outside myself, I go along beside it, I can assess it, condemn it or be proud of it. But in the act I *become* something for the first time: I find my being in it, live in it and do not stand alongside it. If I were to seek to look at myself and my act, I would destroy the act as an act, and degrade it into a 'work'.[30]

A work is that worldly by-product of the act which alone is truly existence; it is that actuality which I have brought into being, and which I can now, controlling it, behold or not behold, be proud of, take security in the thought of, etc. What I have done is not at all constitutive for what I essentially am; I am only in the act in which I *"become something."* That is, my being is only in the moment of the act itself, not in what ensues from it. But is it not simply common sense that the identity of a human being, his "self," is constituted by what he has done? If I have written a book, does not that come to constitute part of my *identity?* Is not my self at least partly the self which I have *made* of myself, through good deeds or evil? If I am not what I have thus made of myself through my "works," have I any identity at all? Bultmann will answer again that this kind of question merely betrays our failure to think through in a radical way the fact that man is a maker of decisions, a potentiality to be. If we see that, then we will see that all these things done have nothing to do with existence: "Existence is not something which a man possesses and which he can observe on occasion; man is himself existence."[31] As potentiality to be, man is no product of his acts which he could distance from himself, reflect upon, seek to control, or possess. He is simply *identical* with his act, taken independent of any effect or product or actuality which might ensue from it; he is identical with *pure* act thought of as the moment of acting, the moment of decision.

It is in the light of Bultmann's notion that man as potentiality to be has his true being only in the moment of act that we are to understand him when he talks about freedom as *surrender* ("obedience").

---

[30] *Essays,* p. 175.
[31] *FU,* p. 316.

As true obedience, 'faith' is freed from the suspicion of being an accomplishment, a 'work'. As an accomplishment it would not be obedience, since in an accomplishment the will does not surrender but asserts itself; in it a merely formal renunciation takes place in that the will lets the content of its accomplishment be dictated by an authority lying outside of itself, but precisely in so doing thinks it has a right to be proud of its accomplishment. 'Faith'—the radical renunciation of accomplishment, the obedient submission to the God-determined way of salvation, the taking over of the cross of Christ—is the free deed of obedience in which the new self constitutes itself in place of the old. As this sort of decision, it is a deed in the true sense: In a true deed the doer himself is inseparable from it, while in a 'work' he stands side by side with what he does.[32]

Since the true deed brings nothing into actuality, it remains precisely identical with itself as deed: it is *pure* deed, *pure* decision, and thereby stands apart from everything worldly, every accomplishment. To be anything more than pure decision is, if it is a renunciation at all, "a merely formal renunciation" which "does not surrender but asserts itself," that is, conceives itself in terms of the worldly, the actual, the *done*. For this identification of itself in terms of the done, Bultmann uses the metaphor of pride (the opposite of surrender); for what one is proud of is usually what one has done. The radical renunciation of accomplishment, the deed pure of all actuality, is the free deed of obedience in which the new self is identical with itself as potentiality to be. There is no element in it which can be *controlled*; it has achieved perfect 'existence'.

To see how radical this renunciation or surrender is, it is instructive to compare it with stoicism, in which the self also renounces control over the world:

> *The difference from stoicism,* then, lies in the motivation of freedom as inner independence and so, too, in the conception of the self. Here the question arises whether Paul has conceived of man's self more profoundly and radically; whether, when the question is thought out to its logical conclusion, the stoic can realize only a schematic, ideal picture of man as a rational being, in taking up a neutral attitude in the encounters of history,

---

[32] *TNT*, I, pp. 315f.

BULTMANN (...)   R.O. ... 1977, 84, 85.

whereas the Christian view is open for the fullness of the possibilities of life in history. We may further ask whether freedom is understood more radically if the law behind it is the law of reason, a law which is at the disposal of thought, so that man—as the stoic actually tries to do—can gain a peculiar security, such as is never attainable for the Christian, who is subject to the incontrollable law of grace; for grace can never be possessed, but can only be received afresh again and again. But in reality are not insecurity and radical freedom identical; and finally, is it not a fact that man always comes into his present situation as in some way under constraint, so that real freedom can only be received as a gift?[33]

The stoic gives up trying to control his *environment,* and resigns himself to whatever fate it may hold for him. He has given up control over *it.* But in so doing, he defends himself against that environment by locking himself, as it were, into his mind; by attempting to become pure mind he makes himself independent of the environment and invulnerable to it. And by making himself so independent, he makes himself *secure.* He thinks of himself as pure mind, and as subject only to the laws of reason, not to those of nature. Now it is clear that the stoic has achieved this security by an act of renunciation, but it is also clear that it is not total renunciation, for he still hangs on to what he can achieve through his mind for his security. He renounces control over the physical environment, but not over *himself.* He has made himself secure by closing himself off to certain of the possibilities of life. But this is not true freedom. The person who *acts* in accordance with his true being as potentiality to be abandons not just this or that aspect of control over his own life, but abandons *every* ploy for securing himself, and thus becomes open in advance to *every* possibility which "life in history" could offer. He frees himself not only from the "world" as environment, but also from the "world" as his will. This is a freedom even from one's own striving to be free, a total letting-go, a renunciation even of renunciation, radical openness, a paradoxical willing not even to assert one's own will. Thus Bultmann's radical dichotomy between existence and world also constitutes a formal demand as to the nature of that "grace" which is a necessary cor-

---

[33] *Essays,* pp. 309f.

relate of the free act of faith: it will have to be something which by its very nature cannot in any way be "controlled" by man; it will have to be something which *cannot* be reduced to the actuality of worldly being. But that is another story, to be discussed at length in the third chapter.

II. 'World' as physical nature

Everywhere man is busy shaping the physical universe into a place where he can dwell in comfort and security. He cuts down weeds and plows the fields, that they may bring forth fruit for him to eat, and he builds storage places, so that in the times between harvests he will have wherewithal to nourish his body. He domesticates animals so that he will not depend for meat upon chance comings and goings of game. He hews down trees and builds a house to protect him from dangers of the environment. Modern science is but an extension and sophistication of the activities, basic to man's life on earth, in which he subdues the physical universe and through this mastery makes himself a secure home. Medicine attempts to eradicate the dangers besetting man from disease, agronomy trys to find ever better means of feeding him, and architecture looks for better methods of housing his fragile body.

But what are obvious necessities for man's physical life become the ground of a false self-understanding. For man is tempted to think that he himself is something that he can thus secure with cleverness and industry, whereas his true self is something which by its nature can *never* be made secure. So to try to make it secure, to understand oneself in such a way that one attempts to do so, is *eo ipso* to have become the possession of an alien reality: "By means of science men try to take possession of the world, but in fact the world gets possession of men."[34]

However, it is only because the physical universe is of such a nature as to offer man a security contradicting his authentic self that Bultmann thinks of it as world. Thus his dichotomy 'existence'/'world' is not a positing of two alien "substances" after the manner of the "anthropological dualism of Hellenistic

---

[34] *JCM,* p. 40.

mysticism."[35] Attributing his own view to Jesus, he says,

> Jesus knows only one attitude toward God—*obedience*. Since he sees man standing at the point of decision, the essential part of man is for him the will, the free act, and in this connection the dualistic anthropology which sees two natures, flesh and spirit, active in man, has no meaning. For on will, on free act, depends man's existence as a unit, as a whole; reflection on the antithesis of spirit and flesh has no place here. It is not the physical in man which is evil in him—the *whole* man is evil if his will is evil.[36]

So the question is not one about two mutually separable *parts* of man, one "natural" and the other "spiritual"; it is for Bultmann a question of the *essence* of man, that is, of which aspect of his being is his *authentic* aspect. And his answer is that authentically man is *will* (potentiality to be, decision-maker).

It is understandable, but nevertheless a mistake, therefore, when Austin Farrer criticizes him by saying,

> Dr. Bultmann seems to have no difficulty with the belief that personal existence can kick off the body and survive; his unbelieving existentialist teachers would hardly follow him there.[37]

If we stick close to Bultmann's use of words like *authenticity* and *essence* we will see that there is no reason why man's true nature as will would have to be *separable* from everything about him which is not his true nature. Speaking of the dual possibilities of man's understanding his self in terms of the world or in its authenticity, he says,

> One will have to designate the relation between the two modes of self-understanding as a *dialectical* one, inasmuch as factically the one is not given without the other. For man, whose authentic life takes place in decisions, is also a corporeal being. Responsible decisions are made only in concrete situations, in which corporeal life is also at stake. The decision in which man chooses himself, that is, chooses his authentic existence, is always at the same time the decision for a possibility of the corporeal life. The responsibility for himself is always at the same time the responsi-

---

[35] *JW*, p. 48.
[36] *Ibid.*
[37] *KM*, p. 222.

bility for the world and its history. For the sake of his responsibility man requires the objectifying look (*Blick*) into the world into which he is set as into his disposable "field of operation" (*"Arbeitswelt"*). Whence also comes ever again the temptation or seduction to regard the "field of operation" as the authentic reality and to miss what is really essential about existing (*die Eigentlichkeit des Existierens*), and to secure one's life by having the disposable at one's disposal.[38]

Bultmann's doctrine does not at all imply that one could escape from the world in the sense of having a life in which there was actually no corporeal aspect. The question is entirely one of essence, and therefore of how an individual is going to *understand* himself. The question is whether man will understand his "field of operation" as *merely* a field of operation, as of a radically different nature from his true self, a mere context in which he realizes his true self; or whether he will understand himself as *continuous* with that field of operation and thus as essentially a natural being.

The fact of the matter is that physical nature is not a very important aspect of Bultmann's concept of world. What importance it has it gains primarily from being something like a paradigm of the controllable.

III. 'World' as general truth

Certain kinds of *sentences* also fall under the category of 'world' for Bultmann, namely various kinds which he lumps under the heading 'general truths.' Under this category he includes (1) "truths which are familiar to everyone, because they originate out of human reflection on man, his situation (even if that be so-called 'frontier-situations'), his problems, his pleasures and his sufferings"; (2) "ethical norms or imperatives, since these originate in man's knowledge of being under a demand"; (3) sentences which "are valid for man at any time"; (4) sentences setting forth "a so-called Christian picture of the world or sentences of a Christian dogmatics."[39]

Contrasting with such general truths is what Bultmann

---

[38] *GV*, III, p. 132.
[39] *Ibid.*, p. 167.

calls 'address,' and only language which is address can be, in
encountering man, the occasion for his true freedom. General
truths can only contribute to his bondage to his old self. But it
cannot be simply the address-character of a sentence which distinguishes the freedom-occasioning discourse from worldly language, for as Bultmann acknowledges, sentences of the kinds
listed above can be employed *in* or *as* address, and this would not
be enough to render them non-worldly. What distinguishes
worldly from non-worldly address?

> Precisely this, that ethical imperatives and proverbs are general
> truths which each person can speak, and insofar as they are ad-
> dress, can address to himself. This is shown by the fact that the
> "Ten Commandments" can be learned by heart, as can "Chris-
> tian" truths, dogmatic sentences such as the so-called confes-
> sions of faith. What has been heard and learned becomes a pos-
> session, and the riper a man becomes in the experience of life,
> the more richly does he come into possession of it. Then a man
> needs no one to address him here and now; he can say it to him-
> self. And that is not all! If we disregard dogmatic sentences for
> a moment, then it holds that he could in principle have done so
> without any moment of initiation at all. For when a man has
> once heard this or that general truth in training and instruction
> or in the course of human affairs, then he is only made aware
> on a given occasion of something which he himself could have
> said to himself. He adopts it only because it is "evident" to him,
> that is, because he recognizes its general validity.[40]

From this account it is quite clear that what makes commandments, dogmatic sentences, proverbs, and the like, as such
counter-authentic is the same thing that made physical nature
so: their content can be possessed, known, mastered, judged,
criticized, employed in a variety of ways. That is, they are at our
disposal, within our *control*. The kind of discourse appropriate to
human freedom will, on the contrary, have to be such as to be
radically incapable of being at the disposal of men. It will have
to be something which cannot be known in the sense that once
knowing it I could tell someone else what I know (or even
that I could sit down and reflect on what I know); it will have to
be something which in principle and by its very nature could

---

[40] *GV*, III, p. 170.

not be judged, criticized, or employed in argument. It has to be something which will escape learning and cannot be gained by either informing or training:

> Man cannot speak the address of Christian proclamation to himself; he can always only let it be spoken to him—always and again let it be spoken. For he cannot carry its truth with him as a possession. Such a mistaken opinion would turn Christian truth precisely into a general truth. For in the case of faith, which lays hold of Christian truth, the truth has to be laid hold of ever anew—and indeed with a struggle; for it is precisely not "evident," but rather paradoxical, an offense to "natural" man.[41]

But let us now look in some detail at those things which Bultmann calls general truths, first at what would usually be called descriptive propositions, and then at imperatives.

Bultmann contrasts the Greek view of freedom with that of the New Testament, in the following way: according to the Greek view, a man gained his freedom through an insight into the cosmos and thus into himself as a being with a certain place and station in that cosmic whole. Thus a *Weltanschauung,* a conceptual picture of the world, was essential to salvation. The New Testament, by way of contrast, sees salvation as an act of surrender so complete that it is at the same time a renunciation of all security and control which man might himself have. But the world-view which forms the organ for Greek salvation is, as something which man can possess in the way of thoughts, something over which he has control; it is a source of security, for it is in the realm of ideas what his log cabin is in the way of physical materials: it protects him from the wide open spaces and closes him off from the multitudinous dangerous possibilities of life—it enables him to settle down and find himself "at home" in the universe. A *Weltanschauung* is not only unnecessary to true freedom; it is essentially a means of escaping from it:

> A *Weltanschauung* is a theory about the world and life, and about the unity of the world, its origin, purpose or worth—or again its worthlessness—about the meaning of it all—or again, about its meaninglessness. . . . In a *Weltanschauung* it is a question of understanding my life and my destinies on the basis of a

---

[41] *GV*, III, p. 170.

general conception of the world—always as an instance of the general rule. In a *Weltanschauung* I simply escape from the reality of my existence, which is actually real only in the 'moment', in the question involved in the 'moment' and in the decision called for by the 'moment'. We can see in the longing for a *Weltanschauung* an escape from the enigma and from the decisive question of the 'moment'. It is man's escape from himself; it is the effort to find security in generalizations, whereas insecurity is what characterizes the real nature of human existence.[42]

Bultmann contrasts such a *Weltanschauung* with the New Testament teaching on creation:

But for the New Testament the idea of creation is not a cosmological theory which teaches us to see every individual existence and event in the framework of the unity of the whole, and so leads man to conceive of himself as an organic member in the cohesion of the whole: on the contrary, the idea of creation means that God is continually Lord over me as the one who gives me my life, before whom I am as nothing, and to whom I am under the obligation of giving honour in fulfilling his will and acknowledging his grace.[43]

Now one might ask why an understanding that God is continually Lord over me as the one who gives me my life is contradicted by my having a *Weltanschauung* according to which he is the source of the whole physical universe and I, being a part of that universe, am also derived from him. Why is it that such a "picture" of the way things are, into which I fit, contradicts my "fulfilling his will and acknowledging his grace"? If it is true that the Greek view of salvation simply *consisted* in my seeing where I fit in the order of things, cannot Christian piety at least *involve* such sight? Bultmann's answer seems to be no. But if this answer seems paradoxical, it is only because we have not seen in radical enough fashion what man's authentic being, and therefore his true salvation, is. "Fulfilling his will and acknowledging his grace," if it is to be truly *human* salvation, must be that radical surrender in which I renounce *all* control and give up *every* security. So if I found security in believing that the world is a great

[42] *Essays*, p. 8.
[43] *Ibid.*, p. 76.

system created and cared for and destined for ultimate good by God, I would be contradicting my nature as potentiality to be.

Reality, according to Bultmann, is divided into two spheres, on the one hand "the sphere of visible, concrete, tangible, and measurable reality," and on the other that of "unseen, intangible realities."[44] The former is the sphere of what can legitimately be talked *about,* "the 'being to hand' (*Vorhandensein*) of worldly phenomena which may be apprehended in objective thought."[45] Here objective, descriptive language is appropriate and can be successful. To the invisible sphere belong the realities of God and the human self. (And since, as we have seen, the human self simply *is* its acts, these acts are also among the invisible realities.) Here objective language is inappropriate and always fails: "It is as impossible to speak meaningfully about God as it is about *love.*"[46] Jesus anticipated this fundamental insight about the limits of objectifying thought and description:

> In the thought of Jesus, however, man is not seen in this way from outside, thus himself acting as observer; instead, the observer's standpoint is abandoned. Man is seen in his essential being, in his life, which is lived in specific decisive moments in the present, which cannot be understood through a general description of humanity. A man has no control in his ideas over this essential self, for he cannot stand to one side and observe it, he *is* it.[47]

If man is to be seen "in his essential being" then "the observer's standpoint" must be "abandoned." No man can observe another in his essential being, nor can he even observe himself, because this implies the "observer's" standpoint, a seeing "from outside." To the ordinary thinker, this seems an odd thing to say. The observer's standpoint—*"abandoned"?* What then is left of man's "being" to see? If Bultmann were to make a distinction between different *kinds* of observation, we might find him understandable. We could see readily enough how the kind of observation which looks for an understanding of people's emotional life in terms solely of physiological processes would miss seeing man in his

---

[44] Cf. *KM,* pp. 18f.
[45] *Ibid.,* p. 194.
[46] *FU,* p. 53.
[47] *JW,* p. 207.

"essential being." And then, by contrast, the kind of observation which is at the basis of the work of Dostoievsky or other great describers of human life, we would take to be a more adequate use of the "observer's standpoint." But great novelists are undeniably observers; the existence they describe (their characters') is not always their own; and even in the case of autobiography, the descriptions of the existence would surely involve standing to one side and observing oneself, remembering one's thoughts, one's feelings, what one said and did, and what happened to one. No, Bultmann's position is clearly more radical than this. He is denying the possibility of an objective observation, and thus of an objective description, of existence *at all*.[48] He is not suggesting that we need a *better* observer's standpoint than is attained in, for example, physiological psychology; he is saying that the observer's standpoint must be *abandoned*.

Why is it so? Why does Bultmann force us into a rigid dichotomy between what is observable and describable on the one side, and man's true being on the other? Is it not a daily occurrence and even a necessity in our lives that we observe and describe *human beings*? But again Bultmann's answer to our naive questioning is that we have simply failed to grasp in a radical way what it is for man to be a potentiality to be. To be truly himself he must be radically open to possibility, radically insecure. He must have renounced all control, not only of his physical environment, but also of his ideas. He must have abandoned all placing and grasping of himself which could possibly provide a kind of knowledge which he could possess, and in which he could thus rest to some extent secure. Objective observation and description, as providing such possessable and controllable knowledge, must therefore *as such* fall on the side of 'world' in antithesis to 'existence.' Any existence which has been described has *ipso facto* been transformed into world.

To objectify existence is something like a logical contradiction because it would involve a self-understanding containing an element of security. As we have already begun to see, the kerygma—that kind of language in face of which authentic "ex-

---

[48] Bultmann does, of course, have a stake in preserving the possibility of an objective description of "existence" along the lines of Martin Heidegger's *Being and Time*. For an analysis of how Bultmann attempts to overcome this paradox, I refer the reader to chapter six.

istence" can become an event—must be correspondingly non-objectifiable. Speaking of this kerygma, Bultmann says,

> Again, this event which comes to the man cannot be an occur-rence to be looked at objectively, a part of the world of objects constituting man's environment, which can be observed and analyzed in order to establish the fact that it is the event of for-giveness, to which the man can now relate himself. For the act of forgiveness between God and man, as between man and man, escapes observation.[49]

The kerygma cannot be something which can be looked at ob-jectively; it must be something which "escapes observation." It is for this reason that

> if the death and resurrection of Jesus are asserted as redemptive acts, in the sense of cosmic events which affect mankind in gen-eral so that the individual can rely upon them, this is not the meaning of Jesus—neither sin nor forgiveness is really taken seriously. Not sin, for it is thought of as a universal human attri-bute; nor forgiveness, for it is conceived as a mere event in the world of external objects, on which man by his very theories and proofs exercises judgment, asserting that divine forgiveness can and must be thus and so.[50]

Again, to our ordinary ways of thinking this juxtaposition of ideas seems enigmatic. It is not immediately self-evident why we should not rely on the redemptive acts of God. Are we not taught to *depend* on God's grace as something always available to us, even when we neglect him and do without him? Does the Christian not take the death and resurrection of Jesus as the immovable ground of his comfort and peace, the deeds of God done quite independently of our paltry "responsibility," indeed as the ground of a certain security against our sin and death, as a source of *assurance?* Again, it is not immediately obvious why thinking of sin as a universal human attribute necessarily in-volves not taking it seriously. *Must* I cease to take my sin se-riously just because I recognize that every other man is also a sinner? Or again, it seems paradoxical to hold that to think of

---

[49] *JW*, p. 212.
[50] *Ibid.*, p. 213.

the death and resurrection of Jesus as cosmic events involves thinking of forgiveness as "a mere event in the world of external objects." There does not seem to be any contradiction involved in thinking of the death and resurrection of Jesus as having happened at a particular location in space and at a particular time in the history of the world, and at the same time as having happened *for me*. Many things happening in space and time have tremendous significance for us as persons; to say that an event is "cosmic" in this sense is not to assimilate it necessarily to the status of a "mere event" like the falling of a twig in a remote forest. Or again, just because the event of forgiveness is something that can be thought about does not mean that man "exercises judgment" over it in any invidious sense, or that he by his own powers decides how and what divine forgiveness can and must be. Indeed, his reflection about it *may* be quite humble and reverent, taking a quiet and appropriate joy in it.

But if our thoughts take such a turn, if by clinging thus to our ordinary ways of thinking we find enigmas and paradoxes in Bultmann's thought, it will again be because we have not grasped in thoroughness his basic idea. If we understand rightly that man's true being is radical insecurity, then we will also see what his "redemption" is, namely that he should cast off every security which falsifies that truth of his nature. And in that case we will see that the redemptive act of God simply *cannot,* on pain of contradicting man's true nature, be anything upon which he could rely. It is this idea too which explains why it is impossible both to take sin as a universal human attribute and to take it seriously. For taking sin seriously can mean nothing other than giving up all the securities which constitute my sin, including the security of knowing who I am by virtue of a description which has general validity and which I can therefore possess. Taking my sin seriously must involve casting off every objective description of myself, including that of sinner. This idea is also the clue to why a "cosmic" event cannot have significance for me as a person. For true human being, as potentiality to be, a cosmic event simply *is* a "mere event in the world of external objects." As something that can be seen and talked about ("objectified") it must be something *actual;* and for a man to understand *himself* in terms of something actual is to close off some of that openness to possibilities which as potentiality his true self is. This idea also enables us to see how thinking about God's grace is identical with exercising judgment over it in an invidious sense. There is no way to think *about* it without falsifyng it as God's grace. For it could not be God's grace if it were not appropriate to our salvation, and our salvation is the renunciation of "control" in the most radical sense possible. And that, of course, includes the kind of control we can have over an idea. God's grace, therefore, by the nature demanded of it by human authenticity, cannot be transformed into an idea; so to objectify it in thought has to be impiety. It is really this concern, to take away from man everything "objective," and therefore every kind of knowledge which could be a source of security for him, which motivates the de-objectivizing interpretation of the New Testament which Bultmann calls demythologizing:

> Demythologizing is the radical application of the doctrine of justification by faith to the sphere of knowledge and thought. Like the doctrine of justification, de-mythologizing destroys every longing for security. There is no difference between security based on good works and security built on objectifying knowledge. The man who desires to believe in God must know that he has nothing at his disposal on which to build his faith, that he is, so to speak, in a vacuum.[51]

Sometimes Bultmann's critics, sensing his constant submission to the existence/world dichotomy, accuse him of subjectivism, of making faith purely an inner experience and of denying the objective reality of God and his grace. But this criticism, if not erroneous, is at least ill-expressed. For it has been one of Bultmann's abiding concerns to *overcome* the subject/object thought pattern which seems to him fundamental to Greek thought and to modern science. The reason is that this thought pattern sees man (the subject) merely as experiencer or thinker, a kind of passive receptacle for data. What is thus passively received in experience is the object. This pattern of thought must be overcome, for it misses the true nature of existence: we leave out the fact that decision in every moment is constitutive of man's true being. Or to put the same thing another way, the failure of the subject/object dichotomy is that it conceives both object and subject in terms of world. Speaking of man's desire to see

---

[51] *JCM,* p. 84.

himself with the help of something like the Greek world-view, Bultmann says,

> But that very view is the primary falsity (*proton pseudos*) and it leads necessarily to mistaking the truth of our own existence, since we are viewing ourselves from outside as an object of scientific investigation. Nor is there any gain if we label ourselves 'subject' in distinction to the other objects with which we see ourselves in interaction. For man is seen from outside even when he is designated 'subject'. Therefore the distinction between subject and object must be kept separate from the question of our own existence.[52]

To think *about* man at all (here, to conceive him as 'subject') is to falsify his true nature by objectivizing him. So the two dichotomies are not parallel, but criss-cross one another. The human self (called in this terminology 'subject') can be either existence (when it is authentic, deciding in the moment) or world (when it is objectified, thought about, described, known, etc.). Likewise what the human self encounters (called in this terminology 'object') can be either existential (when it is something non-objectifiable like the kerygma or God) or worldly (when it is something either rightly or wrongly objectified in knowledge, description, etc.). For this reason Bultmann can speak of God and the kerygma as objective without being objectifiable[53] and of existence as non-objectifiable without being subjective.

Besides objective descriptions, Bultmann also includes ethical norms or imperatives under the category of general truths. This designation may seem a little strange, since imperatives are not truths at all, but it is clear what he has in mind. An ethical imperative can be learned, and then when it is thus in a man's possession, he can carry it, as a source of orientation for his behavior, into the concrete situations of his life. In this way he knows, on the basis of his past learning of the imperative, and of its universal sway, what he should do: he is not left utterly on his own without a firm base of orientation, but acts with a

---

[52] *FU,* p. 59.
[53] Whether ultimately we can make sense talking about an object of encounter which is in principle non-objectifiable is a question which will concern us at various points in chapter three and Part II.

certain sense of security that what he is doing is right. When a man comes into the concrete situation thus armed with a definite standard, the range of possibilities which are open to him has been narrowed beforehand. So to adhere to ethical standards is to contradict one's true nature as existence.

> A man cannot control beforehand the possibilities upon which he must act; he cannot in the moment of decision fall back upon principles, upon a general ethical theory which can relieve him of responsibility for the decision; rather, every moment of decision is essentially new. . . . For man does not meet the crisis of decision armed with a definite standard; he stands on no firm base, but rather as it were alone in an empty room. This it is which shows the requirement of the good to be actually the demand of God—not the demand of something divine in man, but the demand of God who is beyond man.[54]

Every demand which is capable of giving a man *orientation* as to what to do, every specific prescription for the way he should lead his life, is worldly. By contrast with such demands, the demand of God is distinguished by the fact that it gives him no principles to guide him, no definite standard. It leaves him without "a firm base, but rather as it were alone in an empty room." A man is *truly* responsible only in responding to the demand which leaves him totally alone and without guidance, for only then is his existence unviolated by world.

Bultmann does not deny that decision is made in concrete situations of life where knowledge of the empirical possibilities and of the consequences of this or that action is relevant. But he does seem to deny that a knowledge of such possibilities is relevant to the decision itself, if it is truly responsible. The following enigmatic passage seems to make sense only if we posit a distinction between the "how" of a decision and the "what" of it, and say that only the "how" determines whether the decision is authentic:

> The crisis of decision is the situation in which all observation is excluded, for which *Now* alone has meaning. *Now* man must know what to do and what not to do, and no standard whatever from the past or from the universal is available. *That* is the

---

[54] *JW*, p. 85.

meaning of decision. It does not, of course, mean that man lacks insight into the empirical possibilities of his conduct or its consequences as empirical processes. Decision is not dice-throwing; its character becomes plainer, the more clearly the empirical possibilities are understood. Decision means that the choice between the possibilities is not determined by insight into them but is free and responsible. Anyone who sees man in the crisis of decision and recognizes this as the essential of human existence, assumes that man knows what is good and evil *now;* as has already been said, he knows, not on the basis of any past experience or rational deductions, but directly from the immediate situation.[55]

When Bultmann says that "decision is not dice-throwing," he seems to mean that it does matter in *some* sense which of the concrete possibilities is chosen in the decision. But when he says that "decision means that the choice between the possibilities is not determined by insight into them but is free and responsible," he seems to be saying that the choice's being authentic depends on its *not* being made on the basis of an assessment of the possibilities. Only if "all observation is excluded," along with "any past experience or rational deductions," is the choice free, and thus responsible. So *what* is decided would seem to be ultimately irrelevant to whether the decision is a responsible and right decision. The "what," the actual empirical possibility which gets chosen, is only an *occasion* for the making of the decision to be one's true self, namely a maker of decision in radical independence of the empirical world, as well as of the 'world' of ethical norms. This seems to be Bultmann's meaning when he says, "the distinction between right and wrong decision is identical with that between nature and decision."[56] The "right" decision is simply the only one which is *real* decision, the one in which one chooses oneself as decision-maker and thus distinguishes oneself from all that is not potentiality (nature). Ethical principles contravene this pure "how" by prescribing a more or less specific "what," and misguide the individual to choose this or that possibility rather than himself as possibility-as-such.

---

[55] *JW,* p. 88.
[56] *KM,* p. 121.

IV. 'World' as the past

Another aspect of Bultmann's division of reality is the dichotomy between existential and worldly time. The kind of temporality which characterizes nature, as well as history in the sense of an objectively observable sequence of causally connected events, and the psychological development of human personality, is a time in which past, present, and future can be represented as a sequential continuum. In this kind of time there is development (change through time) and stability (sameness through time). Therefore for something to be *in* this kind of time, it must be something determinate and characterizable; it must be *something* which either does or does not develop through time. For example, a forest, or a psychological personality, or a political system, has enough describable determinacy to be characterizable with respect to *its* past, *its* present, and *its* future; consequently these are worldly phenomena. But existence is not on such a continuum. It is neither static, nor does it develop. The past is not its whence, and the future (as something which may *actually* come about) is not its whither. Consequently its present is not *between* its past and future, as nature's is, but is rather the 'moment' which is the whole of its reality:

> On each several occasion existence is mine and can only be taken over or achieved by me; that means: existence is on each several occasion *event* in the decisions of the moment. It is not to hand, but is something which happens on each several occasion.[57]

What has to happen on each several occasion is a decision in which the past is denied to be constitutive of the individual's authentic nature and the future denied to be anything into which the self might develop. But it is clear that this denial of worldly time's past and future is at the same time a denial of being in the present, since in worldly time the present is what it is with respect to something's past and future. As Bultmann says, "what we never are here and now—precisely that is our true being."[58] Thus worldly time even as present is denied, and existence is

---

[57] *GV*, III, p. 117.
[58] *EF*, p. 281.

collapsed into the 'moment' of decision. The past as a whole becomes decision-fodder as what is rejected in the decision, and the future becomes the emptiness into which the existence, now radically insecure from having cut itself off from every mooring in the past, plunges. The moment is thus a dynamic moment by virtue of the decision in which the self kicks away its past and hurls itself into the dark void.

Something which is in worldly time is in it simply by having actuality, by being at all. Worldly time comes automatically, as it were. But since existence's most fundamental characteristic is that of potentiality, nothing which is authentic to it comes automatically with being; a man has to *become* his authenticity. And so it is with authentic time (what Bultmann calls man's "historicity"): a man *is* not in existential time, but rather *becomes* temporal in the moment of decision. If we conceive worldly time as moving in the manner of a river which flows regardless of what man does, carrying his little boat along as he progresses towards death, existential time is dynamic in quite a different way. Here the "movement" occurs only in the act of decision, and not at all apart from such a moment. Here the movement from the past through the present into the future occurs only as man kicks off from the security of his little boat and plunges into the deep where all external orientation is foregone, and he floats in the turbid darkness of his radical freedom. The kicking away from the past and the plunging into the future conceived as total unsupporting openness *is* the movement of existential time.

This achievement is identical with the abandonment of worldly time. This means that past events, even those which have been traditionally thought of as religiously significant, must be categorized as 'world':

> [Jesus'] coming is not understood when it is critically attested and a 'position' taken in regard to it. Then it would be seen as an object, understood as 'world' instead of as an eschatological event. A reconstructed 'life of Jesus' is 'world'. As the fact, 'Jesus', which is universally demonstrable, Jesus is made into world. But the living Jesus—that is, Jesus as eschatological fact—is not visible at all to the world.[59]

---

[59] *FU,* p. 177.

As we will see in chapter three, the Jesus who is the eschatological fact escapes being world by not being an event of the past *at
all,* but by becoming identical with the word of the kerygma
which, when rightly heard, is also not in the worldly time continuum, but in the moment. How thoroughly dichotomous Bultmann's division of reality is becomes clear in his inability to see
how any succession of events in time could have significance for
persons. Oscar Cullmann, in his *Christ and Time,* describes the
New Testament view of salvation-history as being essentially
the history of the world, divided into two large parts, that preceding and that succeeding the life, death and resurrection of
Jesus of Nazareth. In a review of Cullmann's book Bultmann
finds this conception highly confusing, and says,

> It seems, at least, that history for the author is nothing other
> than the succession of events in time (and, naturally, also in
> space); thus not even once is there a distinction made between
> truly historical processes and events of nature.[60]

If we give our imagination a little rein, we can perhaps hear
Cullmann responding: "It is not I, but Bultmann, who does not
know the difference between historical processes and events of
nature. For it is he who seems to want to assimilate the life,
death, and resurrection of Jesus to events such as the digestive
processes of a cow. These latter may come close to being 'nothing other than the succession of events in time,' but the history
of Jesus our Lord, simply by being something of the past, is
not so limited. Is it not precisely as something of the past, as
something that happened, that it has for us the existential significance that it has?" But, alas, such a response from Cullmann
would only betray his failure to think through radically man's nature as a decision-maker. For to see in a thorough-going manner
that man is potentiality is to see that *everything* which is actual,
which can be characterized as belonging to the sequence of the
time-continuum, is alien to his true being. Indeed it is to see that
the life, death, and resurrection of Jesus, *as past events,* are precisely as alien to his true nature as the digestive processes of a
cow. The relation between existential and worldly time is a dichotomous one: becoming authentically temporal involves un-

---

[60] *EF,* p. 232.

derstanding oneself as not temporal in the worldly sense. It is to understand oneself as radically unidentifiable in terms of what has happened and what may happen, as alien to all such.[61]

But the form of the past perhaps most likely to drown man's true life in the alien being of the "world" is his own past, what he has *done*.[62] What is alien about the past is that it is something effected, accomplished, established, attained, whereas our true being is to be never what we already are:

> But since our action always does produce some effect, it carries within it the hidden temptation to estimate ourselves from what has been done and to attach ourselves to what has been done. In fact we are continually yielding to this temptation and so lapsing into the past—what is done is always past. When we estimate ourselves really from what is accomplished, though the accomplishment may be in the future, even our future action is already past, branded by sin and death. It confronts us actually as a work, as an established, attained position.[63]

The contrast with this living in the alien reality of the already established is the moment of decision in which we kick off the already-is and dive into the never-to-be of the beyond which alone is our truth:

> God's Beyond and the Beyond of my real 'I' belong together. For humanism God's Beyond is spirit of which man with his spirit partakes. Man can give form to that spirit in the direction which his life takes and in the creation of culture. For the Christian understanding, God is always the hidden one and the coming one. God's Beyond is his constant futurity, his constant being-out-before. With this transcendent God man has communion only in openness to the future, which is not at man's disposal or under his control. He has communion only in readiness to enter the darkness of the future hopefully and confidently, as Luther often has said. This readiness to enter the darkness of the future confidently is nothing else but readiness for my transcendent self which stands before me.[64]

---

[61] Though one does not *belong* to the sequential continuum, it goes without saying that one continues, "dialectically" of course, to live in it.

[62] *Essays,* p. 81.

[63] *FU,* p. 256.

[64] *Journal of Religion,* 1952, p. 83.

It is important to note that when Bultmann speaks of authentic decision as openness to the future, he is not using the word *future* in quite the ordinary way. This is why he often specifies it more carefully, calling it "God's future." The reason the future can stand in such absolute opposition to man's inauthentic life in his past, is that Bultmann thinks of the future as radically indeterminate, unknowable, and uncontrollable. Now, although we cannot know or control our ordinary future with the same certainty as the past, it nevertheless remains true that we have considerable knowledge of it and control over it. So Bultmann's future is an idealized future of which *nothing* can be known, and over which we can have *no* control. It is a future which is "darkness," a future which never comes: it is a *constant* futurity, a *constant* being-out-before. This is why, answering the question why men flee from authentic life, Bultmann can say that man "cannot bear to look into the *void*."[65] The Kingdom which is always "coming" but never comes is a void darkness likened to death:

> . . . the Kingdom of God and death are alike in this—that both the Kingdom and death imply the end of earthly existence as we know it, with its possibilities and interests.[66]

It is not difficult to see why the future, in order to be man's authentic temporal mode, has to be empty: if his being is potentiality, then any actualization would be a violation of his reality. A future which *came,* which got accomplished, effected, established, would be the death of him as possibility. It would be a violation of his freedom, of his being-in-decision, his responsibility. This is, in the last analysis, why Bultmann rejects an actualizing consummation:

> The crux of the matter is the extent to which man is conscious of his responsibility in his decisions, or the extent to which he pushes off responsibility on historical or natural conditions. His responsibility is always responsibility for the world and its future, as Gogarten has so often stressed. A cosmological escha-

---

[65] *Essays,* p. 81 (my emphasis).
[66] *Ibid.,* p. 54.

tology would reduce this responsibility; indeed, it would permit such responsibility to vanish entirely.[67]

V. 'World' as personality

Our ordinary thought and speaking about persons provide various ways of answering the question "Who is so-and-so?" One of the most important of these is reference to "personality." By personality we mean the more or less stable dispositions which serve to explain a person's behavior in any given instance. This is one of the ways we distinguish one person from another, and thus can treat people as individuals. Personality traits are such things as habits ("characteristic" ways of behaving), perceptual dispositions, personal abilities which result from training and nurture, traits of moral character such as are named with virtue- and vice-words, confirmed emotions, the kind of wisdom and understanding which are the fruit of years and struggles and experiences of life. As identifiable by personality traits, we think of a person as persisting, as developing or failing to develop.

It will be obvious by now why this everyday feature of our concept of person will have to fall on the world side of Bultmann's dichotomy. For to think of man as persisting is to see him not as having the totality of his temporality in the decisive plunges of the moment, but as floating along on the continuum of worldly time. It is to think of him not as radical potentiality, but as at least partly done, accomplished, effected, already here. It is to think of him not as radically different from everything in his past, but as being constituted as a self partly in continuity with it. It is to transgress his being as complete insecurity, for to have a personality is to have at least the security of knowing who one is.

"Jesus," according to Bultmann, "is not interested in character building, personality values, and the like."[68]

> The view of Jesus as a great character or a hero is simply the opposite of Jesus' conception of man; for man as a 'character' has his centre in himself, and the hero relies on himself; in this

---

[67] *The Theology of Rudolf Bultmann,* ed. Charles W. Kegley (New York: Harper & Row, 1966), p. 267.

[68] *JW,* p. 105.

the greatness of the man consists; this is the aesthetic point of
view. Jesus however sees man in his relation to God, under
the claim of God.[69]

To see a man in his relation to God is not to see him as a 'character.' But what if it is a man's character to love God? What if,
after many years, the love of God has become such an abiding
disposition of his heart, that it structures his very character?
Does it *then* mean that he "has his centre in himself"? Would
not such love as a quality of his personality precisely mean
that he has his center not in himself, but in God? But thinking
in this way is, as so often, to have forgotten Bultmann's radical
conception of the self as potentiality. For a self to have its being
in something which is continuous through time, such as a quality, is a transgression of the self's true nature, of its freedom,
even if that quality is a love for God. As Bultmann says,

> The Christian view of freedom indicates that freedom, as free-
> dom of the individual, is not a *quality*, but can only be an *event*
> at any given time.[70]

A disposition, as such, remains with a person and can be thought
of as a possession; but if man's action is to be free and authentic, it must be cut off from any such remnant of it which might
be thought of as belonging to the person. Action must be *pure*
action, must have an "absolute character":

> The demand for asceticism really rests on the assumption that
> man through his behavior can attain a certain ideal or saintly
> quality which remains with him as a possession. The emphasis
> shifts accordingly from the behavior, the action, to that which is
> achieved thereby. Action loses its absolute character as the mo-
> ment of decision, when subordinated to the view-point of the
> end, the ideal.[71]

The picture which Bultmann here paints for us is that of someone setting out deliberately to attain for himself a "saintly quality which remains with him as a possession." So he calculates

---

[69] *JW*, p. 216.
[70] *Essays*, p. 310.
[71] *JW*, pp. 100f.

his actions with this end in mind: when he helps the widow, or gives his last penny to the poor, or remains steadfast with a friend through a time of trouble, he does so with a view to how holy he is going to become, to what lovely qualities his soul will take on. And he looks forward to the fruits of his sacrifice as to a kind of treasure in whose possession he can find security. The picture is clearly one of piety gone awry. But surely not everyone who develops holy dispositions by the way he has comported himself in the past takes such a distorted view of them; surely *really* to have the qualities of soul called holiness is to be self-forgetful, to take no pride in one's dispositions or actions, but to think only of the other's good. But holiness (Christian freedom) is surely no less dispositional for that. The difference between it and that false piety which Bultmann pictures for us is surely not that it is not dispositional at all while the false piety is, but rather that it and false piety are *different* dispositions. Or to put it another way, the reason that we cannot understand ourselves as holy on the basis of our dispositions is not that they are our *dispositions,* but that they are in fact not holy. It is not a logical question (a question of action versus disposition) but a question to be answered with an "empirical" judgment (whether the action or disposition is in *fact* holy, judged against Christian criteria).

But if Bultmann's view that faith is not a quality of personality at all, but logically *must* be absolute act in the moment, remains paradoxical to us and presses from us the kind of protest to which I've just given expression, it is because we have not yet learned to think of man strictly as potentiality. If we learn to do so, we see that any quality of the soul, any persistent trait of personality, is in radical antithesis to existence, regardless of how saintly it may be. He who understands himself in terms of his character never finds his real self:

> For Christian thought the *essential nature of the self* is not the mind in the Greek sense—rational self-possessed thoughts—but the self understood as the 'I' existing in history; that is, man is understood as a being who becomes himself in his concrete decisions in relation to what at any given time confronts him, whether other men or fate. In these decisions he *develops;* he gains his character. But for this very reason, his way is pointed out as that of the man who is already conditioned by his pre-

vious decisions. To this extent he is not really free, but tied to his past. Hence he never finds his real self.[72]

To be conditioned by one's previous decisions *via* the character which emerges as their consequence is in antithesis to human freedom, and this not just because the decisions of the past were evil, but simply because, as character, they have now ceased to be *decision,* pure openness; they are, rather, now something actual, something *done.* That the antithesis between human freedom and character is for Bultmann a logical one, rather than one based on the goodness or badness of the character in question, is clear from the fact that even authentic decision cannot build a character which is the true self:

> However, even though in decision he has become a new man, has gained his real self, he does not hold on to it as to something he owns. Forthwith it stands once more before him, transcendent and future. The progression and sum of the moments of decision can, when seen from an objectivizing point of view, be understood as character development. From the point of view of faith, however, the moments cannot be understood as a nexus of development or progress, for the reason that each new moment puts me into question, demands of me a decision. The adjective 'Christian' can never qualify the substantive character. Only the decision of each new moment can be called 'Christian'. Each encounter of each moment intends to renew me, to free me from myself as I have come out of my past to each moment. There is here no continuous security whatsoever. I can never look back on what I have attained and claim my faith as a possession. Never can I state my act of decision as a Christian piece of work. Decision cannot be objectivized as a piece of work definable as Christian. For it is not the timeless eternity of the idea which determines the moment but the encounter which approaches me. As an eternal future God's eternity robs man of every lasting condition, of every security of possession, of every security of what he has become.[73]

Even the character which results from the authentic decision becomes, in the next moment, world; it becomes something of the sort that can be seen from an objectivizing point of view, some-

---

[72] *Essays,* p. 309.
[73] *Journal of Religion,* 1952, p. 84.

thing of the sort that can be possessed. Even the true self achieved in the moment of decision must, in the next moment, be denied to be my real self. The authentic self has absolutely *no* continuity whatsoever, for it constitutes itself anew in each moment precisely as the denial that anything continuous can constitute it. Its *total* being consists in its decisive momentary dying away from anything that might identify it and thus make it "substantive." This dying away from the substantive *is* the self, for all else, all that is not this pure act, is inauthentic. All else—and that means all personality, all that is actual and continuous about my life, anything about myself that I could objectify in memory—is that alien kind of being called 'world'.

We have now examined in five of its salient aspects the dichotomy which informs and unifies Bultmann's theology. Our next question must be, "What is the relation between this dichotomy and the New Testament?" Is it to be found in the New Testament? If not, is it at least consistent with it? Let us now turn to a consideration of these questions.

2

Existence, World, and the New Testament

In what follows I am not trying to say, at least in anything like a complete way, what the New Testament "means." I am not writing a short theology of the New Testament.

I shall follow two "hermeneutical principles." First, I come to the text with a very specific question: Does the thought of the New Testament writers exclude the things which Bultmann's dichotomy excludes? And second, in asking this question, I will assume that the authors are, in the broad features of their thought, self-consistent. Thus if we find a more or less pervasive element in an author's thought, we can, on this assumption, treat it as not excluded by his more general way of thinking, but rather as capable of integration into the latter. For example, if John repeatedly pictures people as coming to belief in Jesus on the basis of "signs," my assumption warrants the conclusion that John was not just making a stupid mistake, but that his *thought* allowed a grounding of belief on the basis of signs.

I am not assuming the "unity of the New Testament." If my argument is successful, however, I will have shown a certain purely negative unity in it: all the major authors do not exclude the kinds of things the existence/world dichotomy excludes: they all stand in contradiction to Bultmann's fundamental idea. On this they all agree. I here leave open the question whether they agree on anything else.

I. Assurance

In the foregoing chapter I have tried, though sometimes with difficulty, to let my thinking be guided by Bultmann's notion of man's authentic being as potentiality to be and of its radical opposition to the being of the world. But now we must take leave of this guide so as to look independently at the New Testament. Does it also see man radically as a decision-maker, to whose true being all security is a mortal threat? Do the biblical authors see faith as a venturing into utter darkness, as being left totally alone and without orientation as in an empty room, as casting oneself into the void? Do they guard as carefully against all assurances of the truth of Christian faith as would be demanded by the existence/world dichotomy? Do they treat faith as something by nature opposed to all argument and proof, as a decision from which we fall away *ipso facto* when we seek reassurance? Or are they also, on occasion, interested in providing believers with a certain security and assurance that their belief is not in vain?

A variety of assurances of the truth and appropriateness of faith are offered in the New Testament, and they appear in all the major authors. The security of faith which is offered is not absolute either in the sense of covering all possible doubts, or in the sense of making some particular doubt completely impossible. The assurances which these authors hold out to believers are *ad hoc,* directed toward particular kinds of doubt, and aim not at Cartesian certainty but only at enough certainty to make *belief* possible. Let us now look at some of the types of assurance which the New Testament authors think appropriate to Christian faith.[1]

First, there are the authors' uses of what we may call, somewhat loosely, "historical" assurances. In the prologue to the Gospel of Luke the author declares the purpose of his writing to be that his reader "may know the truth concerning the things of which you have been informed," and stresses the reliability of his account of these things by claiming to have been informed

---

[1] I will not here be concerned with whether the assurance offered is historically and logically acceptable as assurance for *us,* but only with whether the view of faith includes the possibility and propriety of such assurances.

"by those who from the beginning were eyewitnesses and ministers of the word" and himself to have "followed all things closely for some time past" (cf. Luke 1:1–4). He is also careful to establish the dates of the birth of Jesus (2:1ff.) and the commencement of the gospel story with the activity of John the Baptist (3:1ff.) by reference to the reign of secular rulers.[2] It is difficult to see why Luke would be so solicitous about these things if he thought the object of Christian faith not the sort of thing for which assurances of a historical kind were in principle appropriate. The same author reports that the resurrected Jesus reassured his doubting disciples by presenting them what we could call empirical evidence:

> "Why are you troubled, and why do questionings rise in your hearts? See my hands and my feet, that it is I myself; handle me, and see; for a spirit has not flesh and bones as you see that I have." (Luke 24:38–40)

In another writing the same author says,

> To them he presented himself alive after his passion by many proofs,[3] appearing to them during forty days, and speaking of the kingdom of God. (Acts 1:3)

Reconstructing a speech of Peter's, Luke has Peter say, in the middle of a summary of the events of Jesus' life,

> And we are witnesses to all that he did both in the country of the Jews and in Jerusalem. (Acts 10:39)

---

[2] Bultmann comments on these passages: "Luke betrays the effort to write as a historian and to find points of contact for his narrative in various world-historical dates. Yet this is not really based upon a genuine historical interest, but is only the endeavor to bring home to educated Gentiles the universal significance of the gospel story" (FC, p. 70). The disjunction, typical of Bultmann, is sophistical: there is no reason why Luke should not have *both* a genuine historical interest and a concern to highlight the gospel's universal significance. An historical interest can be genuine without being motivated by the mere technical curiosity characteristic of some modern historians.

[3] The Bauer-Arndt-Gingrich *Lexicon* gives the meaning of *tekmerion* as "convincing, decisive *proof*," and suggests that *en pollois tekmeriois* should be translated as "by many convincing proofs."

A similar kind of evidence is proffered by the author of the Gospel of John, in relating the story of Jesus' death. The soldiers, finding that Jesus was already dead, did not break his legs, but pierced his side with a spear, whereupon blood and water flowed forth. Then the author says, "He who saw it has borne witness — his testimony is true, and he knows that he tells the truth—that you also may believe" (10:35).[4] Although John has reservations about Thomas' need for empirical evidence by which to buttress his faith in Jesus, he nevertheless accepts Thomas' faith, so buttressed, as true faith in Jesus:

> Then he said to Thomas, "Put your finger here, and see my hands; and put out your hand, and place it in my side; do not be faithless but believing." Thomas answered him, "My Lord and my God!" Jesus said to him, "Have you believed because you have seen me? Blessed are those who have not seen and yet believe." (20:27–29)[5]

These passages would seem to indicate that a view of faith which makes it radically insecure and unsusceptible of any assurance is contrary to the thinking of John's Gospel.

To some who are wavering in their belief that they will be raised from the dead, the Apostle Paul argues that if there is no resurrection of the dead, then Christ was not raised; but on the contrary Christ has been raised, and there is good reason to believe it:

---

[4] Bultmann does not deny that this claim of an eye-witness' testimony intends to buttress the gospel reader's faith; however, he holds the verse not to be from the evangelist's pen, but from that of a later redactor (cf. *GJC*, pp. 678f.).

[5] Bultmann agrees with this interpretation: "The answer of Jesus by all means confirms that in the statement of Thomas faith speaks" (*GJC*, p. 695). But he holds that John's real view is that a miracle is always "a concession to the weakness of man," who, because of the nature of faith, fundamentally "ought not to need it" (*ibid.*, p. 696; cf. p. 233). It is worth noting that this view, which he utters under the watchful eye of the text, is considerably weaker than the one to which he gives expression when thinking on his own. Indeed, it is remarkable how often his interpretation of a text, under the pressure of the demands of exegesis, will come very close to our own rather ordinary reading. These two Bultmanns have led many a critic on a merry chase!

> For I delivered to you as of first importance what I also re-
> ceived, that Christ died for our sins in accordance with the
> scriptures, that he was buried, that he was raised on the third
> day in accordance with the scriptures, and that he appeared to
> Cephas, then to the twelve. Then he appeared to more than five
> hundred brethren at one time, most of whom are still alive,
> though some have fallen asleep. Then he appeared to James,
> then to all the apostles. Last of all, as to one untimely born,
> he appeared also to me. (I Cor. 15:3–8)[6]

Another objective ground for belief assumed throughout
the New Testament to be appropriate is miracles associated with
Jesus, either as performed by him, or in his name by his disciples. In addition appeal is often made to the central miracle
of the New Testament, the resurrection of Jesus himself from
the dead.

Matthew and Luke record the story of John the Baptist's
query regarding Jesus' identity. Jesus answers by directing John's
disciples' attention to the extraordinary things to be heard and
seen in association with Jesus' ministry:

> Now when John heard in prison about the deeds of the Christ,
> he sent word by his disciples and said to him: "Are you he who
> is to come, or shall we look for another?" And Jesus answered
> them, "Go and tell John what you hear and see: the blind re-
> ceive their sight and the lame walk, lepers are cleansed and
> the deaf hear, and the dead are raised up, and the poor have
> good news preached to them. And blessed is he who takes no
> offense at me." (Matt. 11:2–6)[7]

The most natural reading of all our Gospels is surely to look at
them as telling a story the elements of which accumulate to

---

[6] Bultmann acknowledges that this passage proposes a kind of historical assurance for belief. In a dispute with Karl Barth he says, "I can
understand the text only as an attempt to make the resurrection of Christ
credible as an objective historical fact." But instead of drawing the
obvious conclusion, namely that Paul's view of faith contradicts Bultmann's, he concludes that Paul is contradicting himself! (*FU*, p. 83).

[7] On the assumption that reference to Jesus' miracles implies churchly
literary creation, Bultmann considers the Baptist's question to be a "community product," and the use of Isaiah to be part of Christian polemic
against the disciples of the Baptist, who denied the Messianic character
of Jesus' miracles (*HST*, pp. 23f.).

answer the central question: Who is Jesus? As in any other
story through which an individual is identified, Jesus' identity
here emerges and is established through what he does and says
and undergoes. In all the Gospels his miracles are treated as
signs of his identity; but in John the connection between his
miracles and his identity as the Messiah becomes an explicit
theme. After the first miracle recorded in John's Gospel the
author says,

> This, the first of his signs, Jesus did at Cana in Galilee, and
> manifested his glory; and his disciples believed in him. (2:11)

The healing of the son of the official at Capernaum has the
same effect: when the man pleads with Jesus to heal his son,
Jesus replies, "Unless you see signs and wonders you will not
believe" (4:48). Then Jesus sends the man home, with the
assurance that his son will live. Finding his son well, he asks
the servants what time it was when he began to mend. The
servants tell him it was the seventh hour, and John remarks:

> The father knew that was the hour when Jesus had said to him,
> "Your son will live"; and he himself believed, and all his house-
> hold. (4:53)

After recounting the story of the feeding of the five thousand,
John comments:

> When the people saw the sign which he had done, they said,
> "This is indeed the prophet who is to come into the world!"
> (6:14)

After the raising of Lazarus, John reports that

> many of the Jews therefore, who had come with Mary and had
> seen what he did, believed in him; but some of them went to
> the Pharisees and told them what Jesus had done. (11:45)

John also attributes to Jesus these words:

> If I am not doing the works of my Father, then do not believe
> me; but if I do them, even though you do not believe me,
> believe the works, that you may know and understand that the
> Father is in me and I am in the Father. (10:37–38)

Whether the reference here is to miracles or non-miraculous deeds, it is clear that deeds performed by Jesus and observable by men are considered capable of being the basis for a belief in his identity. At the end of his Gospel, John makes a general comment about the deeds of Jesus he has reported and the faith of those to whom he has addressed himself:

> Now Jesus did many other signs in the presence of the disciples, which are not written in this book; but these are written that you may believe that Jesus is the Christ, the Son of God, and that believing you may have life in his name. (20:30–31)

John does not, of course, think that all belief on the basis of miracles is true belief, the kind in which the believer has "life."

> Now when he was in Jerusalem at the Passover feast, many believed in his name when they saw the signs which he did; but Jesus did not trust himself to them, because he knew all men and needed no one to bear witness of man; for he himself knew what was in man. (John 2:23–25)

But in light of all the passages from John in which he presents an authentic belief undergirded by signs, it is clear that the deficiency of such belief as the above is not that it takes security in the miracle; but rather that it fails, one way or another, really to acknowledge who Jesus is.[8] Instead of worshiping him and trusting him for eternal life, it perhaps makes him an object of idle curiosity, or seeks to turn him into a revolutionary king (6:15). On the other hand, *some* assurance that he is who he claims to be seems to be not only appropriate, but indispensable to faith.

The author of Acts seems to affirm a similar view of the relation of Jesus' miracles to his identity, for he records that in calling for belief Peter spoke, in his sermon on Pentecost, of

> Jesus of Nazareth, a man attested to you by God with mighty

---

[8] Bultmann does not, in his comment on this passage, dispute this interpretation. After saying that true faith should not have to rely on miracles, he continues, "This is not, of course, to say that faith aroused by miracles is false, but that such faith is only the first step towards Jesus; it has not yet seen him in his true significance, and is therefore not yet fully established" (*GJC,* p. 131).

> works and wonders and signs which God did through him in
> your midst, as you yourselves know. . . . (Acts 2:22)

But in that author's view it was not only the miracles of Jesus
himself which attested to him; also the miracles of his disciples
might be a basis for belief in him. Speaking of Peter's raising
Tabitha from the dead, he says, "And it became known throughout all Joppa, and many believed in the Lord" (9:42). He also
tells the story of the proconsul of Salamis, whose magician
sought to turn him away from the faith. Through Paul the hand
of the Lord made the magician blind for a time, and Luke says,
"Then the proconsul believed, when he saw what had occurred,
for he was astonished at the teaching of the Lord" (13:12).

All four evangelists treat the miracles of Jesus as signs of
his identity. But if they treat the miracles as signs, then these
authors must not think them wholly ambiguous; but if they are
not wholly ambiguous, then the miracles are being treated as
the sort of thing which is capable of being a source of assurance
that Jesus is the Messiah. Taken in isolation from other aspects
of Jesus' story (and thus from other aspects of his character)
such as his teaching, his treatment of the downcast, his death
and resurrection, the miracles would, of course, be ambiguous.
Not just anyone healing a paralytic, much less changing water
into wine, is thereby manifested as the Son of God. But the
miracles lose their ambiguity as signs as they are kept in close
connection with such other elements in the story as Jesus'
teaching with authority, forgiving men's sins as God, and showing his extraordinary mercy towards sinners and outcasts.

The New Testament writers also refer to the resurrection
of Jesus as a source of assurance for faith. In Luke's account of
Paul's preaching in Athens he has Paul saying,

> The times of ignorance God overlooked, but now he commands
> all men everywhere to repent, because he has fixed a day on
> which he will judge the world in righteousness by a man whom
> he has appointed, and of this he has given assurance to all men
> by raising him from the dead. (Acts 17:30–31)

Paul uses a similar appeal to assure those who grieve as men
without hope:

> For since we believe that Jesus died and rose again, even so,

through Jesus, God will bring with him those who have fallen asleep. (I Thess. 4:14)

He also indicates that it is part of the logic of Christian faith that amid persecution (perhaps even unto death), the believer takes courage in remembering the resurrection of Jesus:

> We are afflicted in every way, but not crushed; perplexed, but not driven to despair; persecuted, but not forsaken; struck down, but not destroyed; always carrying in the body the death of Jesus, so that the life of Jesus may also be manifested in our bodies. . . . Since we have the same spirit of faith as he had who wrote, "I believed, and so I spoke," we too believe, and so we speak, knowing that he who raised the Lord Jesus will raise us also with Jesus and bring us with you into his presence. . . . So we do not lose heart. (II Cor. 4:8-16)

The authors of the New Testament also seek to effect conviction of the truth of Christianity in either non-Christians or wavering Christians by the use of *arguments*. The author of Acts sometimes uses verbs like *argue, prove,* and *persuade* to describe the activity of Paul in his missionary work. Describing Paul's work in the synagogue at Thessalonica, he says,

> And Paul went in, as was his custom, and for three weeks he argued with them from the scriptures, explaining and proving that it was necessary for the Christ to suffer and to rise from the dead, and saying, "This Jesus, whom I proclaim to you, is the Christ." And some of them were persuaded. . . . (Acts 17:2-4)

Such would also be an accurate characterization of Paul's speech in the synagogue at Antioch of Pisidia in Acts 13:16-41. We have an extended example of this kind of argument in the Epistle to the Hebrews, which is an elaborate proof of the pre-eminence of Christianity over Judaism with the purpose of reassuring Jewish Christians who were on the verge of giving up Christian faith and returning to Judaism (cf. Heb. 10:32-39). In all four of the Gospels arguments both explicit and implicit are made to establish the identity of Jesus as Messiah by showing him to be the fulfillment of Scripture, though it is in John that this becomes something like a theme (cf. 2:22; 7:38; 12:37-41; 13:18; 15:25; 17:12; 19:24, 28, 36-37; 20:9).

Another kind of assurance which the New Testament finds appropriate to faith is provided by what we might call "teachings." As a type of this we might take the little remark made in the sixth chapter of Mark's Gospel:

> As he landed he saw a great throng, and he had compassion on them, because they were like sheep without a shepherd; and he began to teach them many things. (6:34)

This is hardly the picture of people being saved by a decision in which all security of orientation is cast away and the individual floats upon the void of pure possibility. For those who may waver in the faith because of suffering, Paul offers the assurance of God's sovereignty and the goodness of his predestinating will:

> We know that in everything God works for good with those who love him, who are called according to his purpose. For those whom he foreknew he also predestined to be conformed to the image of his Son, in order that he might be the first-born among many brethren. And those whom he predestined he also called; and those whom he called he also justified; and those whom he justified he also glorified.
>
> What then shall we say to this? If God is for us, who is against us? He who did not spare his own Son but gave him up for us all, will he not also give us all things with him? Who shall bring any charge against God's elect? It is God who justifies; who is to condemn? Is it Christ Jesus, who died, yes, who was raised from the dead, who is at the right hand of God, who indeed intercedes for us? Who shall separate us from the love of Christ? Shall tribulation, or distress, or persecution, or famine, or nakedness, or peril, or sword? (Rom. 8:28–35)

The purpose of such teaching as this is clearly to give orientation to those who may be disoriented by tribulation and difficulty. It aims to give us a certain "distance" on our immediate situation, and it does this by giving us something like a *Weltanschauung* (though certainly not a very complete or systematic one), a larger picture of the economy of God's universe which orients us by showing us where we fit. Our immediate circumstances may look quite desperate, but Paul's picture offers us objectivity about ourselves and the world, by showing us how these fit together. It is perhaps of a function something like this that Paul speaks when later in the letter he says that the Scriptures give us "encouragement":

> For whatever was written in former days was written for our instruction, that by steadfastness and by the encouragement of the scriptures we might have hope. (Rom. 15:4)

After the discourses of the fourteenth and fifteenth chapters of his Gospel, the fourth evangelist remarks, by the mouth of Jesus, on the purpose of their teachings: "I have said all this to you to keep you from falling away" (16:1). Bultmann's picture of salvation as radical insecurity makes a neat contrast with the "refuge" and "strong encouragement" and "sure and steadfast anchor of the soul" of which the author of the Epistle to the Hebrews aims to make his readers aware by his teaching:

> Men indeed swear by a greater than themselves, and in all their disputes an oath is final for confirmation. So when God desired to show more convincingly to the heirs of the promise the unchangeable character of his purpose, he interposed with an oath, so that through two unchangeable things, in which it is impossible that God should prove false, we who have fled for refuge might have strong encouragement to seize the hope set before us. We have this as a sure and steadfast anchor of the soul, a hope that enters into the inner shrine behind the curtain, where Jesus has gone as a forerunner on our behalf, having become a high priest forever after the order of Melchizedek. (Heb. 6:16–20)

And of course, what makes these teachings capable of steadying a person's faith and hope in God is precisely that they can be *learned*, and in that sense possessed by the individual; they become a part of his personality and outlook in such a way that they equip him for life. But that is no more than to say that they are really *teachings*, and not merely a dispensable linguistic occasion for an act of faith, or an expression of such an act.

We have discerned in the New Testament four kinds of assurance (on the basis of history, miracle, arguments, and teachings) all of which are integral to its view of faith and contradictory of Bultmann's concept of human authenticity. So far, it looks as though the picture of the Christian life in the New Testament is, in Bultmann's terms, hopelessly "worldly."

II. Ethical principles

Does the New Testament regard fixed ethical principles as a threat to true human responsibility? Does it deny all principles (that is, descriptions of determinate, conceptualizable modes of behavior) to be capable of constituting the authentic human existence?

From beginning to end the New Testament is packed with teachings, more or less specific, about how people should and should not behave; and they look like learnable guidance and orientation for comportment in life. But Paul and Jesus were both, on occasion, willing to summarize the whole of ethical teaching in one or two commandments. Matthew records:

> And one of them, a lawyer, asked him a question, to test him. "Teacher, which is the great commandment of the law?" And he said to him, "You shall love the Lord your God with all your heart, and with all your soul, and with all your mind. This is the great and first commandment. And a second is like it, You shall love your neighbor as yourself." (22:35-40)

And Paul says,

> The commandments, "You shall not commit adultery, You shall not kill, You shall not steal, You shall not covet," are summed up in this sentence, "You shall love your neighbor as yourself." (Rom. 13:8)

Is it the purpose of these summaries to say that the specific commandments which they summarize are merely ambiguous expressions, that what they actually prescribe is no longer to be taken as a content actually commanded? Do the summaries serve to radicalize the law so as to leave the individual totally without orientation or guidance about what to do, casting him back upon himself as radical decision-maker?

The very fact that the New Testament is so full of specific ethical teachings seems to contradict such a suggestion. Jesus not only summarizes the law, he also expands and specifies it. Such would seem to be the clear purpose of much of the Sermon on the Mount, as well as of a large portion of the rest of Jesus' teaching. Jesus' demand upon his disciples is not a mere demand for obedience, without any explanation of what obedience consists in. His ethical teachings about treatment of the brother (Matt. 5:21ff.), about sex (5:27ff.), about oathmaking (5:33ff.), about vengeance (5:38ff.), about the practice of piety (6:1ff.), and so on, are surely designed to give us a conceptual grasp of the *logic* of that law. That the general law has a logic at all means that it is not completely ambiguous, that it excludes certain kinds of things and demands certain kinds of things, in principle. And the person who *knows* the logic of the law consequently possesses a guide for his conduct. Does Jesus find it contrary to faith's openness and freedom for a man to go into a situation armed with the principle "You shall not commit adultery"? Does he demand that I be completely open, open to *every* possibility, and thus also to the possibility of adultery? To ask such a question is to have answered it. To be faithful would seem to require *closedness* to certain possibilities.

Neither does Paul's summarizing of the law intend to render the law ambiguous, thus guarding man against the security of a possessable prescription and freeing him for total "responsibility." Paul seems to think it quite unambiguously wrong for a man to be living with his father's wife (I Cor. 5:1f.). He is similarly unopen about the possibilities of greed and idolatry, of being a reviler, a drunkard, or a robber (5:11). He takes it as a command from the Lord that married people should not divorce (7:10ff.). He is quite willing to give a fuller description of love than merely to affirm that it is commanded (cf. I Cor. 13:4–7).[9]Thus whatever Christ's being the end of the law may

---

[9] Saying that faith sets a man "free for a real historical life in free decisions," Bultmann goes on: "This is made clear by the fact that the demands of God are summed up in the commandment of love, that is, in a commandment which does not consist in formulated statements and therefore can be depicted only in a negative way, as for instance in I Cor. xiii" (*HE,* p. 45). This statement is quite confused. First, we can note that a negative statement is no less "formulated" than an affirmative one. (Nor is a negative principle any less a principle than an affirmative.) Second, even if negative form implied non-formulation, it would not be a significant point, since statements in negative form always have near equivalents in affirmative form, and could thus easily be rendered in formulas. For example, "Love does not insist on its own way" could be formulated, "Where wills conflict, love yields." But third and most obviously, half of the statements in I Cor. 13 are not negative. However, from this fact Bultmann does not draw the obvious conclusion that his above argument has failed, but takes their affirmative form as expressing another

mean for Paul, it is clearly not that the Christian life has become totally "open" and ambiguous with respect to specific,
conceptual, prescriptive content. "All things are lawful for me"
(6:12) cannot mean that all possibilities of conduct are equally
open to the Christian. For Paul the Christian life is richly determinate and describable; and in *that* sense is still fully under
the law.

Thus from the point of view of ethics, the New Testament
does not seem to regard man's true being as radical potentiality,
but rather as something definite and describable. It sees him as
authentic in the *limitation* and *circumscription* of possibilities
of behavior. It assumes throughout that a man can be *taught*,
via language, what conforms and does not conform to the will
of God; that is, that he can possess in his person, and carry into
situations, a determinate knowledge of good and evil.

III. Time

Is the past, simply as past, a threat to man's true nature,
according to the New Testament? Is any self-understanding
essentially involving reference to events accomplished in the
past necessarily one which denies man's authentic being? Is
man's authentic future thought of as radical openness, a darkness and a void, pure indeterminate possibility? The contradiction between the New Testament and Bultmann's view of man
is so obvious at this point that it hardly requires discussion. He
himself indirectly admits it often enough in his work. But to get
a clear impression of the contradiction, it may be handy to make
a few remarks.

In the New Testament the past is obviously of enormous
importance to faith. If the specimens of preaching which we
have from Acts are at all accurate, it is clear that a fundamental
logical feature of preaching is that it is *report,* news, an account
of "things which have been accomplished among us," as Luke
puts it (1:1). All four of the Gospels also have the character
of report; they are realistic narratives, primarily of Jesus' pas-

---

existentialist emphasis: "When Paul says 'Love is patient and kind; love
bears all things', and so on, then it is evident that the concrete commandments of love grow out of definite situations, encounters with one's fellow-
men, and that obedience is rendered in decisions here and now" (*ibid.*).

sion and resurrection, but also of enough of what he said and did during his ministry to give us an idea who it is who thus dies and is raised. The importance of this past to the New Testament writers is punctuated for us by the fact that one kind of assurance they offer the believer is of a *historical* nature, as I noted in an earlier section. Whatever else the celebration of the Lord's Supper may be, it is at least a *memorial* of Jesus: "Do this in remembrance of me" (I Cor. 11:24). The reason, of course, that faith in the New Testament is connected in a fundamental way with report, narrative, history, and memorial is that faith is conceived as faith in Jesus of Nazareth: "If you confess with your lips that Jesus is Lord and believe in your heart that God raised him from the dead, you will be saved" (Rom. 10:9). It involves the belief that "while we were yet helpless, at the right time Christ died for the ungodly" (Rom. 5:6). Faith is conceptually determined self-understanding, the terms of which involve a reference to something which took place in the past: to the question "Who am I?" the believer answers "I am one for whom Jesus of Nazareth died." Whatever else faith may be for the writers of the New Testament, it is at least this.

The New Testament authors picture the future of the children of God in rather a wide variety of ways, though all their conceptions involve resurrection in some sense (e.g., Matt. 22:30ff., John 6:44, I Cor. 15), and a becoming holy (e.g., Luke 20:36, I John 3:2, Eph. 1:4–5). One thing they all have in common is that for them the future can be grasped in *hope*. That is, the future is not utterly void, but there is something to be hoped for. It is conceived not as *pure* possibility, but as the possibility of *something*. To speak of "hope" in the void future which alone is authentic to man regarded as radical potentiality can only be an act of violence to our language; for a hope which expects only the void is not hope.

Thus it is clear that the New Testament understanding of time is just as "worldly" as our everyday experience, and stands in contradiction to Bultmann's view of man as radical possibility.

IV. Character and dispositions

Does the New Testament regard confirmed character traits as an inherent threat to the authenticity of man? Does it see all personal products of training such as dispositions and capacities as contrary to man's true being? Is faith not at all something into which the individual matures and grows, but rather a momentary act in which he decisively casts off every accretion to his personality and understands himself as radical openness and potentiality?

Paul seems not to think it contradictory that Christians can grow in love and holiness and in those capacities of judgment which they involve, when he says,

> And it is my prayer that your love may abound more and more, with knowledge and all discernment, so that you may approve what is excellent, and may be pure and blameless for the day of Christ, filled with the fruits of righteousness which come through Jesus Christ, to the glory and praise of God. (Phil. 1:9–11)

The author of Hebrews sees holiness and righteousness as the possible fruit of the discipline and training involved in suffering:

> It is for discipline that you have to endure. God is treating you as sons; for what son is there whom his father does not discipline? . . . our earthly fathers disciplined us for a short time at their pleasure, but he disciplines us for our good, that we may share his holiness. For the moment all discipline seems painful rather than pleasant; later it yields the peaceful fruit of righteousness to those who have been trained by it. (12:7ff.)

And through his suffering, even Jesus Christ *learned* obedience:

> Although he was a Son, he learned obedience through what he suffered; and being made perfect he became the source of eternal salvation to all who obey him. . . . (Heb. 5:8–9)

Paul also depicts a kind of personal growth in the Christian life, which can surely only be described as a growth of character, originating in sufferings:

> More than that, we rejoice in our sufferings, knowing that suffering produces endurance, and endurance produces character, and character produces hope, and hope does not disappoint us, because God's love has been poured into our hearts through the Holy Spirit which has been given to us. (Rom. 5:3)

And in a somewhat mysterious passage, he speaks of the Christian's growth into the likeness of the Lord:

> And we all, with unveiled face, beholding the glory of the Lord, are being changed into his likeness from one degree of glory to another. . . . (II Cor. 3:18)

James expresses a similar idea when he says,

> Count it all joy, my brethren, when you meet various trials, for you know that the testing of your faith produces steadfastness. (James 1:2–3)

The very idea that the Christian life involves steadfastness, that the man of faith is not "like a wave of the sea that is driven and tossed by the wind," seems to suggest that faith can be a perduring trait rather than something that arises in the moment. The mature Christian life seems to be one which is *confirmed.* This is surely what the author of Colossians has in mind when he connects being "rooted" and "built up" and "established" in the faith with *teaching:*

> As therefore you received Christ Jesus the Lord, so live in him, rooted and built up in him and established in the faith, just as you were taught, abounding in thanksgiving. (Col. 2:6)

Paul also connects the steadfastness of Christian hope with instruction:

> For whatever was written in former days was written for our instruction, that by steadfastness and by the encouragement of the scriptures we might have hope. (Rom. 15:4)

It would seem that the reason a person has to be steadfast in order to be really hopeful is that a wavering hope — one which was only momentary and not a relatively stable characteristic of the person — is not really hope at all.

St. Paul characterizes the life of the Christian (at least the ideal one) thus:

> But the fruit of the Spirit is love, joy, peace, patience, kindness, goodness, faithfulness, gentleness, self-control; against such there is no law. (Gal. 5:22–23)

The most natural way to categorize these features of the life of faith would seem to be to call love, joy, and peace *emotions,* and the others *virtues.* The language of emotion and virtue is sprinkled liberally throughout his writings:

> Let love be genuine; hate what is evil, hold fast to what is good; love one another with brotherly affection; outdo one another in showing honor. Never flag in zeal, be aglow with the Spirit, serve the Lord. Rejoice in your hope. be patient in tribulation, be constant in prayer. (Rom. 12:9–12)

> Love is patient and kind; love is not jealous or boastful; it is not arrogant or rude. Love does not insist on its own way; it is not irritable or resentful; it does not rejoice at wrong but rejoices in the right. Love bears all things, believes all things, hopes all things, endures all things. (I Cor. 13:4–7)

> So if there is any encouragement in Christ, any incentive of love, any participation in the Spirit, any affection and sympathy, complete my joy by being of the same mind, having the same love, being in full accord and of one mind. (Phil. 2:1–2)

But emotions and virtues such as love, joy, peace, patience, kindness, are not momentary feelings, impulses, or acts, but are (at least when the individual is mature — steadfast) confirmed and established traits of *character.* That is, they are individualizing dispositional qualifications of the *person,* actualized qualities of the soul. It may be that in most people who call themseves Christians (and are Christians, in one sense) these emotions and virtues have not taken very deep root; but it seems quite clear that for Paul they constitute a considerable aspect of the life of faith, ideally. He does not have any inclination at all to say that in an act of authenticity the individual must cast away as inauthentic the love, joy, patience, and self-control which have become confirmed and actual traits of his character. These are rather the substance, the actuality of faith in his life. To cast them away in an act of affirming himself as potentiality would be something quite foreign and contrary to Christian faith; it would be not faith, but the abandonment of faith.

Bultmann is the last person who would ever knowingly mix scholarship and comedy. Yet, in light of the preceding considerations surely only the soberest stoic will be able to resist a little smile when he reads:

> Above all, Heidegger's existentialist analysis of the ontological structure of being would seem to be no more than a secularized, philosophical version of the New Testament view of human life. For him the chief characteristic of man's Being in history is anxiety. Man exists in a permanent tension between the past and the future. At every moment he is confronted with an alternative. Either he must immerse himself in the concrete world of nature, and thus inevitably lose his individuality, or he must abandon all security and commit himself unreservedly to the future, and thus alone achieve his authentic Being. Is not that exactly the New Testament understanding of human life? Some critics have objected that I am borrowing Heidegger's categories and forcing them upon the New Testament. I am afraid this only shows that they are blinding their eyes to the real problem. I mean, one should rather be startled that philosophy is saying the same thing as the New Testament and saying it quite independently.[10]

We are struck with the charming naivete of such a statement, for we have begun to get a perspicuous view of the tension which exists between the New Testament and the idea governing Bultmann's thought (an idea he here attributes, perhaps rightly, to Heidegger). And we have seen that this strain is not a peccadillo, not a little incongruity isolated at this or that particular point in the analysis, but rather a massive contradiction involving fundamental features of the New Testament and reaching into every corner of it. The existence/world dichotomy stands in contradiction to the New Testament's understanding of the nature and significance of Jesus, the nature of faith and the shape of the Christian life, the function of miracle, the nature of history, the estate of preaching as report and news, the uses of argument and teaching, the relation between time and existence, and the nature of ethics, to mention only some fundamental things. The difficulty is this: at every point the New Testament regards human life in ways which Bultmann's terminology would have to call "worldly."

But Bultmann's naivete is not so great as at first it might

---

[10] *KM,* p. 27.

appear. He is well aware of the New Testament's resistance to existentialism. Indeed, it is possible to read almost the whole of his scholarly and theological productivity as an effort to mediate the contradiction which we have discerned. This mediation takes the general form of claiming that what the New Testament says cannot be taken at face value, and has its hub in that cluster of things called "hermeneutics."

How does Bultmann overcome the contradiction between his basic philosophical principles and a natural reading of the New Testament? The answer, crudely put, is that he does not read the New Testament "naturally." Indeed, it is his view that modern men *cannot* read it in a straightforward manner and understand it, since any attempt to do so confronts them immediately with the enormous barrier which he calls the "hermeneutical problem." The problem is that we cannot understand the New Testament without an "interpretation," because it expresses itself in a conceptuality utterly foreign to us. It is as though in a foreign language which needs to be translated. In its untranslated state, the New Testament confronts us as opaque. The reason is that its conceptuality can be understood only by someone who holds what Bultmann calls the "mythological world view," whereas all our concepts are determined by the "modern scientific world view" which in various ways contradicts that of the New Testament. This ploy gets rid of worldly elements in the text in two ways. First, although Bultmann obviously does not appeal directly to this aspect of the "problem" he has set up, in principle at least it would seem to allow the New Testament to mean anything that the hermeneutician might find expressed in it. For if it is in a completely foreign language, then we ordinary people are at the mercy of the specialist who knows how to "translate" it for us. And if he finds that its true meaning excludes worldly elements, we who are utterly in the dark without the translation are hardly in a position to dispute him. In the essay where Bultmann proposes the kind of translation of the New Testament required for modern man's understanding of it, he issues a warning which gives us an idea just how inaccessible its real meaning is to ordinary readers. The task of translation, he says, "will tax the strength of a whole theological generation."[11] But if the true

---

[11] *KM*, p. 15.

meaning of the text is discernible only with the full-time work of a whole generation of specialists, then it must be very deeply hidden indeed, and the kind of reading I have given in this chapter is hopelessly naive. Second, since the mythological is defined as a conceptuality in which the other-worldly (transcendent) is expressed in terms of this world, then since the New Testament is "in" a mythological conceptuality anything in it which has a worldly character can be regarded as expressing something *else* — i.e. something non-worldly or transcendent. Thus such elements in the New Testament as the atoning death and resurrection of Jesus and the hope of a future life become candidates for a "translation" in which the hermeneutician tells us what they *really* mean.

So the next question in logical progression will be, "Does Bultmann's hermeneutical attempt to reconcile the existence/world dichotomy with the New Testament succeed?" In chapter four it will be our task to examine his notions of the mythological and scientific world views and the corresponding conceptualities, with a view to seeing whether the "problem" which justifies Bultmann's particular kind of translation is really a binding one. In chapter seven we will take a hard look at the concept of understanding which is associated with his theory, and then in chapter eight at the concept of an existential interpretation. And since such a conception of interpretation rests on a rather odd view of language, we will have to precede that latter investigation, in chapters five and six, with the project of teasing out and analyzing the implicit theory of meaning which lies behind Bultmann's hermeneutics. But I have so far almost entirely neglected another foundational element in Bultmann's thought, that element which he stoutly holds up as distinguishing him from the secular existentialists — his christology. So it is to the subject of Jesus Christ and the kerygma that we must turn our attention in the next chapter.

3

The Kerygma

The existence/world dichotomy and the picture of human authenticity which it involves belong among Bultmann's debts to the work of philosophical existentialism. But as a Christian theologian he wishes to distinguish himself sharply from such philosophers. For the most part he agrees with the picture of authenticity they paint; but he parts company with them when they suppose that man can actually *achieve* this authenticity apart from the grace of God offered in the Christian kerygma. Accordingly, our account of the foundations of this theology will not be complete without a discussion of Bultmann's thought about the grace of God. In the present chapter I shall discuss the kerygma in two connections: (I) authenticity and the kerygma (Bultmann's contention that secular existentialism cannot achieve its end on its own), and (II) Jesus and the kerygma.

I. Authenticity and the kerygma

Although Bultmann never tires of saying that the word of grace escapes our control, coming to us from beyond ourselves and independent of anything we do, nevertheless when he argues for the importance of the Christian gospel he does not base his argument *a posteriori* on features of that gospel, but rather argues *a priori* from a certain notion of human authenticity. A description of Bultmann's kerygma can be derived, by conceptual argument alone, from his notion of what it is to be a human being. Indeed, it is his concept of authenticity which legislates, paradoxically, that the word of grace must meet us as something utterly beyond our control or calculation.

The argument, which has several variants, takes the form of showing that without the kerygma the concept of authenticity is internally contradictory. We have seen that man's true being is potentiality, the opposite of everything perduring and actual (in particular his self as constituted by his past), a kind of "humility" which is radical openness to whatever may come, an acknowledgment of one's finitude so complete that one lives purely out of transcendence.

Now the secular existentialists have a variety of ways of talking about this decisive self-constituting withdrawal from the world. 'Death,' 'despair,' 'nothingness,' 'frontier-situations,' are the various names they give to the phenomena in face of which life out of transcendence is grasped. But Bultmann questions whether such a picture is coherent:

> 'La vie humaine commence de l'autre côté du désespoir' (Sartre) . . . . The question seems to me to be whether the existentialist pronouncement that in despair (Sartre), in looking at the nothingness which is in an imminent threat (Heidegger), or in the frontier-situation of failure (Jaspers) man comes to himself by taking his 'being' independently upon himself — whether this must be understood as the summit of human *hubris,* or as the expression of humility and radical openness.[1]

That is, if by a simple *act of will* in the face of despair, for example, one affirms that one's true life is not in the actual but rather in what one is potentially, then Bultmann questions whether that act can be what it purports to be. Has one thus really become pure potentiality, or has one not rather fallen back into the most "worldly" sort of existence by attempting to to grasp for oneself this life out of the transcendent? As Bultmann says,

Despair reaches the point which is the *dos moi pou sto* beyond

---

[1] *GV,* II, p. 290.

everything relative, so that the ear can hear the call of absolute
authority in the concrete situation of the day. The question is
whether man hears this call or seeks to be himself on his own
resources in a fanatical heroism. . . . In religious language, becoming aware of a transcendent authority — an ordinance based
on the transcendent—is *faith in God the Creator*.[2]

The question is whether, without the kerygma, man's every
attempt to live out of transcendence — to grasp a positive
life on the other side of despair over everything worldly — is
not a seeking "to be himself on his own resources in a fanatical
heroism." The question is whether one can have a true "faith
in God the Creator" (Bultmann assumes that what the existentialist seeks can be so described — "in religious language")
apart from a hearing of the word of grace. Bultmann's answer
is that this is not possible: "Christian faith believes that man
does not have the freedom which is presupposed for historical
decisions."[3]

The argument seems to go something like this: if man's
authentic being is potentiality, then his becoming anything actual
and established is a fall from his true being, which is only in
the moment of decision itself, not in the product of decisions.
His true life is in an ever-coming future, not in his past. So in
becoming something actual he falls into "security" and thinks
to have "control" over his life, and thus denies his true nature.
But a difficulty arises in the fact that this becoming actual is
both a consequence and a presupposition of the acts and decisions of our everyday life. By doing something we become
something concrete — namely, the person-who-has-done-such-
and-such. It is this actual, and thus inauthentic, "I" which must
be renounced if the individual is to grasp himself in his authenticity.

In fact, I am always determined by my own past by which I
have become what I am and of which I cannot get rid, of which
in the last resort I am unwilling to be rid, although uncon-
sciously. For everyone refuses to give himself up without reser-
vation. Certainly everyone can be conscious of his responsibility

---

[2] *GV*, II, p. 291.
[3] *HE*, p. 149.

and has a relative freedom in the moments of decision. But if
he recognises that this freedom is only a relative one, that
means that his freedom is limited by himself as he is coined by
his past. Radical freedom would be freedom from himself.[4]

But since it is precisely this actual "I," who carries his past into
every new situation, who must do the act, even the purest act of
self-renunciation will have to be inauthentic, for it will be an
act of the "I" as actual rather than as radical potentiality. Thus
the self as potentiality is always implicated in its actuality insofar
as it *does* anything on its own. It is in a kind of logical bondage
to itself. The act in which a man becomes authentic will have
to be more radical than stoic renunciation of will, because in
his act of renunciation the stoic cannot help asserting his will,
and thus drawing upon his actual self. What is required is a
renunciation of the act of renunciation, but insofar as it is the
self on its own who acts, we are involved in an infinite vicious
regress — the required act fails of accomplishment on something
like *logical* grounds. The only way this bondage in regress can
be broken is by the coming to the individual of an *offer* of his
being as potentiality as an utterly free gift.

> The man who understands his historicity radically, that is, the
> man who radically understands himself as someone future, or
> in other words, who understands his genuine self as an ever-
> future one, has to know that his genuine self can only be offered
> to him as a gift by the future. . . . Man has to be free from
> himself or to become free from himself. But man cannot get
> such freedom by his own will and strength, for in such effort
> he would remain 'the old man'; he can only receive this free-
> dom as gift.[5]

What is needed is a word which confronts man as the demand
to be pure potentiality, but which does so by telling him that he
is *already* that (i.e., that that is where his true life resides). It
is a word which not only demands that he cast himself upon the
void, but demands this precisely by promising him that the void
will (in its own peculiar way) hold him up—that he will find

[4] *HE*, p. 149.
[5] *Ibid.*, pp. 149f.

himself there. What the offering, or gift-character, of the kerygma enables is that a man no longer needs (futilely) to assert
his will in the attempt to constitute himself potentiality. For his
being is now simply bestowed on him by the kerygma, and thus
his strivings after authenticity are enabled radically to cease.
He has been freed from the bondage in infinite regress which
held his acting self in thrall, because he has now been enabled
to perform (paradoxically) the radically pure act of self-renunciation in which his self is constituted as unmixed potentiality.

For Bultmann the Jewish law has two distinguishable failures. One is that it falsely seems to be *describing* man's authentic
life, thus delimiting his possibilities and depriving him of his
true nature as openness. I shall discuss Bultmann's thoughts on
this matter in chapter ten. But what concerns us presently is a
certain self-contradiction which Bultmann discerns in the concept of God's law *as law*. Though the commandment rightly pictures the authentic life of man as life out of the transcendent, in
independence from the "world," it sets forth the achievement
of that life in a mode which contradicts the very picture it presents. The difficulty lies in *commanding* radical *submission,* for
the response to a commandment can only be to do something
(on one's own), which is precisely the opposite of submission.
According to Bultmann, it is this insight which lies behind
Paul's teaching about the law, for he

> recognizes that man fails to fulfil the will of God, not only by
> violating the commandments of law, but even in fulfilling them,
> because man imagines that he is able by fulfilling the law to
> make a claim on the grace of God. For this means trusting in
> his own power and failing to realize that man as a whole is a
> prisoner of sin and has to become an entirely new person.[6]

The person who tries to live by commandment (even the commandment to give up all self-assertion) always ends up asserting
himself, and thus only compounding his inauthenticity:

> St. Paul demonstrates this in the case of the Jews. In their
> search for righteousness they missed the very object of their
> quest. They looked for justification from their own works; they

---

[6] *HE,* p. 99.

wanted to have a ground for glorying before God. . . . If the authentic life of man is one of self-commitment [living as potentiality independent of the worldly, actual self], then that life is missed not only by the blatantly self-assertive but also by those who try to achieve self-commitment by their own efforts.[7]

But it is of course not just those, like the Jews, who possess formulated commandments, who will mire down in this self-contradiction, but anyone who tries by his own acts and efforts to become independent of his actual self.

In Heidegger's case the perversity of such an attitude is less obvious because he does not characterize resolve as self-commitment. But it is clear that the shouldering of the accident of his destiny in the facing of death is really the same radical self-assertion on man's part.[8]

For as a result of his self-assertion man is a totally fallen being. He is capable of knowing that his authentic life consists in self-commitment, but is incapable of realizing it because however hard he tries he still remains what he is, self-assertive man. So in practice authentic life becomes possible only when man is delivered from himself.[9]

The only way that what is commanded in the law (or pictured forth in existentialist philosophy) could ever *conceivably* be achieved is that it cease to be flatly commanded (or striven for) and come rather to be offered and received as a free gift.

Bultmann sometimes gives the same argument in more psychological terms by noting that man's life is a restless search for recognition and security.[10] In pursuing recognition, man seeks to establish the worth and meaning of his life; in his search for security, he seeks to establish that life itself against the dangers which abound in it — pain, failure, and ultimately death. The real object of his search is of course his authenticity, the consummation of his being as potentiality; but he always gets diverted by worldly objects and thus falls into inauthenticity. His quest fixes him on things like money, fame, achievements,

---

[7] *KM*, p. 29.
[8] *Ibid.*, p. 30.
[9] *Ibid.*, p. 31.
[10] Cf. *Essays*, pp. 36ff.

a position of authority, lots of pretty daughters, an enormous house, and so on. Such things tend to give a person a place in the world, a sort of metaphorical house in which to live; they compass him about on all sides and establish his locus within the larger world in such a way that it becomes difficult for him to doubt who he is. He is recognized as a man of worth by himself and others, and he has a bulwark against the contingencies which beset a perishable being like himself.

Now if it is true that man's authentic being does not belong to the world, then it is clear that *these* forms of recognition and security will have to be cast off if he is to find his true self. But if his authentic being also involves *necessarily* a striving after recognition and security, then it will not be enough simply to demand him to give up all recognition and security. Such a demand will have to take the form of offering him a kind of recognition and security which casts out the worldly kind. The reason the kerygma is capable of giving rise to authenticity is that it offers a kind of recognition and security which comes from "beyond," condemning the world, but by doing so does not simply condemn the striving for these things, but in its own peculiar way fulfills it. In confronting the kerygma one finds recognition,[11] only of a paradoxical and transcendent sort; one is offered security, the paradoxical security one has in living out of a void future.

What kind of kerygma is it, the idea of which can be deduced from Bultmann's notion of authenticity? One can discern several features which it must have.

(1) Obviously it must meet man with the demand to decide for his authenticity, that is, to understand himself as pure potentiality.

(2) But since man's being is of a radically non-worldly kind, the phenomenon over against which he makes this decision will have to be from beyond the world; it must be transcen-

---

[11] The idea Bultmann is trading on in speaking this way is that of God's love for the individual to whom the gospel comes. Whether the existence/world dichotomy does not reduce the encounter with God to an encounter with mere "transcendence" (even though on a concrete historical occasion), and thus do away with all personal characteristics such as recognizing and loving, is a question we will have to defer until chapter nine, when we discuss Bultmann's concept of God.

dent, or as Bultmann often says, employing biblical vocabulary, it must be a word of God.

(3) But if it is to be a transcendent word, it must be beyond man's control in every sense; it must by definition resist man's employing it in a worldly fashion; it must not offer him any security other than the paradoxical security of the void.

(4) This means that as a word it must be ambiguous, must not provide the believer with any knowledge.

(5) It also means that it must be what it is only in the moment; it must not be an object which perdures through time and is capable of being possessed or criticized or scrutinized.

(6) Thus it must be something which is always only encountered on concrete historical occasions.

All the above features might be present in the phenomena in face of which a secular existentialist pretends to grasp his authentic being. But for Bultmann there is one more feature of the kerygma which, he argues, sets the Christian radically apart from the philosopher:

(7) The kerygma must offer authenticity as a "gift."

This argument is designed to show that the Christian kerygma is required for authenticity. We want to know whether it succeeds; but as a preliminary, we can ask whether it serves a more modest function: does it show that *a* kerygma is required for authenticity? What distinguishes an encounter with the kerygma from an encounter with the transcendent as nothingness or despair, is that in the kerygma authenticity is bestowed as a "gift." But what precisely is *offered* in Bultmann's kerygma? This is in a way the major question to be answered in the second section of this chapter, and we cannot answer it until we have looked closely at the connections between Jesus and Bultmann's kerygma. But so far (on the basis of his *a priori* argument for the necessity of the kerygma) his answer seems to be that what is offered is a recognition and security which are to be found, paradoxically, in abandoning every striving after recognition and security. On this account the goodness of the kerygma is nothing more than the positive fruit of the decision to understand oneself in independence from the world. But if the "offer" is only the promise of life which is *intrinsic* to the act of dying to the world, then it would seem inappropriate to say that anything is *offered* in this kerygma. That is, if nothing more is offered than is already contained in the demanded act of authenticity, then it is misleading to speak here of a "gift." What is "given" would seem to be nothing but an aspect of what is demanded. It is a little like one person's offering another some money, where the "offer" amounts to pointing out that he who works gets the bread. For someone who hasn't grasped the happy consequences intrinsic to work, this insight may come as a freeing piece of "good news." But it is hardly a bestowal of free bread. If there is a gift here at all, it is the gift of an insight; but it is the nature of an insight that it does not *have* to be a gift, for one might very well come to the insight on one's own.

So if the kerygma does not offer anything more than the "security" and "recognition" which are logically entailed by the act of radical renunciation, it becomes fatuous to say that the kerygma with its gift-character is necessary to authenticity. For then the only thing the kerygma offers is what authenticity itself offers, and the "Word" is thus nothing more than a cryptic description of the benefits of authenticity. The kerygma as good news is only a highlighting of an aspect of the authentic self-understanding; and as such it is not really news at all; it does not offer anything that is not already contained in the demanded act. The advance that such a kerygma would make on a mere command is only that it makes clear the benefits of obeying the command. Can Bultmann mean to say that the secular existentialist must fail to perceive that it is precisely life which is to be found in his dying to self?

But even if we admit that a kerygma of some sort is a necessary condition for authenticity (and I think the foregoing considerations show that we do not need a kerygma in any very robust sense of the word), the question remains why it would have to be the Christian one. Bultmann says,

> Here then is the crucial distinction between the New Testament and existentialism, between the Christian faith and the natural understanding of Being. The New Testament speaks and faith knows of an act of God through which man becomes capable of

self-commitment, capable of faith and love, of his authentic life.[12]

But why could a philosopher not just *make up* a kerygma with the seven features we derived above? We could imagine him following the existentialist analysis of Being all the way, acknowledging Bultmann's charge that a man has to be confronted with an offer of life out of the transcendent — and then we could imagine him simply formulating such an offer. He could then "preach" this offer to his fellow philosophers, and have them in turn preach it to him, and in each case it would come from the "beyond" (since they would be preaching in the name of the transcendent) and would confront them in their concrete Now. One could imagine one philosopher proclaiming good news to another in the word, "I call you to a decision, whether you will have your life in the world, or receive it as a gift from the future, for I proclaim to you in this very moment that your true life is already to be found only in the beyond."

Why would such a "kerygma" not be just as capable of occasioning authenticity as the Christian one? Why would it not express just as much the "love of God" as Bultmann's characterization of the Christian kerygma?

> The event of Jesus Christ is therefore the revelation of the love of God. It makes man free from himself and free to be himself, free to live a life of self-commitment in faith and love. But faith in this sense of the word is possible only where it takes the form of faith in the love of God. Yet such faith is still a subtle form of self-assertion so long as the love of God is merely a piece of wishful thinking.[13]

The reference to "wishful thinking" makes it look as though not just any word which claims to be a word of the transcendent can be the occasion for authenticity. Is it perhaps because he does not speak with authority that the philosopher's word is not really kerygma? What then are the criteria by which we distinguish a piece of wishful thinking from the real kerygma of God?

When the revelation is truly understood as God's revelation, it

---

[12] *KM*, p. 33.
[13] *Ibid.*, p. 32.

is no longer a communication of teachings, nor of ethical or historical and philosophical truths, but God speaking directly to me, assigning me each time to the place that is allotted me before God, i.e., summoning me in my humanity, which is null without God, and which is open to God only in the recognition of its nullity. Hence there can be only one "criterion" for the truth of revelation, namely, this, that the word which claims to be the revelation must place each man before a decision — the decision as to how he wants to understand himself: as one who wins his life and authenticity by his own resources, reason, and actions, or by the grace of God.[14]

But this "one 'criterion' for the truth of revelation" is also fulfilled by our imagined philosopher's kerygma. The reason is that the answer to the question of authority is not an "objective" one at all, but is arrived at only internally to the act of decision in face of the kerygma. Bultmann asks, "how do we meet the objection that . . . I obey an authority which is actually constituted by my obedience?" and answers,

> The objection that the authority is of my own making proceeds from the presupposition that I must myself make a resolve to have faith, as if I had been offered an option. But faith does not depend on a resolution about which I can deliberate. Faith is immediate decision; that is, in hearing I *have* already *decided how* I hear. The objection overlooks the fact that I am a historical being, that the *Word of the proclamation does not confront me in a detached situation as a fortuitous happening, but confronts me as I live within a definite historical situation.*[15]

It seems that the reason faith does not erect its own authority is not that it has external (more or less public, objective) criteria which are given from outside the particular act of faith, but simply that it does not reflect enough for any real question of authority (criteria) to arise. The authoritativeness of the Word is identical with its demand of an unreflective response, a pure act of decision in which nothing is conceptually determined, asserted, believed. (The conceptual indeterminacy of the kerygma is obviously required by the existence/world di-

---

[14] *MC*, p. 69.
[15] *FU*, p. 139.

chotomy, for to have one's authenticity specified is a contradiction.) That is to say, the question of authority, in the sense
of the question, "Which kerygma is the right one?" is *logically*
excluded by the nature of faith. Speaking of "when and how
man gains the right to speak of forgiveness," Bultmann says,

> The act of forgiveness! Is there any such act? Is there a criterion
> to determine when it occurs, how it is accomplished, so that a
> man may become sure of forgiveness? Obviously not a sub-
> jective spiritual experience can be meant; there can be in ques-
> tion only an event which confronts man, which happens to him
> from without; an event which manifests itself as an act of God,
> because it confronts man as authority. It presents the claim of
> God to him and thus it identifies the forgiveness as divine, be-
> cause it is pure gift, delivering man while judging him.[16]

What then does Bultmann mean here by "authority"? One
knows that the Word is an act of God "because it confronts
man as authority." But what gives it this authority? What identifies it "as divine"? Nothing more, it seems, than "because it
is pure gift, delivering man while judging him." Thus if one is
confronted by pure gift, a word which delivers one from one's
old worldly self by bringing upon it a judgment which calls it
radically into question, then that *is* the authoritative word: and
standing in obedience to that word, standing under its judgment
and allowing oneself to be delivered by it, gives man "the right
to speak of forgiveness." But if *this* is the nature of the authority
of the Christian proclamation, our imagined philosopher's kerygma does not differ from it in the least.

Why could a philosopher not simply make up a kerygma?
So far there seems to be no reason why he could not. So if
Bultmann's *a priori* argument for the necessity of the kerygma
establishes anything at all, at least it does not establish a requirement for the *Christian* kerygma. Traditionally the Christian
proclamation was thought to be unique, irreplaceable, and authoritative because of the identity of the one whom it proclaimed: Jesus of Nazareth, the Christ, the Lord, the Son of
God. It was indispensable because he was indispensable. To
the question, "What right has this message to be regarded as

---

16 *JW,* pp. 211f.

the only authentic one?"[17] there was possible an answer which proceeded *a posteriori* from the narrative of the Christian story. Can Bultmann, in spite of the existence/world dichotomy, give any analogous account of the uniqueness of Christianity? Let us now turn to that question.

II. Jesus and the kerygma

Possibly the most perplexing part of Bultmann's theological work is his teaching about Jesus Christ. A fertile bewilderment has sucked barrels of ink through the pens of critics and sympathizers alike, as they have endeavored to understand this crucial juncture in his thought. As we read the relevant pages in his work we often get the impression that the only way to make sense of them will be to take utterly seriously his thought about distinguishing what is said from what is meant and measuring the former by the latter; for if we do not, the conclusion seems inevitable that he is contradicting himself in a most unsubtle way. Schubert Ogden reported in 1961 a "growing consensus" among the learned that on this central point Bultmann's theology was infected with an internal inconsistency. He himself stated the contradiction thus: on the one hand, "Christian faith is to be interpreted solely in existential terms as man's original possibility of authentic self-understanding," and at the same time it "has a necessary connection with a particular historical event."[18]

Having surveyed the foundations of Bultmann's theology we might expect some symptoms of unease at this point, for it is evident that the biblical teaching about Jesus Christ is at once the center of Christianity (to which Bultmann desires with all his heart to remain true) and one of the aspects of Christianity most difficult to reconcile with the existence/world dichotomy. These symptoms can be read in either of two ways. Ogden and others hold Bultmann strictly accountable for what he says, and find a rather gross contradiction internal to his thought and right at its center. As our analysis proceeds we will be impressed again and again with how imprecise Bultmann's thinking

---

[17] *Essays,* p. 16.
[18] *Christ Without Myth* (New York: Harper & Row, 1961), p. 117.

is. But such a flatfooted contradiction as Ogden discerns, at such
a central position in the thought of a man of Bultmann's stature,
seems to me *prima facie* implausible. I shall therefore choose
an alternative way of reading these symptoms, namely to see
Bultmann's talk as ambiguous and misleading, but not necessarily as inconsistent, at least in this gross sense.[19] I believe that
this kind of reading is in a way more sympathetic than Ogden's,
since it means bending over backwards to see the real shape of
Bultmann's thought. Clarity will be served by an "interpretation" in which we try to make distinctions which he did not
state explicitly, clarify what ambiguities there are, and then try
to say what he means.

a. Christology and critical history

Bultmann protests against earlier ways of understanding
the person of Jesus Christ, in particular the Greek-influenced
Chalcedonian explanation in terms of two "natures"[20] and liberalism's preoccupation with Jesus' character or "personality."[21]
Bultmann is surely right in protesting that these ways of understanding Jesus are not true to the New Testament. But this protest in behalf of the Bible is misleading because it obscures the
thoroughgoing way in which he himself stands in opposition to
the New Testament understanding of Jesus.

In a time when it is stylish to emphasize the differences
between parts of the Bible, it goes unquestioned that the Synoptic Gospels are a very different sort of document from
John's. But it is striking to note that all four Gospels are designed to answer the question, "Who is this man Jesus?" And
their answer, namely, that he is the Son of God, is given in
a manner which is not only formally identical in the case of all
four Gospels, but is also the same as our everyday manner of
identifying any person whose life among us is over. That is,

---

[19] My basic view of Bultmann is not that this thought contradicts
itself, but that it contradicts the *New Testament*. Though he does no doubt
contradict himself on specific points here and there, a large perspective
on his thought presents a picture which is highly consistent and even
systematic.

[20] *Essays*, p. 286.

[21] *FU*, p. 268.

Jesus is identified by telling what he did, and what he said, and what happened to him. His identity becomes known to us through his story. We do not, for this purpose, need a full biography. Nor is it necessary to the truth of his identity as, for example, a miracle-worker, that any particular miracle story be historically accurate. All we need is that it accurately represent the sort of thing which he actually did. What the Gospels give us is an account of typical things he said and did during a crucial period of his life (his ministry), and also the passion and resurrection narrative, in which what he undergoes provides the decisive marks of his identity as the lamb of God who is simultaneously the Lord. The Synoptics and John, when viewed from this angle, agree not only formally, in their method of identifying Jesus for us, but also in the substance of that identification: he is the Son of God, who in giving his life takes away the sin of the world. Though Paul does not provide us with narrative (since he was writing letters, most of which were pointedly occasional, one could hardly expect him to do so) it is far from obvious that he did not presuppose his congregations' knowledge of certain traditions of the sort provided us in the Gospels. And it cannot be doubted that he assumes the identity of the earthly Jesus and the exalted Christ. On the two aspects of Jesus' story which pre-eminently identify him — his death and resurrection — Paul is as emphatic as the Gospels.

Bultmann's work has the effect that the identity of Jesus, thus given, is lost. This happens from both the theological and the historical side of his work. The existence/world dichotomy, which rules that something past or a definite person cannot be a constitutive element in an authentic self-understanding, is well served by the results of Bultmann's historico-critical labors on the Gospels. Their upshot is to deprive Jesus of the identity which the New Testament ascribes to him: the christologically decisive elements in the narrative are creations of the primitive church, expressions of their faith, "interpretation," "secondary construction."

Narrative elements such as Jesus' miracles, his offering people forgiveness of sins in the manner of God, his demeanor of authority both in teaching and generally in dealing with men, his speaking (in particular, referring to himself) in such a manner as to imply that he is the Messiah and Son of God (and thus to demand faith in his person), the positive intention with which he is pictured as going to Jerusalem and the cross, and his being raised from the dead — such narrative elements as these go together to manifest Jesus' identity.

The strong tendency of Bultmann's work is to excise such elements, and thus to divest Jesus of the identity which the Gospels claim for him and which makes him a possible object of faith. Bultmann eliminates miracles in one fell swoop via a transcendental deduction of their impossibility.[22] That a man should pronounce the forgiveness of sins directly as though having the authority to do so is, in the context of Jewish piety, tantamount to the claim which John the Evangelist expresses with the words "I and the Father are one." Thus to tell the stories in Mark 2:1–12 and Luke 7:36–50 would be part of claiming an extraordinary identity for Jesus. But Bultmann contends that the part of the Markan story which refers to Jesus' forgiving sins was constructed by the early church as a defense of its own right to forgive sins.[23] His view of Luke 7:48 and the following verses seems to be that it too is embellishment.[24] Since these are the only two cases of Jesus' forgiving sins which the tradition has preserved for us, one is encouraged to suspect that Jesus did not forgive sins in that manner at all. Bultmann treats sayings in which Jesus implicitly claims Messiahship as "secondary formulations." He will not admit the historicity of self-references implying more than that Jesus is "the prophet sent by God at the decisive hour."[25] "The 'I-sayings' were predominantly the work of the *Hellenistic Churches,* though a beginning had already been made in the *Palestinian Church.*"[26] For Bultmann it goes without saying that Jesus' predictions of his death and resurrection are such secondary constructions.[27] He admits that "there are no possible grounds for objecting to the idea that Jesus could have spoken in the first person about himself and his coming." But he can admit this because such speaking "need be no more than what befits his prophetic self-con-

---

[22]   Cf. *FU*, pp. 247ff. I examine the validity of this argument in chapter four.
[23] *HST,* pp. 14ff.
[24] *Ibid.,* p. 21.
[25] *Ibid.,* p. 151.
[26] *Ibid.,* p. 163.
[27] *Ibid.,* p. 152.

sciousness";[28] that is, such speaking does not imply the claim of an identity which would make him a possible object of faith. And lastly, of course Bultmann is famous for his hypothesis that that element of the narrative which the early church took to be the decisive indication of Jesus' identity, namely, his resurrection, is only the picturesque way in which the unsophisticated disciples expressed their newfound authenticity.

No one of these elements (not even Jesus' resurrection) would, by itself, be sufficient to provide a well-established claim of his identity as the Son of God and Messiah. Nor (beyond saying with Paul that if Jesus was not raised our faith is futile) is it possible to say precisely the absence of which, or how many, of these elements would constitute a decisive denial of Jesus' identity. But we can certainly say that if *none* of these elements in the narrative is true of the historical Jesus, the claim of his identity as the Son of God is disestablished; and this seems to be the effect of Bultmann's reflections. As one reads his allegedly historical account of the tradition about Jesus, the cumulative effect is that those elements of the narrative which for the New Testament writers formed the basis for the claim that Jesus was the Son of God (not a *proof,* at least in the strong sense) have disappeared.[29]

---

[28] *HST,* p. 153.

[29] This is an essay on Bultmann's theology, so it cannot be my purpose here to dispute his historical judgments on historical grounds (even if I had the competence to do so). My intention in the foregoing is only to show the relation between the New Testament's understanding of Jesus and Bultmann's; and to show that he has, through historical and other methods, eliminated what was of supreme importance to the New Testament writers, namely Jesus' identity as Son of God and Messiah. But I suppose it is evident that I am more confident about the historical trustworthiness of the New Testament's picture of Jesus than Bultmann is.

I cannot overemphasize that in a biographical sense he does not *wish* to deny that Jesus is the Son of God; whatever the *logic* of his position may amount to, Bultmann the Christian theologian wants to be faithful to the christology of the New Testament. A major theoretical element of his conviction that he can do so is his more or less implicit beliefs about meaning and language, to be treated in chapters five and six. But there is also an historical explanation of his confidence. Professor Hans Frei has pointed out to me that Bultmann stands in a tradition stretching back as far as Locke, passing through Schleiermacher, Ritschl, and Herrmann, and reaching into our own era in Brunner, the early Barth, the Niebuhrs, and many others. This mediating theology has always attempted to steer

b. The connection between Jesus and the kerygma

If one reflects about the possible species of connection between Jesus of Nazareth and the preaching of the Christian church, there seem to be, broadly, three which emerge. I shall call these kinds of connection the logical, genetic, and analogical.

If, as seems to be quite evidently the view of the New Testament, preaching has the character of report, story, or narrative, then the connection between the preaching and the person it is about is a *logical* one. That is, when a story ceases to be about the person it is about, it also *eo ipso* ceases to be the story it is. For example, Abraham Lincoln's story is not replaceable by another story because he is a unique individual. His story is the means of identifying him, and his identity determines whether the story is indeed his story; so the connection between the individual and his story is an internal or logical one. Similarly, if the kerygma is seen as a report or story, then the identity of the kerygma's subject determines the identity (uniqueness, irreplaceable character) of the kerygma. It is the report it is because of who it is about: as report it is tied necessarily to Jesus of Nazareth, because it is a report about him.

Another connection between Jesus and the kerygma is that a true *genetic* (historical-causal) account of the existence of the kerygma in the world requires reference to him. Here a different kind of necessity characterizes the connection. If one leaves out the report-character of the kerygma, then the particular man Jesus being the referent of the genetic account is

---

a course between a christological reductionism in which Jesus becomes a cipher for some aspect of our present existence in faith, and a realistic historical christology of which Chalcedon (metaphysically understood) is usually taken as the paradigm. Common to this long tradition has been an underlying confidence that there is possible some third alternative between asserting that Jesus was and is himself the Son of God, and asserting that his being the Son of God amounts to a state of the believer's consciousness or an act of his existence. To us it may seem a piece of impossible logic for Bultmann to deny what he does and still assert that "The word of God is not some mysterious oracle, but a sober, factual account of a human life, of Jesus of Nazareth, possessing saving efficacy for man" (*KM*, p. 44). But if we consider the unconscious persuasive weight of such a powerful and populous theological ancestry we can at least appreciate how he can, psychologically, hold such things together without bad faith.

merely an accident of history. What is necessary in the account is only that *somebody* have been the genesis of the kerygma, not that it have been Jesus of Nazareth. Here the relation between Jesus and the kerygma is analogous to the relation between J. C. Penney and his chain of stores. If one wants to explain the historical rise of the stores, one has to go back to somebody, and upon investigation it turns out to be Penney. But it would not have to have been that particular individual, for any number of people might have started the business. And this is further shown in the fact that the business can go along fine without Penney's name being mentioned at all. This, then, is a different relation than that between an individual and a report about him. Whereas the particular man Abraham Lincoln stands in a necessary relation to the report about him, so that to cease to speak of the individual is to cease to give the same report, the particular man J. C. Penney stands only in an accidental relation to the business which bears his name.

Another possible connection, which would probably not occur to us without Bultmann's help, is that Jesus was to the original disciples as the kerygma is to us; that is, the relationship is *analogical*. The reason we would probably not think of this without Bultmann's help is that it depends on a rather odd assimilation of words and a person. Thus Bultmann assimilates these things by speaking of both Jesus and present-day preaching as "events" which are "encountered." It is almost as though the words themselves constitute an event which one encounters, rather than communicating something which one might, speaking somewhat oddly still, "encounter." We will have more to say of these oddities later. Such an account of the connection could be combined with a genetic one, in that Jesus' standing to the original disciples in a certain relation (e.g., his preaching or the spectacle of the cross being for them the "eschatological event," as present-day preaching is for us) occasioned the rise of the kerygma, and is thus a filling out of the genetic connection. Here again if we leave out the report-character of the present-day kerygma, it would not stand in any necessary relation to Jesus. And the reason is that although one *could* draw the analogy (perhaps as a matter of historical interest), one would not *need* to do so. As long as the kerygma stands to us in the required relation (that of the eschatological event), there is no need to refer to Jesus.

Corresponding to his elimination of the christological identity of Jesus of Nazareth is Bultmann's rejection of the first of these three kinds of connection between Jesus and the preaching of the church. The kerygma does not inform us, nor report or narrate anything to us.

> The forgiving word of God is neither a general, universal truth nor a piece of information about the grace of God; nor is it a report or record about the history of Jesus Christ. It is the word of God only as the word spoken ever anew in the moment of the Now.[30]

The kerygma does not offer any knowledge about Jesus, but demands an immediate, unreflective decision: "One does not acquire knowledge about the Messiah; one either acknowledges him or rejects him."[31] "To *have faith in Christ,* therefore, does not mean to hold particular opinions about his nature, although one can certainly have such opinions."[32] If we ask how we know, in the absence of any knowledge about Jesus or opinions about his nature, that it is in fact *Jesus* who is the object of our faith, the answer is that it is *not* he: "It is the Christ of the kerygma and not the person of the historical Jesus who is the object of faith."[33] Indeed, in a certain sense, the farther we are removed from the historical specifics of Jesus' life, the closer we approach the true meaning of the gospel:

> In John the original meaning of the gospel comes out in fullest clarity, in that the evangelist while making free use of the tradition *creates* the figure of Jesus entirely from faith.[34]

But although the kerygma does not communicate any knowledge about Jesus, and although faith is at its most authentic when it "creates the figure of Jesus entirely," Bultmann can still aver:

---

[30] *Journal of Religion,* 1952, p. 85.
[31] *GV,* I, p. 203.
[32] *FU,* pp. 276ff.
[33] "The Primitive Christian Kerygma and the Historical Jesus," *Kerygma and History,* ed. Carl Braaten and Roy Harrisville (Nashville: The Abingdon Press, 1962), p. 17.
[34] *FC,* p. 70 (my emphasis).

From the discrepancy which I emphasize between the historical Jesus and the Christ of the kerygma it does not at all follow that I destroy continuity between the historical Jesus and the primitive Christian proclamation.[35]

The question we have now to ask is whether, having denied that Christian preaching is report, Bultmann will be able to give an account of the connection between Jesus and the kerygma which will preserve the necessity of reference to Jesus. We have seen that his *a priori* argument for the necessity of the kerygma does not establish the need for anything peculiarly Christian. Can he, by an *a posteriori* connection between the kerygma and Jesus of Nazareth, preserve the uniqueness of the Christian revelation?

Once he has so sweepingly denied historicity to those elements of the gospel narrative which would, if historical, justify Jesus' disciples in their claim that he is the Messiah, Bultmann has created the enormous difficulty of explaining how it could have entered their heads to do so. He succinctly expresses both this "great enigma" and his proposed solution of it in these words:

The great enigma of New Testament theology, *how the proclaimer became the proclaimed,* why the community proclaimed not only the content of his preaching, but also and primarily Christ himself, why Paul and John almost wholly ignore the content of his preaching — that enigma is solved by the realization that it is the fact, '*that* he proclaimed', which is decisive.[36]

This, then, is the fact about the historical Jesus which explains why the disciples made the extraordinary move, after his death, of proclaiming not just his message, but his *person* as the savior of the world: "*that* he proclaimed." The *content* of Jesus' preaching "does not differ from pure Judaism, from the pure prophetic teaching,"[37] nor did he teach about the significance of his own person; and yet his disciples were not unjustified in preaching him as the Messiah. Speaking of Paul's gospel in contrast with the preaching of Jesus, Bultmann says,

---

[35] Braaten, *op. cit.*, p. 18.
[36] *FU,* p. 283.
[37] *Ibid.*

But is not precisely this binding of God's grace to the person of Jesus a limiting of it of which Jesus himself knew nothing? While it is true that Jesus did not demand faith in his own person, he did demand faith in his word. That is, he made his appearance in the consciousness that God had sent him in the last hour of the world. But this means that the decision to which he summons men by his proclamation is the definitive decision; that precisely the fact that he now summons men to repentance is the final proof of God's grace. . . . If Paul, like the earliest community, saw in Jesus the Messiah, he did nothing other than affirm Jesus' own claim that man's own destiny is decided with reference to his person.[38]

But if "Jesus did not demand faith in his own person," what does "Jesus' own claim that man's destiny is decided with reference to his person" amount to for Bultmann? He says that Jesus demanded faith in his word, and evidently since he was the one who spoke the word, demanded a decision "with reference to his person." The trouble is that in that sense every preacher in the world demands a decision with reference to his person. But we feel no inclination on that basis to preach, for example, Harry Emerson Fosdick as the Mediator of God's reconciliation of the world to himself. Is it perhaps that Jesus was the first one who spoke this particular word? That would differentiate him from other preachers, but not in such a way as to warrant Paul's demanding faith in *him* now. He could be revered as the father of Christian preaching, but surely not as the Lord in whom faith is demanded. And besides, Bultmann has told us that his particular word does not differ from pure Judaism and the prophets, so in reality he is not even the first. Is it perhaps that "he made his appearance in the consciousness that God had sent him in the last hour of the world" which differentiates him? But this too could be said of every preacher, once we have done a Bultmannian reinterpretation of the expression "last hour."

The proclaimer must become the proclaimed, because it is the fact *that* he proclaimed which is decisive. The decisive thing is his person (not his personality), *here* and *now*, the event, the commission, the summons. When the primitive community

---

[38] *EF,* pp. 195f.

called him Messiah they were confessing that he was the decisive
event, the act of God, the inaugurator of the new world.[39]

The decisive thing is his person, but the only decisive thing
about his person seems to be that he is the proclaimer in the
here and now. Indeed, it looks as though what Bultmann means
by "person" is nothing more than the fact that the word confronts me factically in the concrete here and now, that is, that
it is a "historical" word. *That* is the significance of Jesus'
"person." But the difficulty we are left with is that in that sense
every preacher in the concrete here and now is "Jesus." The
effect of Bultmann's reducing the historical presupposition of
the christological kerygma to the bare "that" of Jesus' preaching is a redefinition of the word *Jesus*. The word has now become a cipher for the concreteness, the "historical," the here-
and-now character of the kerygma, the fact that it confronts me
in the moment.

We will find that this is often the largest part of what
Bultmann's use of the word *Jesus* amounts to. But it also remains true that he believes there was an apocalyptic preacher
by this name who must stand as a historically decisive feature
of any account that rightly represents the genesis of the Christian church and its preaching. He trades on this use of the
word, and often slides back and forth between this and the
other in a very confusing manner. Sometimes it is as though he
is trying to ride two horses at the same time, one leg on each;
and what gets stretched very thin by their divergence is his
capacity to make determinate sense. For example, in the following passage about Jesus' cross:

> It is not the *what*, the content, of his proclamation that is put in
> question by his death on the cross. What is put in question is
> his legitimacy as the proclaimer, the *that*, the fact that it is
> really he who is the messenger of God bringing the final decisive
> word.[40] Therefore what is important is the acknowledgement

---

[39] *FU*, p. 284.

[40] If the proclamation is the word which both demands and enables
a person to understand himself as not belonging to the world, how could
its "legitimacy" be called into question by the death of its proclaimer?
What could conceivably render the preaching of such a message illegiti-
mate? If it is not the content of the message which is made dubious by

of the *crucified* as the coming Messiah. To adhere to his person thus also involves adherence to his death and the recognition of it as an essential part of the saving act — not as something appended to that act, but as something that decisively determines everything else.[41]

Thus the "Jesus" who is merely the concreteness, the nowness of the eschatological preaching, the significance of whose "person" is the mere contentless "that" this message is proclaimed, who thus has the status of a formal feature of present-day proclamation, is in some sense the person named Jesus who died upon a Roman cross, and who had actually preached an eschatological message which occasioned the decision of authenticity in his disciples. That is, he is a historical figure about whom we do know more than just "that" he preached:

> Characteristic for him are exorcisms, the breech of the Sabbath commandment, the abandonment of ritual purifications, polemic against Jewish legalism, fellowship with outcasts such as publicans and harlots, sympathy for women and children; it can also be seen that Jesus was not an ascetic like John the Baptist, but gladly ate and drank a glass of wine. Perhaps we may add that he called disciples and assembled about himself a small company of followers — men and women.[42]

We will see a little later how these two elements in Bultmann's use of *Jesus* serve on the one hand to preserve the paradoxical

---

his death, what *is* made dubious? Could such a death call into question the right of the particular man Jesus to proclaim that message? Meaning that if someone else had proclaimed it, the proclamation might not have been legitimate? It is hard to see how the death on a cross could call into question the proclamation of that message; if anything, it would seem to be quite congruent with it. But if Jesus' death is *capable* of calling into question the legitimacy of *his* preaching *that* message, then something about the *man* must be in principle capable also of legitimating his preaching; but then we have something more than a bare "that"; we also have the question the early church was so careful to answer, the question of the "who," of the identity of Jesus. It is this confusing teetering between the "that," which is a merely formal characteristic of the proclamation-situation (namely that it is concrete), and something approaching an identity for Jesus, which I am trying to point out.

[41] *FU*, p. 238.

[42] Braaten, *op. cit.*, pp. 22f.

character of Christian preaching (that the eschatological phenomenon confronts me as an ambiguous, worldly phenomenon), and on the other to avoid the impression that the disciples arbitrarily began preaching Jesus as the Christ without any warrant at all.

But if Bultmann admits, and even trades on the fact, that we have firm knowledge of some details of Jesus' life, why does he insist that the only connection between Jesus and the christological kerygma must be the bare "that"? Is it simply that he is skeptical about the historicity of the christologically relevant features of the narrative? There is more to it than this, for it seems that he would hold firm to the bareness of the "that" even if the christologically relevant features were vindicated historically:

> The Christ-kerygma is a christological kerygma. Is Jesus' preaching also a christological proclamation? This would still not be implied, even if it were true that Jesus regarded himself as the Messiah and demanded faith in himself. . . . Even then the faith demanded by the christological kerygma would be of a *totally different kind*.[43]

To explain this surprising passage, we must go back to the existence/world dichotomy, which legislates that truly human existence is achieved only in a decision in which the individual becomes independent of every world object. This means that a figure of past history (or even, as was in question for the earliest disciples, an individual man of their present history) cannot be a constituent part of an authentic self-understanding. He may be an occasion, an ambiguous phenomenon in face of which the authentic decision is made; but he cannot, in his describable determinateness, be the *object* of joy, trust, hope, and the like. That would be, *eo ipso*, inauthenticity, the precise opposite of true faith. So when Bultmann speaks of "the faith demanded by the christological kerygma," it is human authenticity governed by the existence/world dichotomy of which he is speaking. And of course if one requires faith to be *that*, then the historical Jesus, no matter what he claimed or who he was, cannot be the object of faith; for he is something within the

---

[43] Braaten, *op. cit.*, p. 28 (my emphasis).

world. Thus we can see that Bultmann's denial of the material unity between Jesus and the kerygma, his reduction of the features of Jesus' life to a bare "that" which becomes nothing more than a formal characteristic of the present-day proclamation-situation, follows with logical necessity from the existence/world dichotomy and has, ultimately, nothing to do with historical research. If historiography were to establish that Jesus spoke every word which is attributed to him in all four Gospels, and performed miracles which no man before or since ever performed, and was crucified and raised from the dead bodily on the third day, even then Jesus *could not* be the object of "faith."[44] A Jesus with an identity would be counter-existential.

The effect of the existence/world dichotomy is to demand that the *person* of Jesus, in the ordinary sense of that word, should disappear from the kerygma: this is the real motivation behind Bultmann's denial that the kerygma is a report or story, and his reduction of Jesus to a contentless "that." He is fond of quoting Melanchthon to the effect that *hoc est Christum cognoscere, beneficia eius cognoscere.*[45] But for him this is more than a remark about what it is to know the person of Christ — namely, that one must have a personal knowledge of his work (*beneficia*) in one's own life. For him it is a denial of the possibility of distinguishing the person of Christ from his work,

---

[44] Norman Young in his book *History and Existential Theology* (Philadelphia: Westminster Press, 1969) finds it "difficult to see" why, in the face of compelling arguments from some of his students, Bultmann staunchly rejects any richer connection between Jesus and the christological kerygma than the bare presupposition of the contentless "that" of Jesus' history (cf. pp. 118ff.). But Young's difficulty rests on failing to grasp the real basis of Bultmann's theology; he takes the peculiar Bultmannian understanding of history to be fundamental, whereas if he had perceived that Bultmann's primary allegiance is to the existence/world dichotomy, he would be quite clear why Bultmann *cannot* accept any more Jesus-content than a bare "that." Anyone who reads Bultmann's responses to his critics cannot help noting the striking way he refuses to budge from his established positions. The fault is always with the critics, who are forever "misunderstanding" him. In the early 1920's he achieved the insight that man's true being is radical openness to the future, and that he realizes his being only by casting off every security, constantly venturing away from his past. For the next fifty years Bultmann held that idea fast with unmoving determination.

[45] *FU*, p. 279.

a collapsing of the person of Christ into his work of justification. It is an attempt to have Christ's work without his person, in the normal sense of *person*. "Faith certainly depends wholly on the person of Jesus, but in such a way that his person and his work are seen as one."[46] "The saving efficacy of the cross is not derived from the fact that it is the cross of Christ; it is the cross of Christ because it has this saving efficacy."[47] And according to Bultmann's reading of John's Gospel, "Jesus as the Revealer of God reveals nothing but that he is the revealer. . . . John . . . in his Gospel presents only the 'that' of the Revelation without describing its content."[48] But if Jesus has no identity other than that of revealer or justifier — that is, if he is not a person in the sense of having a determinate story — then *Jesus* is merely a cipher for the kerygma or an aspect of the kerygma. And if that is the case, then it is fatuous to make the distinctiveness of the Christian proclamation ride on its relation to "Jesus." To know Christ's benefits has lost all connection with knowing Christ; the words *Jesus* and *Christ* have taken on a new meaning, which is only in some ways similar to the old one, and indeed a meaning to which a secular existentialist could have no objection, if he rightly understood it.

c. *The measure of what is said*

But still, Bultmann wants to hold tightly to some kind of connection between Jesus and our present-day preaching. I believe that if we look closely at what he says, we will see him shifting back and forth in odd and somewhat confusing ways between what I have called the analogical and the genetic kinds of connection. Broadly speaking, the historical Jesus has two kinds of theological importance for Bultmann.

First, Jesus was, paradoxically, the concrete world phenomenon who was at the same time the eschatological event for the first disciples. That is, it was in face of that specific preaching and the spectacle of that particular man's death that the earliest disciples achieved the act of authenticity; and thus the historical-factual side of it is essential to this "event."

---

[46] *FU*, p. 277.
[47] *KM*, p. 41.
[48] *TNT*, II, p. 66.

I do not regard the factual character of history and of Jesus as in any way irrelevant for faith and for theology. I say, rather, Christian faith declares the paradox that an historical event (precisely, Jesus and his history) is at the same time an eschatological occurrence. If the historical fact were stricken out, then the paradox would be abandoned.[49]

Speaking as an interpreter of Paul and John, Bultmann says,

the kerygma contains the paradoxical assertion that a historical event — the historical Jesus and his history — is the eschatological event (the end of the age and what it implies). It is therefore obvious that the kerygma presupposes the historical Jesus, however much it may have mythologized him. Without him there would be no kerygma.[50]

But this paradox of a concrete world phenomenon which is at the same time the end of my world (the eschatological event) is reduplicated in present-day preaching, and thus there is an *analogy* between the historical Jesus and that preaching. "The proclamation of Jesus' messengers is an eschatological event, just as much as his own ministry."[51] In interpreting the eschatology of the Gospel of John, Bultmann expresses well his view of preaching:

Accordingly, if the *crisis* is consummated *in the present* (that is, at the definite time when the response is made to the sending of the Son, in answer to the Word) then it is not consummated *at any time one chooses to take a position* in relation to the concept of God, to the idea of a redeemer, to eternal norms and orders, to the 'intellectual content' of the Word, to concepts which 'interpret' the world or the 'meaning of life' or the like. On the contrary, it is consummated in a *specific* present, a specific *now*, as the response to an *historical fact*.[52]

The historical-factual side of the original eschatological event was Jesus, and our present-day preaching similarly must have

---

[49] *The Theology of Rudolf Bultmann,* ed. Charles W. Kegley (New York: Harper & Row, 1966), pp. 274f.
[50] Braaten, *op. cit.,* p. 18.
[51] *GJC,* p. 197.
[52] *FU,* p. 174.

such a side if it is to reduplicate the paradox. Sometimes Bultmann speaks as though the world phenomenon side of the paradox is adequately fulfilled by the fact that the kerygma is spoken
by the mouth of a human preacher. Thus one might (rather
misleadingly) call this world phenomenon character of the
present-day preaching "Jesus," since it plays the same role as
Jesus did long ago. (Bultmann does seem to do this, though he
usually does it in ambiguous association with the genetic use,
which makes it seem less arbitrary, as when he says, "The Now
of the kerygma is not purely fortuitous, but identical with the
advent of Jesus and his passion."[53] At other times he seems to
be saying that the world phenomenon side of the paradox is
provided in the fact that the present-day kerygma actually
mentions Jesus. But if the point is only to preserve that side of
the paradox, mention of Jesus would not seem to be necessary,
but only one way to accomplish that end, and indeed a super-
fluous one if it is already accomplished by the humanness and
specific occasionality of the preacher's mouth. Thus at such
points Bultmann would seem to be verging on the genetic use
of *Jesus*.

The second kind of connection that he trades on is the fact
that Jesus of Nazareth is the one with whom it all started, the
genetic origin of the kerygma and faith, and as such is a kind
of warrant for preaching. And he says, "We observe that this
society [the early church] owes its existence and its spiritual
possessions to the work of Jesus."[54] The presence among men
of the eschatological event began with Jesus:

> The incarnation should not be conceived of as a miracle that
> happened about 1950 years ago, but as an eschatological hap-
> pening which, beginning with Jesus, is always present in the
> words of men proclaiming it to be a human experience.[55]

Reference to the original eschatological event of which Jesus
was an element, keeps subsequent instances of that same event
from being arbitrary:

> The living Word of God is never a word of human wisdom but

[53] *KM*, p. 115.
[54] *FC*, p. 60.
[55] *MC*, p. 69.

an event encountered in history. The fact that it originates in an historical event provides the *credentials* for its utterance on each specific occasion.[56]

In answer to those who accuse him of abandoning the *extra nos* dimension of the salvation-occurrence, Bultmann says,

> We can make our answer . . . in the single affirmation that God meets us in his Word, in a concrete word, the preaching instituted in Jesus Christ. . . . This living Word of God is not invented by the human spirit and by human sagacity; it rises up in history.[57]

Although Bultmann's use of the word *history* in the above passages is ambiguous, and could have reference both to the *origin* of Christian preaching and to its character as *occasional,* nevertheless his speaking about its originating, its being instituted, and its being given credentials, would lead us to think that he is at least making reference to the historical genesis of the kerygma. Thus reference to Jesus as the origin of this preaching helps to keep the preaching on the track of a tradition, and guards against the accusation that either we or the earliest disciples simply made it up. Reference to the genetic relation thus aims to fulfill the function of a kind of authority.

We have gained some insights into Bultmann's use of the word *Jesus,* and in particular into the connections which he allows, and those he does not allow, between Jesus of Nazareth and the "christological kerygma." We are now in a better position to read some of those perplexing passages which tempt us to accuse him of self-contradiction — to read them in such a way as to distinguish what he says from what he means, and to measure the former by the latter. Let us now look at some hard passages, and try to discern what he means.

What could be the role of Jesus in the following passage (in which he is, however, not mentioned)?

> The new life is a *historical possibility created by the saving event and it is a reality wherever it is grasped in the resolve to*

---

[56] *KM,* p. 207 (my emphasis).
[57] *JCM,* pp. 78f.

act. Precisely this resolve is *faith,* the faith which believes in God's act of salvation as it happened in Christ and as it is taught in the proclamation of the Church, and which obeys it. Through this saving act the new life is offered as possible for men. Of themselves they do not have this possibility; it is therefore not enough to have it called to their attention by some illuminating instruction. For they are sinners before God, imprisoned by their past, by what they have done as well as by what they have left undone. They gain the new life only through the forgiveness effected in Christ. They do not gain that forgiveness through an idea of the grace of God. Forgiving must be an event; it is an event which actually has occurred — as the proclamation asserts — in Christ in whom God reconciled the world to himself.[58]

What interest us in this passage are the expressions "as it happened in Christ" (past tense), and "an event which actually has occurred." We have learned that for Bultmann faith does not believe in something which happened in the temporal past, but only in something which happens in the 'moment' — the word of the kerygma. Therefore when he uses the past tense in cases like this, what he must mean to express is the fact that God's grace is prevenient, that is, that I encounter it as already there, that as I come it always has preceded me. God's grace can for Bultmann only be in the temporal Now; but as we have seen in discussing his arguments for the necessity of the kerygma, the structure of human authenticity demands that it be *extra nos,* and thus have this formal feature in common with the temporal past. We have also learned that the kerygma does not have the character of report or historical narrative. So when he says that the proclamation "asserts" something "which actually has occurred," we must take this as a somewhat awkward way of saying that the proclamation, by its very nature as the prevenient grace of God, *expresses* its own prevenience. (For literally the kerygma does not, *as the grace of God* at any rate, assert anything at all; as Bultmann never tires of telling us, the kerygma does not give us any information.) So much for what Bultmann must mean insofar as the kerygma is the grace of God. But he probably does also want to suggest here some connections between the "Christ" and Jesus of Nazareth. These

---

[58] *FU,* p. 276.

connections cannot be essential to the kerygma as the grace of God, but they can bear on it in analogical and genetic ways. Thus when he speaks of "God's act of salvation as it happened in Christ" he certainly wants to associate the present-day proclamation with the fact that the historical Jesus was the first eschatological phenomenon. Jesus was for the original disciples what the proclamation is for us today, and as such he is the one to whom we look back as the originator of faith and the proclamation. But what makes Bultmann's talk so confusing is that he constantly elides the essential features of what he takes to be the Christian kerygma, with the inessential (genetic and analogical) associations which Jesus of Nazareth has with that kerygma.

Some of his objectors have seen in his making the preaching, rather than the referent of the preaching, the object of faith, a denial that what happened in Judaea 2000 years ago is once and for all the event of salvation. He replies that, far from denying the once-for-all and historical character of the event of Jesus Christ, in his existential interpretation

> the *ephapax* is understood as never before in its true sense of the "once" of the eschatological event. For it does not mean the datable uniqueness and finality of an event of past history, but teaches us in a high degree of paradox to believe that just such an event of the past is the once-and-for-all eschatological event, which is continually re-enacted in the word of proclamation. This proclamation is a word which addresses me personally, and tells me that the prevenient grace of God has already acted on my behalf, though not in such a way that I can look back upon this act of God as a datable event of the past, but in the sense that God's having acted is present as an eschatological Now.[59]

This is a pretty example of the ambiguous way Bultmann uses language, especially time categories, to slip through the groping fingers of his critics. It is indeed a confusing array, but I think if we read between the lines a bit it is possible to make sense of it. It is clear that the critics are right in thinking Bultmann to deny that the (in principle) datable and reportable history of

---

[59] *KM,* p. 209.

the man Jesus is the event of salvation. Thus when he says that just such an event of the past is the once-and-for-all eschatological event," what he has to mean is that the worldly event was the backdrop onto which, through the eyes of faith, was superimposed the address which encountered the original disciples as the eschatological event. Now since Bultmann makes but fails to state the above distinction, "once-and-for-all" also has the ambiguity that it applies, in different ways, to the event both as eschatological and as worldly. As worldly it is once-for-all in the sense of over and done and completely accomplished and never to be re-enacted. But as the event or phenomenon in face of which authentic existence can arise, Bultmann can speak of this event as identical with the one which he thinks happens in the preaching in the village church on Sunday morning. And in this sense it is infinitely repeatable and not once-for-all in the world-historical sense. But the eschatological event is also, in its own way, once-for-all, in the following three senses:

(1) It is always *einmal* in that what is encountered and the decision which responds to it are always in a concrete situation and at a particular moment (this is a sense in which Bultmann, often to everybody's confusion but his own, uses the word *historical*).

(2) Since it is defined as the end of an individual's "worldliness," there are no essential variations on it, and so one can think of the eschatological event as being only one event, regardless of how many such encounters might be counted in the history of the world.

(3) To make the decision which is the eschatological event is by definition to make it "for all" — if in making the decision the individual held back something worldly in his self-understanding, say his money or some particularly glorious achievement, then by definition the eschatological event would not have occurred.

When this word addresses me, telling me "that the prevenient grace of God has already acted on my behalf," the *already* does not refer to an earlier moment of time at which God so acted, but expresses rather a kind of logical priority: my act of decision is not one accomplished simply out of the resources of my own personal life, but is dependent on this word of address in that it is a *response* to it. Accordingly, it would have been more precise for Bultmann to say, not that the word *tells* me that the grace of God has already acted on my behalf, but rather that the word of forgiveness addressed to me *expresses* the priority of God's "act." The only priority which the grace of God has here is that entailed by the fact that it encounters me. The temporal priority of Jesus of Nazareth, though it is a convenient analogy and ambiguity, has nothing to do with the "already" of God's grace, but only with the genetic-historical account of the rise of the kerygma.

In the following passage Bultmann is obviously using words eccentricly:

> Buri is, of course, right in that God's creative operation is not confined to the historical personality Jesus of Nazareth, in so far as we understand 'historical personality' here as an objectifiable historical phenomenon. But it is a different matter if the historical person of Jesus of Nazareth is understood as the Eschatological Event which is present in the Word of preaching at any given time.[60]

If the kerygma is not a report about Jesus, in what sense is "the historical person of Jesus of Nazareth" present in our contemporary preaching? Surely only in the sense that an "event" analogous to the one which occurred in Jesus' preaching and the spectacle of his death can also occur in "the Word of preaching at any given time." That both Jesus and the present-day preaching are the Eschatological Event seems to be what warrants Bultmann's saying that the historical Jesus is present in preaching. And if he were pushed to answer why he picks on the historical Jesus rather than, for example, the historical John Wesley (whose preaching, if true, was also the Eschatological Event), we can suppose that he would fall back on something like the genetic connection: Jesus' preaching was the original Eschatological Event. But how confusing it is for Bultmann to use the words *the historical person of Jesus of Nazareth* in this odd way. For, having denied an identity to Jesus, having reduced him to a presupposed contentless "that," having denied that he reveals anything other than that he is the

---

[60] *Essays*, p. 288.

Revealer, there is no way that Bultmann can mean that Jesus is a "person" who is present in the Word of preaching.

Defending against those who may think that his "demythologizing" project severs the bond between the church's preaching and the Jesus of history, Bultmann declares,

> The redemption of which we have spoken is not a miraculous event, but an historical event wrought in time and space. . . . the kerygma maintains that the eschatological emissary of God is a concrete figure of a particular historical past, that his eschatological activity was wrought out in a human fate. . . . The agent of God's presence and activity, the mediator of his reconciliation of the world unto himself, is a real figure of history.[61]

In what sense was the historical Jesus the mediator of God's reconciliation of the world to himself? Bultmann's answer must be that he was, for certain of his contemporaries, the Eschatological Event, the phenomenon in face of which they became able to achieve the decision to understand themselves in independence of everything worldly. So much for his contemporaries, but what has that to do with us? The answer is that there is another phenomenon, namely the kerygma, which can have the same effect for us. But the next question is, "What does Jesus have to do with that phenomenon which mediates God's reconciliation to us (besides the fact that this latter is the same sort of phenomenon as Jesus was)?" And the answer is that Jesus has the status of a paradigm of that kind of phenomenon, because he was the first one; he is special because we can trace this sort of thing, historically, back to him. Can we say then that the historical Jesus is our savior? It seems not, at least if we are speaking plainly. The kerygma is our savior, and Jesus is the historical cause of the kerygma. Insofar as the kerygma would never have come into being without Jesus, we are dependent on Jesus for our salvation; but not in such a way as to necessitate mentioning him ever anew in preaching. To that first generation of disciples, Jesus was "the agent of God's presence and activity"; when *we* say he is that, we can only mean that he is the historical cause of God's present-day "agent,"

---

[61] *KM,* p. 44.

which is the kerygma. But again, we must feel that Bultmann could have found less misleading ways to express himself.

When he says,

> to ignore the connection between faith on the one hand and the cross of Christ as a past event on the other would certainly mean surrendering the confession and the kerygma,[62]

he can mean only two things: (1) by "cross of Christ as a past event" he may simply be referring to the world phenomenon side of the paradox which is the Eschatological Event. If this were all he meant, then the expression would be extremely misleading, since the open mouth of the concrete historical preacher will be rightly designated the "cross of Christ as a past event." Therefore we must assume that he also means to use the expression as shorthand for referring (2) to the original Eschatological Event, the early disciples' decision for authenticity as they beheld the spectacle of the historical Jesus dying upon the historical cross. To say that ignoring the connection between this event and present-day faith would "mean surrendering the confession and the kerygma" can only mean that it would be to step out of this particular line of tradition. But to step out of that line of kerygmatic tradition which originated in association with the cross of Jesus would not, on Bultmann's description of faith and kerygma, be to abandon salvation. For as we have seen, the connections which he is able to preserve between Jesus and the present-day kerygma are not such as to disallow the possibility of an equally effectual and formally identical "kerygma" in which reference to Jesus is totally abandoned.

The following is perhaps the most difficult sentence in all of Bultmann's writing to interpret along the lines I have been suggesting:

> The word of God is not some mysterious oracle, but a sober, factual account of a human life, of Jesus of Nazareth, possessing saving efficacy for man.[63]

How can we make this statement consistent with his denial that

---

[62] *KM*, p. 110.
[63] *Ibid.*, p. 44.

the kerygma is a report or historical narrative? For he is obviously here speaking of the kerygma, yet what other than a narrative could be a "factual account" of the life of Jesus of Nazareth? In what sense could the "word of God" be for Bultmann this "account"? We know that the account, insofar as it is the word of God, cannot express any "what" about Jesus which might provide him a particular identity, but only a bare "that." Shall we conclude that the words *factual account* and *human life* are being used eccentricly, and are really meant only to indicate that side of the kerygma paradox which Bultmann usually calls "world phenomenon"; that is, that the account is neither really an account nor really of a particular human life, but that the words are meant to express a formal element of the present-day kerygma which is represented by the preacher's concrete and historically open mouth? I admit that this interpretation is strained;[64] this passage almost tempts one to Ogden's reading. But I know of no other in Bultmann's works as difficult to harmonize with his main thought as this one, and there are countless passages which directly deny what seems to be asserted here. So my inclination is to say that either the above interpretation, violent though it is, is correct; or that he has just made a slip on this occasion and, overzealous to show that he has not given up Jesus, has in fact contradicted himself. But a slip on a given occasion need not be a symptom of a structural inconsistency.

d. Conclusion

Bultmann's "christology" is an attempt at a doctrine of the two natures, now not in the objectivizing mode of Greek thought, but rather in the non-objectivizing existentialist mode. The Chalcedonian formula, "a solution which indeed found an expression that is now impossible for our thought,"[65] held that

---

[64] I warned the reader in the Introduction that our account of Bultmann might seem violent to those whose acquaintance with his works was concentrated in his exegetical or sermonic, rather than in his programmatic and philosophical, works. But having seen how forced a reading of some passages is required to make his christological thought consistent, the reader will perhaps be more inclined to grant that passages in his exegesis and preaching may likewise present us with a hermeneutical problem which at first is not obvious.

[65] *Essays,* p. 286.

the personality of Jesus of Nazareth was constituted of a divine and a human nature subsisting in one soul-substance, thus uniting humanity and divinity in a historical figure. Bultmann's formula is similarly a paradox: "Jesus Christ is the Eschatological Event as the man Jesus of Nazareth and as the Word which resounds in the mouth of those who preach him."[66] Here instead of uniting the humanity and divinity in the crude objectifying mode by attributing the divinity-humanity to a human being,[67] Bultmann attributes it to an "event," namely that in which God's grace is so enacted that he whom it confronts is enabled to grasp himself in the absoluteness of freedom from the world. Here the substance in which the two natures are united is the purely momentary "event" of the proclamation, in such a way that the Christ *is* the preaching. As Bultmann says, Christ's deity "is always only an event at any given time."[68] His is "a christology which is proclamation."[69] The event is a word spoken, a word which, because it demands and enables a decision in favor of transcendence, can be called the Word of God. However, this word is not only a divine word, but also a human one, for in it is mentioned a man, Jesus of Nazareth.[70] Jesus becomes the word of God when he is mentioned in the kerygma; the kerygma is implicated in humanity when it is a word about Jesus.

I must make clear that even on my reading Bultmann is guilty of an inconsistency. But since he never asserts that Jesus of Nazareth is perpetually the object of Christian faith, it is

---

[66] *Essays,* p. 286.

[67] We must remark that there is a more sympathetic way of taking the Chalcedonian formula. Bultmann seems to assume that it must be attributing some kind of quasi-physical properties to Jesus' soul. The problem then might become, how can divine and human essence get mixed together? (We have a similar problem with water and oil.) Not denying that some did take the formula this way, we can hold another reading at least possible. For if it is kept in close association with the biblical narrative, it might be taken as a succinct and perhaps somewhat awkward way of highlighting master features of Jesus' *story:* that he behaved as both God and a man. The non-biblical vocabulary, taken this way, would not be worrisome.

[68] *Ibid.*

[69] *FU,* p. 283.

[70] We have seen, though, filling in this side of the paradox, that Jesus must be replaceable by the preacher's concrete historical open mouth.

not the gross one some critics accuse him of. The inconsistency
has to do with his attempt to use the genetic connection as
credentials for the present-day preaching. On the one hand he
is at pains to deny that Paul has "misused" Jesus and transformed Christianity into something discontinuous with the
teachings of the Lord. He argues that, on the contrary, Paul
and Jesus are in formal agreement about the law and the grace
of God.[71] His motivation here seems to be the feeling that if
Paul and Jesus are really at odds, Paul's gospel is somehow
called into question. But on the other hand he wants to protect
faith from vulnerability to the results of historical research, and
accordingly reduces the theological significance of Jesus to that
of a bare presupposed "that." He wants to hold that nothing
that could be established about the historical Jesus could in-
validate the kerygma. For example, against those who would
make it dependent on the existential self-understanding of Jesus,
he says that we must reckon with the possibility that on the way
to the cross Jesus suffered a moral break-down.[72] The point
seems to be that even if something like this were established
historically, it would not affect the legitimacy of present-day
proclamation. Thus he seems to want to have it both ways: the
kerygma must be invulnerable to historical research, yet the
historical Jesus acts as a kind of credentials for it. Although
this is obviously an inconsistency, it does not seem to me a terribly significant one. The fact is that the central logic of Bultmann's thought makes it queer to talk about the kerygma's historical credentials at all, and as we have seen, when one ex-
amines carefully his remarks about the "authority" of the
kerygma, it turns out not to involve anything of the kind. We
have seen that his rather odd use of the word *Jesus* is, by and
large, consistent, and that it is such as not to involve any logical
necessity for mentioning Jesus of Nazareth in the kerygma. So
I prefer to allow him the little inconsistency of his concern for
"credentials," attributing it perhaps to his tender sentiments
toward traditional Christianity.

In our clarification of Bultmann's account of Jesus and the
kerygma we have seen that Jesus has definite connections with

---

[71] Cf. *EF*, pp. 183ff.
[72] Braaten, *op. cit.*, p. 24.

the kerygma, but that these do not establish his indispensability to present-day proclamation; nor does reference to him have such a status as to procure uniqueness for Christian preaching. What for the New Testament both rendered him indispensable to Christian preaching and rendered that preaching unique and irreplaceable—namely the identification of the historical person as the Son of God and the corresponding characterization of the kerygma as report or narrative—has, under duress from the existence/world dichotomy, dropped out of Bultmann's account. So any desire which he might have had to preserve an ongoing *necessary* relation between Jesus and the kerygma was doomed from the beginning.

In the first chapter we gained a synoptic view of the idea fundamental to Bultmann's thought. In the second we juxtaposed it with the New Testament, and a massive contradiction became evident. Before the interlude on christology which has presently been occupying us, I gave a little preview of the theoretical ploy which attempts a mediation of that contradiction. The next major section of this essay is devoted to a detailed consideration of this mediating aspect of Bultmann's thought.

Part II

Hermeneutics

4

Science
and Mythology

One of the first things to strike any reader of the New Testament (especially if he picks it up fresh) is a certain strangeness about it. True, it is also about universally comprehensible questions, such as the meaning of life, human suffering, love between brothers, human failing, death, and hope. But at the same time, on almost every page there are elements which are opaque, which seem to come from another world. Beside the affinities, there seems also to be a gap separating the authors of the New Testament from us.

It is Bultmann's claim that this gap is constituted by the fact that behind the New Testament writers' beliefs lay a cosmological system which today is neither believed nor believable, because as modern men we hold an alternative and contradictory cosmology. The New Testament cosmology he calls the "mythological world-view," and the one he believes all modern men necessarily to hold (whether or not self-consciously) he calls the "modern scientific world-view." At the beginning of his article "New Testament and Mythology" he describes the ancient world-view succinctly:

> The cosmology of the New Testament is essentially mythical in character. The world is viewed as a three-storied structure, with the earth in the centre, the heaven above, and the underworld beneath. Heaven is the abode of God and of celestial beings — the angels. The underworld is hell, the place of torment. Even

the earth is more than the scene of natural, everyday events, of the trivial round and common task. It is the scene of the supernatural activity of God and his angels on the one hand, and of Satan and his daemons on the other. These supernatural forces intervene in the course of nature and in all that men think and will and do. Miracles are by no means rare. Man is not in control of his own life. Evil spirits may take possession of him. Satan may inspire him with evil thoughts. Alternatively, God may inspire his thought and guide his purposes. He may grant him heavenly visions. He may allow him to hear his word of succour or demand. He may give him the supernatural power of his Spirit. History does not follow a smooth unbroken course; it is set in motion and controlled by these supernatural powers. This aeon is held in bondage by Satan, sin, and death (for "powers" is precisely what they are), and hastens towards its end. That end will come very soon, and will take the form of a cosmic catastrophe. It will be inaugurated by the "woes" of the last time. Then the Judge will come from heaven, the dead will rise, the last judgement will take place, and men will enter into eternal salvation or damnation.[1]

The more specifically Christian beliefs in the atoning death of Jesus Christ, his resurrection from the dead, and the redemption which his work and presence has accomplished and will accomplish for men, necessarily imply the foregoing cosmology, according to Bultmann.[2] That is, it is impossible to hold the beliefs without holding the cosmology. Also, for the modern interpreter, reference to the cosmology constitutes a genetic account for the beliefs: they arose not because the occurrences recounted in the New Testament happened and were witnessed, nor yet because the writers of the New Testament were flagrant liars trying to put one over on the world, but because men in those days thought in these terms. Therefore the beliefs must be radically revised for modern men, who no longer hold the cosmology which is the *conditio sine qua non* for espousing the beliefs in the New Testament. This "interpretation" is called "demythologizing," and is a process in which the "meaning" of the New Testament beliefs is purified of all "objectifying" language — all language about things happening in the world

---

[1] *KM*, pp. 1f.
[2] *Ibid.*, p. 2.

which have in themselves religious significance (e.g., the atoning death of Jesus), all spatial and temporal religious talk such as that about the resurrection of the body, a specific time of judgment, and Heaven. The "meaning" of these beliefs (their significance for the faithful man in the way he decides about his own existence) must be given without the beliefs themselves.

Although Bultmann's description purports to be of a single and unitary cosmology, a system of beliefs which must be either accepted or rejected as a whole, we can discern four distinct elements in his account of the New Testament worldview, each of which has a contradictory counterpart in the modern cosmology. First there is the three-story universe, with Heaven up in the sky (or on the other side of the sky-canopy), our world in the middle, and Hell down under the ground; this view is clearly contradicted by modern geology, which knows more or less what is under the ground, and modern astronomy, which knows more or less what is up in the sky: space goes on and on, and as far as we can see or imagine there is only the natural continuum. Second is the conception of causality, according to which some things which happen in the world do not have causes of the kind we generally (and vaguely) call "natural," but have to be explained by reference to the agency of God or demons; this aspect of the New Testament's belief about the world is contradicted by what Bultmann takes to be a belief implied by the method of natural science, the belief in "the closed causal continuum of the world process." Third is the belief, found in the New Testament, that one can be possessed by the Spirit of God in such a way that one's actions, thoughts and attitudes are influenced by his Spirit, and that one can likewise be possessed by evil spirits; Bultmann seems to think that modern man, in contradiction to this view, sees that he is entirely the master of his own decisions, that he is a center of choice complete in himself and inaccessible to outside influences. Fourthly, Bultmann counts it, somewhat oddly I think, part of the New Testament cosmology that its authors believed that the end of the age, the resurrection of the dead, and the final judgment would come cataclysmically in the near future; this belief is contradicted by the fact that it didn't, and what Bultmann takes to be the modern belief on this matter, namely that it never will. We will soon see that much of the persuasiveness of Bultmann's argument depends on our accepting his lumping together of these four considerably different elements under the single conception of mythological world-view. However, the only way to be clear and critical about Bultmann's argument is to take these elements one by one, examining their status vis-a-vis both the New Testament and modern science. But before I enter upon this more detailed analysis, let me make a few general remarks about our theologian's use of his notion of the two cosmologies.

One of the most important ways the concept of world-view functions for Bultmann is that it enables him to force the question about the beliefs of the New Testament into the form of a sweeping "either/or." Most modern Christians incline, I suppose, to say that certainly there are some things which St. Paul believed which we no longer believe, but that there are others which are still acceptable today without revision. Most, I assume, would not have much use for the gnostic's principalities and powers governing the world, in which it is possible that Paul believed. On the other hand, many would take as being of first importance to believe that Jesus is the Son of God who died for our sins, that he was raised from the dead and presently lives, that we will one day be raised with him to incorruptible life, and so on. One of the prime functions of Bultmann's notion of a world-view is to deny the possibility of just this *ad hoc*, pick-and-choose approach to the New Testament beliefs. The reason is that the world-view theory says that the beliefs are not independent of one another, but have at their basis a system of general beliefs about the world. All the particular beliefs imply the system with something like logical necessity: if you don't buy the system, you can't have the beliefs. Therefore he can present the hermeneutical problem in what he honorifically calls "radical" terms:

> Whatever else may be true, we cannot save the kerygma by selecting some of its features and subtracting others, and thus reduce the amount of mythology in it. . . . The mythical view of the world must be accepted or rejected in its entirety.[3]

Under a term like 'mythical' the choice has of course already been decided beforehand, and any modern man who dares to

---

[3] *KM,* p. 9.

believe the New Testament will be pityingly regarded as having "paid the fearful price of the sacrificium intellectus."[4] This all-or-nothing attitude Bultmann calls "proceeding methodically," and he thus accuses Karl Barth of being arbitrary when he refuses to cover the whole New Testament with the singular wet blanket of mythology, but desires rather to examine the biblical beliefs one by one and to proceed eclectically:

> The purpose of my existential interpretation of myth is precisely to inquire into the possibility of a valid meaning for the mythical picture of the world, and in this I am trying to proceed methodically, while in the case of Barth I can perceive only arbitrary assertions. What, then, is his principle of selection?[5]

As though a man is arbitrary if he has no one single principle of selection covering all the cases beforehand!

Bultmann's motive for "radicalizing" the question about the New Testament's beliefs is (though I think he is only partly conscious of this) the contradiction between existentialism and New Testament thought which I have laid out in the first two chapters. So his problem is this: "How do I, as one having to derive my teaching about faith from the New Testament, hold to the existentialist conception of it?" Answer: attribute these unwanted worldly aspects of New Testament faith to something accidental to the New Testament's real meaning and dependent on historical relativities. Give these undesirable aspects a disparaging name like "mythology" and say that the *whole* New Testament can be so described because it is founded on the "mythological world-view." With such a name people will immediately say "that has nothing to do with us." To clinch the whole thing posit something with an honorific name which logically excludes the mythological world-view and say that people must hold it because of their nature and their generation. Then say that the central meaning of the New Testament — what is left when the worldly chaff has been "interpreted" into something unworldly — is just that decisive self-understanding which Heidegger discerned but failed to grasp as an actual possibility

---

[4] Ogden, *op. cit.*, p. 35.
[5] *Essays*, p. 261.

since he did not acknowledge the kerygma. Thus, if we ask how the concepts of the two world-views fit in a general way into the larger system of Bultmann's thought, the answer is that together they function to protect the existentialist notion of faith against threats from the New Testament: they rationalize the elimination from the modern interpretation of the New Testament of those elements which do not conform to existentialist authenticity. As Bultmann says, it is the nature of "faith" which demands the re-interpretation of the mythological:

> The restatement of mythology is a requirement of faith itself. For faith needs to be emancipated from its association with every world view expressed in objective terms, whether it be a mythical or a scientific one. That conflict is a proof that faith has not yet discovered the proper terms in which to express itself, it has not realized that it cannot be logically proven, it has not clearly understood that its basis and its object are identical, it has not clearly apprehended the transcendental and hidden character of the divine activity, and by its failure to perceive its own "Nevertheless" it has tried to project God and his acts into the sphere of objective reality. Starting as it does from the modern world view, and challenging the Biblical mythology and the traditional proclamation of the Church, this new kind of criticism is performing for faith the supreme service of recalling it to a radical consideration of its own nature. It is just this call that our demythologizing seeks to follow.[6]

Before going into the more detailed examination of Bultmann's claims, let me make one more general remark about his procedure. He gives a ring of plausibility to his assertion that modern man cannot accept the cosmology (and thus the beliefs) of the New Testament by taking some of the stories and expressions with a crudeness which surely outdoes the biblical authors, and probably most of the people of their day. For example it is far from clear to me that the references to the Devil in the Synoptic Gospels are to be taken to mean that there is an individual person, with dark purposes of his own, who lives down under the ground, occasionally emerging from the murky depths to talk to men and do battle with them for the sake of evil. It seems to me not inconsistent with the Synoptic references to

---

[6] *KM*, p. 210.

take them as being, even originally, a picturesque way of speaking about evil in the world and the temptations of individuals. They might indeed arise from a folkish tradition which did not reflect about the objective reality of the Evil One, and thus had no opinion one way or the other about his objective existence. But it would seem a hardy inference to assert from the existence even of the more naive folk-tales (that is, ones which were not self-consciously allegorical or otherwise non-literal) a cosmology of the sort which could be invalidated by modern science. In constructing the so-called cosmology of the New Testament, Bultmann is far more literal and theoretically heavy-handed than ever the New Testament was. One gets the impression from the New Testament that if its writers had a cosmology at all, they sat much looser to it and were less systematic about it than Bultmann's representation of them would have it. But we will finally get clearer about these matters only by going into details. To them let us now proceed.

I. The Three-Decker Universe

If the mythological world-view is to function in such a way as to *necessitate* the existential interpretation of the Scripture, then elements such as the three-decker character of the universe must be foundational for particular beliefs. That is, it must be *impossible* for one holding a contradictory world-view to retain the beliefs in question. Thus Bultmann seems to think that behind any traditional belief in Heaven and the related belief in the resurrection of the dead lies the assumption that the universe is divided into three layers, with Hell down under the ground, Heaven up above the sky, and our own world in between:

> What meaning . . . can we attach to such phrases in the creed as "descended into hell" or "ascended into heaven"? We no longer believe in the three-storied universe which the creeds take for granted. . . . No one who is old enough to think for himself supposes that God lives in a local heaven. There is no longer any heaven in the traditional sense of the word. . . . We can no longer look for the return of the Son of Man on the clouds of heaven or hope that the faithful will meet him in the air. (I Thess. 4:15ff.)[7]

---

[7] *KM,* p. 4.

Now let us experiment with two questions: "Did St. Paul believe in a three-story universe?" and, "In order to believe in Heaven and the resurrection of the dead, did Paul *have* to believe in the three-story universe?"

Early in his writing career, writing his first letter to the Thessalonians, Paul says,

> For the Lord himself will descend from heaven with a cry of command, with the archangel's call, and with the sound of the trumpet of God. And the dead in Christ will rise first; then we who are alive, who are left, shall be caught up together with them in the clouds to meet the Lord in the air; and so we shall always be with the Lord. (4:16–17)

Of all the passages in the New Testament, this is perhaps the one which implies most clearly that heaven is up in the sky—or, perhaps more precisely, on the other side of the sky. Accordingly, when the Lord comes to get his own, he has to descend through the clouds to reach them. However, he doesn't come all the way down to the earth, but stays up in the sky and yells a command for the end of the world to begin. At that point God, who is still up in heaven above the sky (sitting no doubt on his big throne immediately to the left of Jesus' now vacant little one), blows on an enormous trumpet, whose sound shakes everything, including undoubtedly even hell, which not even the earth's crust can protect from God's fury. (Or perhaps it would be more fitting for God to let somebody else blow his trumpet.) The archangel, who is either still up in heaven with God and all the trumpeting, or has perhaps descended into the sky with the Lord, gives out a call also, presumably to a band of angels who will help drag the resurrected up into the clouds through which they'll have to pass on their way to heaven.

Now though my interpretation in the spirit of Bultmann outdoes even St. Paul for picturesqueness, it does seem to me that in this particular account of how the resurrection will occur, Paul assumes that the abode of the blessed is up in the sky, and thus in spatial continuity with the present order of things. Thus something like the three-decker cosmology seems to be presupposed, unless we take the passage as a picturesque way of saying something else, which is not a natural reading. But the question is not whether Paul assumed the three-decker universe in one passage, or one letter, or one period of his career (almost experimentally, as it were), but whether this belief was a firm and abiding and fundamental one for him.

In Paul's slightly later account of the resurrection in I Corinthians 15, he speaks at some length on the subject without referring to any upward or downward movement at all. Bultmann seems to assume that this passage and others must be interpreted in the light of the assumptions which seem clearly made in I Thessalonians 4. But this is to attribute a kind of theoretical consistency to St. Paul which he may not have—it is to assume indeed that his statements necessarily have behind them a "world-view" from which he cannot escape. But if we did not make this assumption, and interpreted I Corinthians 15 as standing in a looser theoretical connection with I Thessalonians 4, it would seem a perfectly natural reading to think of heaven not as being "up there," but as simply the new order which is established at Christ's coming. If we do not make the assumption that Paul was a crypto-cosmologist, then we are free to speculate that perhaps he vacillated in his assumptions about the locality of heaven. If he had been pushed, especially later in his thinking, in a really theoretical discussion of the matter, he might have been reluctant to make hard and fast pronouncements.

Other expressions like "descending" and "ascending" appear in the later writings of Paul, without having as unequivocally a spatial meaning as is evident in the passage from I Thessalonians. For example, in Philippians 2:8–10, Paul says,

> And being found in human form he humbled himself and became obedient unto death, even death on a cross. Therefore God has highly exalted him and bestowed on him the name which is above every name, that at the name of Jesus every knee should bow, in heaven and on earth and under the earth. . . .

Exalted here does not need to have the meaning of "taken up into the sky," and *above* clearly does not refer to a location at a measurable distance from the earth's surface. "In heaven and on earth and under the earth" need be nothing more than a poetic way of saying *"every* knee" again. It may be that Paul held the three-story view of the universe when writing this passage, but the use to which he is putting the relevant expressions is not a cosmological use, and need not even presuppose his being willing or able to use them cosmologically.

In Romans 10:6–8, we read,

> But the righteousness based on faith says, Do not say in your heart, "Who will ascend into heaven?" (that is, to bring Christ down) or "Who will descend into the abyss?" (that is, to bring Christ up from the dead). But what does it say? The word is near you, on your lips and in your heart (that is, the word of faith which we preach).

Here ascending into heaven and descending into the abyss are clearly metaphorical ways of speaking about establishing one's own righteousness by works, as opposed to living by faith in Jesus Christ. Heaven and the abyss need no more be spatially locatable than the word which is "near" us. The passage no more entails that heaven has to be a place reached only by going up and the abyss a place reached only by going down, than it does that a man might actually be able to bring Christ down from heaven or up from the dead. It seems to me that most intelligent Christians in the twentieth century will read expressions of this sort metaphorically without any great difficulty. Those might not be the expressions that *they* would use to say something similar, but they will have no more trouble with them than they have with other poetic allusions to expressions or beliefs which are not a part of their own verbal environment. But we must not make the mistake that Bultmann seems to make, of thinking that if *ascending* and *descending* must be understood metaphorically, then all language about heaven and the resurrection must be understood non-literally.

In Ephesians 1:20–21, the author speaks of God's mighty works of salvation

> . . . which he accomplished in Christ when he raised him from the dead and made him sit at his right hand in the heavenly places, far above all rule and authority and power and dominion, and above every name that is named, not only in this age but also in that which is to come. . . .

That this passage need not be read as entailing the hypothesis that Jesus is sitting up in the sky is evident from the fact that a few verses later Paul avers that by God's action we too are now sitting "with him in the heavenly places" (2:6). The passage can be read as being agnostic about the locality of heaven.

A more difficult passage is found in the fourth chapter of the same epistle. Paul is speaking about the gifts which God has given to the church, and is emphasizing the unity of the church by speaking of the unity of the church's foundation in God and Christ. There he says,

> But grace was given to each of us according to the measure of Christ's gift. Therefore it is said,
>   "When he ascended on high he led a host of captives,
>   and he gave gifts to men."
> (In saying, "He ascended," what does it mean but that he had also descended into the lower parts of the earth? He who descended is he who also ascended far above all the heavens, that he might fill all things.) And his gifts were that some should be apostles, some prophets, some evangelists, some pastors and teachers. . . . (7–11)

Parallel with the tension in the passage between the unity and the diversity of the church is the tension between "Christ's [one] gift" and the many gifts from Christ found in the church. Evidently Paul is saying that the many gifts are possible because of the one gift. Now the one gift of Christ is clearly the redemption of men, the forgiveness of their sins, their reconciliation with God and hope of eternal life, which God has worked through Jesus' presence among men, his death at their hands, and his resurrection and exaltation. In the passage which he quotes from the Psalm, Paul seems to see this connection between the gift of Christ and the gifts which are visible in the church: it is because he "ascended on high" that we men now have the gifts we have. That is, it is only because Christ was raised from the dead and exalted to the right hand of God that his presence, his suffering, and his death are efficacious to our salvation and can be the ground for the gifts found in the church. But the Psalm, in speaking of the gift, only implied, but did not tell, the whole story, reasons Paul: for surely if he was resurrected and exalted, this implies that he was exalted from the lowliness and suffering which was his chosen lot among men, and he was resurrected *from* death and its grave—"In saying, 'He ascended,' what does it mean but that he had also descended into the lower parts of the earth?" (It seems quite speculative to take this passage as evidence for the doctrine that Christ descended into hell.) Thus we can see that it is possible to take verses 9 and 10 as a kind of symmetrical elaboration on a certain version of Psalm 68:18, based on the assumption that it refers to the event by which God wrought the salvation of men—"Christ's gift." To read the passage as a somewhat elaborate way of speaking of something which can be spoken of in other ways—namely, the event of redemption with its elements of Jesus' coming into the world, his death, resurrection, and exaltation—is to relegate the spatial question to an incidental status. To take the passage as necessarily implying the belief that heaven is up in the sky and hell down under the earth's crust is erroneous; and to take it as evidence that Paul believed in a three-decker universe is speculative.

Along with the passage from I Thessalonians 4, the most obvious candidate for a knock-down argument that the writers of the New Testament believed in a three-decker universe is the account of the ascension of Jesus into the clouds in Acts 1. What could Jesus be doing going up into the sky, if not going back to God, to the place where he dwells? But if the scholars are right in holding that the author of the third Gospel is the man who penned the Acts of the Apostles, then it would seem that we have two accounts of the ascension by the same man, only one of which records that spectacular aviatorial event. Luke ends his Gospel with an account of what looks like the final departure of Jesus from among men:

> Then he led them out as far as Bethany, and lifting up his hand he blessed them. While he blessed them, he parted from them. And they returned to Jerusalem with great joy, and were continually in the temple blessing God. (Luke 24:50ff.)

If this is an account of the ascension, it is marked by a notable lack of upward motion. The ascension here would seem to be neither more nor less than the last of the resurrection appearances. But if one man wrote both accounts and let them stand as they were, it would seem that he at least did not believe, in any strong sense, that Jesus went into the sky. It was rather, perhaps, that Jesus being who he was and being associated as he was with the Danielian Son of Man who was pictured as coming on the clouds of heaven, Luke thought it *fitting* that his departure from among men (which certainly would have to be thought

of as an "ascension" to the presence of God) should be represented as a going up into the clouds of heaven (leaving aside
the question whether this was the most strategic way to represent
it, given the trouble this image has caused). Thus, at least as
far as the author of Luke-Acts himself was concerned, it does
not seem quite appropriate to say that he believed that Jesus went
up into the clouds on that first Ascension Day. For him the
language of spatial ascension seems to be not the reporting of an
occurrence, but rather a way of saying something else about
Jesus: that he is the Messiah, and that God has exalted him
King over all.

The upshot of these exegetical excursions[8] is not to deny
categorically that Paul or Luke (and certainly not that some of
their contemporaries) believed in a three-decker cosmology. It is
rather to say that the question whether they so believed is not
so categorically answerable as Bultmann would lead us to
believe.

But even if the writers of the New Testament did believe
that heaven was up in the sky, is Bultmann right in thinking that
without that belief no belief in the resurrection or in heaven is
possible? For his world-view theory is an attempt to force us
into this "either/or": either we believe in the three-decker universe, or we must engage in existential interpretation, which,
since it eliminates all objectifying language, also precludes belief
in heaven and the resurrection (though of course it gives an
"interpretation" of them). Bultmann seems stiffly to identify
belief in the resurrection with a certain "how" of that belief
(represented, perhaps, in I Thessalonians). Now to believe the
resurrection will occur that way does seem to commit us to a
heaven above but in spatial continuity with this order of things.
But it is certainly possible to believe in the resurrection without believing that this is how it will occur, and even the New
Testament does not seem to be very committed to this "how."
Belief in the resurrection is flexible enough to accommodate to
a universe which has no up or down about it, but is just extended in all directions. It is consistent with modern beliefs

---

[8] These comments are not a direct response to Bultmann, because he
gives very little exegetical evidence for attributing the three-decker cosmology to the New Testament writers. And these results are, I think, an
indication why.

about space that heaven be either this order, which will one day be transformed, or a wholly different order, not in spatial continuity with the present universe at all. We can imagine that if St. Paul had been confronted with a refutation of the three-decker universe, he might have adjusted his belief, but would certainly not have felt compelled to give it up and become an existentialist. For his belief in the resurrection of the dead was based not on a conviction about the location of heaven and hell, nor upon the apocalyptic descriptions which were floating around in the Jewish atmosphere of his day, but upon the witness of others and his own experience that *Jesus* had been raised from the dead. Belief in the resurrection does not depend on the three-decker universe, or perhaps on any cosmology at all.

Bultmann's error rests on a confusion of generality and fundamentality of beliefs. The three-story cosmology is a *general* belief with respect to the resurrection, inasmuch as it is capable of giving a certain form to the latter belief. Bultmann, on the other hand, takes it to be *foundational* with respect to the resurrection, and thus a determinant not only of its forms, but of its possibility.

The apostle James wrote, "Every good endowment and every perfect gift is from above, coming down from the Father of lights . . ." (James 1:17). Does this sentence need to be "translated" in order to be understood? Does a three-story cosmology necessarily lie behind it, so that any interpretation must traverse this cosmology, both eliminating it and giving its true meaning? Do the words themselves commit James to draw inferences about the celestial location of God? Bultmann believes that sentences always have their meaning within a context of other possible sentences; and in this he is no doubt right. But he errs in thinking that this context of possible sentences (and correspondingly of beliefs, for one using the sentences on his own behalf) has an inviolable systematic integrity such that one must either accept or reject the system-context *as a whole*. The claim that a cosmology is the requisite sentential context is in error, because the conceptual body in which a sentence has its significance is much more flexible than that. Elements come and go with relative independence of the whole; beliefs and meanings shift and adjust to one another in an enormous variety of ways. The sentences forming the context for the affirmation of James quoted above *might* include some physical talk about God on the other side of the clouds and hell underneath the turf. On the other hand that affirmation might be surrounded by a linguistic context in which the spatiality of heaven was neither denied nor speculated about. If theoretical spatial talk about God did constitute part of the linguistic body which surrounded the sentence in the mouth of James himself, then in consequence of some beliefs which we hold from modern astronomy, the conceptual environment of the sentence in our mouths will differ in this respect. But the spatial implications which might have been drawn by James are undoubtedly only one aspect of the conceptual body in which that sentence had its life for James; so it seems a bit arbitrary of Bultmann to raise that aspect to a place of such central and systematic importance that when it is altered *all* "objectivizing" language in our interpretation of the New Testament can be eliminated along with it.

There is often a blurred boundary between *believing* God to be very far away in space, and *imagining* him so to be. There is something natural to us about thinking of God as "way up there." This seems to be the way children think of him, and I think there are few adults for whom it is not natural to imagine God in this way. Now if we had no idea what was out in space, then this imagining might be connected also with some beliefs and hypotheses, which might evidence themselves in the following way: when asked to speculate on what would take place at the moment of the general resurrection, we might not wince at talking about going up into the sky and through the clouds. But for us, popular astronomy has provided some general information about what is up in the sky, which tends to preclude such hypothesizing—there is space, and space, and more space, seemingly without end. So for us, imagining God to be way up in the sky does not issue in the kind of speculations it might for someone who thought of the sky as a big dome with who knows what behind it. But for the most part neither our nor the New Testament's imagining God to be way up there issues in either beliefs or denials about his spatiality; it is, rather, a way of speaking and a way of imagining whose beliefs and denials are of a completely different order: believing, for example, that nothing can separate us from his love; denying, for example, that evil and corruption and death have the last word in this universe. Our imagining him to be up there, and the language which goes with these images, is and need be (even in the ancient believers) nothing more than an imaginal foothold to give firmness to the steps by which we come closer to loving him with all our heart and soul and mind and strength.

II. Miracles

In the New Testament there are numerous "miraculous" events recounted. Jesus (and later the apostles) heal the sick, the blind are given their sight, and even dead people are raised to life. Water is changed to wine, thousands are fed from a few scraps of food, and Jesus walks on the water and calms the storm with a word. And a central feature of the disciples' preaching after Pentecost was the miracle *par excellence,* that without which there would have been no preaching and no Christian church: the resurrection of Jesus himself from the dead. In all these events as the New Testament recounts them, two elements seem to be bound up inextricably together: they are events which are *extraordinary* in the sense that they are not amenable to explanation by reference to natural causes; and it is because they are extraordinary in this sense that they are to be taken as *attestation* of the authority of Jesus. To see the events as extraordinary is of course not equivalent to seeing them as signs of the presence of the kingdom, so we have warnings against taking them in vain. But it is largely on the ground of their extraordinariness that they are considered to be signs that the kingdom of God is at hand, that Jesus is the Son of God, the Messiah, the Lord.

According to Bultmann, the modern scientific world-view is such that we can no longer believe in events which are inexplicable in principle by reference to the ordinary laws of nature. Indeed, it is not quite right to say that we cannot *believe* in them; for Bultmann's view is that we cannot even *conceive* of them. It is not just that the twentieth century is without miracles to be seen, and so we infer that there were probably no miracles in the first century either. His argument is rather that there is something conceptually wrong with the idea of an event *contra naturam*—it is a self-contradictory concept, a pseudo-idea. Why does he think this is so?

Bultmann believes that it is a fundamental feature of our thinking about the world that we conceive it as a closed system of causes and effects. This foundational characteristic of our thinking gets expressed, Bultmann thinks, in the fact that whenever anything happens, we just suppose that there is an explanation for it in more or less the same terms in which we have explained things before. All our life shows forth our implicit trust that the world is orderly and rational. "We always act in such a way as to entrust ourselves to the regular connection of natural occurrences."[9] From this indisputable fact about our existence Bultmann draws a sort of Kantian transcendental-deductive inference that we *cannot think otherwise* than in terms of this causal nexus, and thus cannot even conceive of an event which is in principle not explicable in terms of it.

> *The idea of the regularity* of "nature" lies either explicitly or implicitly at the basis of all our thinking and acting with reference to the world. It is not merely one way of interpreting or viewing the world . . . but is rather *given with our being in the world*. . . . The idea of the regularity and continuity of nature is not an idea which arose with modern science, but rather, since it belongs to human being as such, is a completely primordial idea which in modern science was merely developed and thought through radically.[10]

Whether modern science in fact draws from its practice the Kantian inference that nature is and must be completely and uniformly subject to law is an allegation which we will have ample opportunity to doubt in due time. But Bultmann, at least, accepts the deduction, and the upshot is that a miracle is neither possible nor conceivable. "An historical fact which involves a resurrection from the dead is utterly inconceivable!"[11]

However, it seems *prima facie* wrong to hold that we cannot conceive of an event *contra naturam*. When we read the story of Jesus healing the paralytic, for example, it seems that we understand well enough what is being represented to us, whether or not we believe that it happened. That is, the paralytic is lying there, and after some conversation with him and with the scribes sitting nearby Jesus says to him, "I say to you, rise, take up your pallet and go home." And the former paralytic gets up and takes his pallet and heads for home. This event is repre-

---

[9] *GV*, I, p. 215.
[10] *Ibid.*
[11] *KM*, p. 39.

sented as *contra naturam* insofar as the story itself prohibits us from looking for other explanations (e.g., the paralytic was faking; Jesus had done physical therapy on him for months preceding, or removed a tumor from his brain; etc.). And however unbelieving we may be, I do not think anyone will deny that he can *imagine* its happening this way—in such a way that all the normal explanations are finally ruled out as inappropriate, and we are reduced to saying something like "Jesus just has the power to do it."

Are Bultmann and the transcendental deductors simply wrong, then? They are wrong, but not simply. It is true that if the world were not in general dependable, our life would be very different, if indeed it would be a life at all. "Our intercourse with other men, when we show them something, ask them to do something, etc., takes for granted this conception of general conformity to natural law."[12] But Bultmann's deduction is to infer from our life's dependence on the regularity of nature to its dependence on the *absolute* regularity of nature: nature must be an inviolably closed continuum of causes and effects, a single "process" whose parts are always fully explicable in principle by reference to its other parts. But this deduction is invalid. It is true that if events not explicable in terms of the causal nexus became frequent and random, if, as Wittgenstein says, we "saw houses gradually turning into steam without any obvious cause, if the cattle in the fields stood on their heads and laughed and spoke comprehensible words; if trees gradually changed into men and men into trees,"[13] then the foundations of our common life and rationality would be taken away. An occasional random event, on the other hand, would not destroy the foundations of rationality; it would only occasion surprise, and perhaps a little embarrassment, and serve to make people with a compulsion to explain everything grateful that so much of our life has regular patterns. The inference from our need for much regularity to the necessity of total regularity, and the corresponding metaphysical picture of all reality as a closed causal continuum, is simply a case of bad logic.

---

[12] *FU*, p. 248.
[13] Ludwig Wittgenstein, *On Certainty*, trans. Denis Paul and G. E. M. Anscombe (Oxford: Basil Blackwell, 1969), 513.

Even totally random events are not ruled out by our life-need for regularity. But it should be said that the miracles of Jesus are by no means even random events. They are, in their own way, subject to regularity: just what one might expect from one who speaks and otherwise acts as he does. That is to say, there are perhaps all sort of things which can count as "explanations," things not dreamt of in the wooden philosophies of Kant and Bultmann.

Bultmann's denial of the possibility of miracles depends on a picture of the world which he thinks is implied by modern science. But the important thing to see about this concept of the world—and its correlate, rationality—is that it is a metaphysical construct, an object of speculative *belief,* and by no means a necessary implication of the natural sciences' use of the concept of cause. From the point of view simply of logic it is clear that Bultmann's picture of the "world" is speculative because it functions as a denial of existence: its point is to deny the truth of the attribution of certain kinds of causes, namely, "non-natural" causes. But even if Bultmann had surveyed all the cases of causation in the world and had not found one in which the explanation that God did it was required (all other explanations being found wanting) it would not follow that only natural causes are rationally applicable, and this for two reasons: (1) the explanation that God did it does not, in Christian discourse, require that all other explanations fail (that is, not everything that God specially does is a miracle in the strict sense); and (2) even miraculous intervention (cases in which the explanation that God did it is required because of the inadequacy of natural explanations) is not logically ruled out for the future by not having occurred in the past. (It should be noted, however, that Bultmann has not checked all past events in the history of the world; and the strength of his belief in the impossibility of miracles seems to have led him—very unscientifically, I might add—to ignore a large body of evidence that some events in the past seem to be inexplicable by reference to natural causes.) The picture of "the causal continuum of the world process" is not to be found among the principles of any science, though it is to be found in naturalistic metaphysics. And now we find it in a theological system, as a ploy for making it look not only justifiable but even necessary[14]

---

[14] Cf. *KM,* p. 7.

to make certain sweeping eliminations from our interpretation of the New Testament. It is a way of making it look as though anyone who believes in miracles, or believes that God raised Jesus Christ from the dead and will one day raise us, is either naive or intellectually dishonest. On the other hand the belief in the closed causal continuum of the world process—a belief for which, unlike that of the resurrection, we do not have and indeed cannot have, any evidence—is praised as modernity and being hardheaded.

Bultmann employs the concept of history in a similar way:

> History necessarily demythologizes to the extent that it views the historical process in an objectifying way and thus understands it as a closed continuum of effects. The historian cannot proceed otherwise if he wants to achieve reliable knowledge of some particular fact — for example, if he wants to determine whether some traditional account is really a valid testimony to a certain fact of the past. Thus he cannot allow that the continuum of historical happenings is rent by the interference of super-natural powers; nor can he acknowledge any miracles in the sense of events whose causes do not lie within history itself.[15]

Here Bultmann conceives of history as a domain of happenings. This domain has an "inside," where the causes for everything that happens in it are exhaustively to be found; and it has an "outside" in the odd sense that one can imagine there being causes for what happens in it other than those which are "inside," but only as long as one does not radically think through the concept of history. Bultmann seems to be thinking of history as a grand machine. When our car will no longer run, we look for the causes of its failures inside the system: we check the carburetor, the spark plugs, and so forth of *this* car. We would think it absurd if someone thought he could find the causes of this car's failure by looking at the spark plugs of another car. History, then, is a system, however infinitely complex it may be, whose events are interrelated in a way analogous to that of the parts of a machine: when something happens in the machine, you look elsewhere within the machine to explain it.

---

[15] *GV*, IV, pp. 132ff.

But the fact of the matter is that we have no idea whether there exists such a thing as history in this sense. The idea of a grand closed system of historical causes and effects is a kind of artificial extrapolation from the fact that things happen and are explicable by reference to other things that happen. *History* is a generic name for accounts and explanations of things that have happened in the past, and also for a set of technical and semi-technical conceptual tools for the production of accounts and explanations of past happenings. As such history is not an objective domain, but a human activity, the rules for engagement in which are determined partly by human purposes and the contexts of human discourse into which the explanations are proposed to fit. Sometimes our purposes in performing historical inquiry make it most expedient to exclude beforehand (and thereafter as long as possible) any explanation in terms of God's activity. Most of technical history is of this sort, and it is this which Bultmann has taken as the paradigm of all rational historical inquiry and from this that he has deduced his metaphysical assertions about a domain called "history." But if history be seen as a human activity, the appropriateness of whose explanations is dependent on human purposes and contexts as much as it is on the sort of thing that has happened, then it may be permissible in historical discourse in some contexts to refer to God as a special agent (to explain something that happened by saying that here God was acting); in other contexts, when explaining even what we might call the same events, the purpose of those engaged in the activity may exclude reference to God as actor. One can "do" political history, economic history, history of ideas, biological history, and so on, and the difference between these activities is not a difference simply of the "objects" of historical inquiry; it is also a difference of the *kind of explanation* which is permitted.

And there is no *a priori* reason, arising from "history" itself, why there cannot also be historical accounts in which it is permissible to refer to God's activity. Indeed, if there are miracles (as there seem to be) one might say that an account of some happenings which left God out of the account would be as inadequate as an account of the rise of industrialism which left economic factors out of account. But even when reference to God as explanatory is not *required* (as it would seem to be where we are dealing with miracles in the strict sense), there is no reason why this kind of explanation would not be appropriate, as long as the activity of explanation was governed by rules. It is, of course, possible that God does not exist, or that he exists but does not ever influence things that happen; in which case historical explanations which referred to him would all be false. But it is a kind of philosophical superstition to think that we already *know* them to be false on the basis of a speculative construct, the grand closed system called "history."

The belief in the closed causal continuum of the world process is, in a certain way, a natural one. That is, if one takes what Aristotle called efficient cause (as opposed, say, to what he called final cause) as the paradigm for causation, and then tries to construct a picture of the whole of reality on its basis, and if one has not been taught to believe in God, then this is the picture which will "naturally" occur to one. One sees the world as an extremely grand and subtle complex of billiard ball connections, so subtle that even the actions, reasons, and purposes of human beings can get assimilated into the picture; and one assumes the rule that no billiard ball will move unless another strikes it. Of course it is not *necessary* that any of the three conditions for this "natural" belief should hold. One might not make the philosopher's leap to the assumption that all causes are like efficient causes, but might allow that causality is as subtle and variegated as our uses of words like *because, hence,* and *since.* Also one might have no inclination to construct a picture of the whole of reality (Bultmann seems to think that we are all metaphysicians, implicitly at least; but this is not clearly the case). Also, one might believe in God in such a way that this belief would give one hesitation about asserting the closedness of the causal continuum. (Indeed we might find a fourth condition for believing in the closed causal continuum to be a theological concern, that is, anti-theological, for this is really a polemical picture of reality; for it might never occur to anyone to say that the causal nexus is closed, unless he had someone in mind *against* whom it could be closed.) But since these are moves which men often make (and in the case of the first two perhaps even typically) when they enter upon reflection, we can say that belief in the closed causal continuum is natural. Bultmann's error is to mistake what is in a way natural for something that is necessary.

But however natural this world-view may be to those who

engage in philosophical reflection, the fact remains that most
people do not hold any world-view at all in this regard, because
even having an opinion about such matters is a rather sophisticated achievement of theoretical imagination. And indeed not
even all sophisticated people have an opinion on the matter.
Bultmann will no doubt reply that he is not talking about an explicit theory of causation, but a pre-theoretical presupposition
of thought. But what does this presupposition consist in? Evidently that in our daily life, as well as in the prosecution of natural scientific investigation, we normally come to questions and
data with the assumption that natural explanations are in principle available. (I say "normally" because not even scientists
always make this assumption—I am thinking of the medical
examining staff at Lourdes.) But such an assumption does not,
as Bultmann thinks the "modern scientific world-view" does, rule
out beforehand the possibility of a case for which no natural
explanation is appropriate. All that is implied by the presuppos-
ing of natural causal relationships is that we will be surprised
if we come across a miracle. And we didn't need modern science
to teach us that; that much we could have learned from the New
Testament. Insofar as it is a necessary presupposition of daily
life, our notion of causality is not a world-view, and does not
exclude miracles; insofar as it is a world-view and precludes
miracles, it is not necessary to our way of thinking, but is a
philosophical construction, an object of speculative belief.

But what about the scientist himself? Surely the *practice*
of modern science forces a belief in the closed causal nexus?
No doubt it would be bothersome if the scientist had to live with
the anxiety that the rules of nature might change from one experiment to the next; the scientist does not reckon with the possibility that God might interrupt the causal regularities upon which
his work depends. If the scientist is a Christian, it would seem
that even his view of God would exclude his believing that God
would interfere in his experiments in an arbitrary way; for the
God of the Christians does not do just *anything* miraculously—
we hear of miraculous cures, but not of miraculous disturbances
of scientific experiments. But the scientist's trust in the regularity of the connections between phenomena in his experiments,
and indeed in his everyday dealings with his telephone and
wife and lawnmower, does not imply that he must hold a belief
about all phenomena whatsoever to the effect that the kinds of

causes which can be observed and calculated in principle are the only ones which are ever operative. The scientist may well trust that in most or even all of his daily dealings in the world "natural" explanations will be sufficient, and yet believe that there can be events which are not so explicable, but which to be rightly explained require reference to God's direct agency.

So there may be such a thing as a belief in the closed causal continuum of the world process, a belief which excludes the possibility of miracles. And it may be more prevalent in the twentieth century than it was in the seventeenth. But it is not, as Bultmann thinks, a necessary consequence of the structure of human thinking, or of being modern, or of using the methods of modern science. Some men may believe in the impossibility of miracles; but no man is compelled to, whether in the first century or the twentieth. And surely one of the ways a Christian in any century distinguishes himself from the rest of the world is to believe that with God all things are possible, and that he has in the past and will in the future do extraordinary things in this world, on behalf of his children. If a man thinks he can't believe in miracles, then that is a point on which he needs to be corrected. The appropriate response to such a man is not to figure a way to make Christianity adapt itself to the impossibility of miracles, but to help the man, who may be in the grip of a strong secular belief, to adapt himself to their possibility. Becoming a Christian might thus entail giving up this aspect of the "modern scientific world-view." However, that would not be a *sacrificium intellectus,* but only the sacrifice of a rather useless belief. For what is more useless than a belief about what can't happen?

However, useless as this belief may be to most of us, it is of considerable theological utility to Bultmann. The concept of freedom which governs Bultmann's entire theology requires a redefinition of "act of God" such that God's acts will have nothing "worldly" about them.

Bultmann believes that if we speak of miracles as demonstrable events, we offend against the thought of God as acting in hidden ways.[16] But as the New Testament describes miracles,

---

[16] Cf. *FU*, pp. 252f.

they are in one sense as demonstrable as any other events. That is, one can ask, "Did it really happen that way?" And evidence can, in principle, be given pro or con. When Paul in I Corinthians 15 lists all the people who witnessed the Lord's resurrection, he is surely attempting to give evidence that the event happened. In another sense, they are not demonstrable, however, for to show that something extraordinary happened is not identical with showing that God did it. Thus it is conceivable (with difficulty) that a person might believe even that Jesus was raised bodily from the dead, without ascribing the event to God's agency. The kind of evidence that can be used to show that one human being, rather than another, performed an act (the kind brought forward in the courtroom, for example) cannot be applied to the question whether God performed a certain act. Speaking about God's performing an act depends on sharing concepts and beliefs which not all men share; and consequently the criteria for judging whether an act performed specially by God depend on these beliefs and concepts. So here we cannot look for a universally acceptable demonstration. But among Christians the character and words of Jesus, along with the extraordinariness of the event of his resurrection, constitute something very much like evidence for the agency of this event: given the event and its context, it is unthinkable that any other than God brought it about.

When he says that to think of miracles as demonstrable events is to offend against the thought of God as acting in hidden ways, does Bultmann mean to say that if a man believes in publicly visible acts of God he thereby commits himself to the belief that *all* action of God is immediately visible as extraordinary? This is surely a *non sequitur,* for Christians who believe in miracles do not typically think that this is the only way God acts. Most of the time the things the pious attribute to God's gracious providence are also explicable, even by the pious themselves, by reference to natural causes and human agency.

But why does Bultmann go to such tortuous lengths to deny that an act of God can be a public event? Why can one not, for example, believe that Jesus' healing of the paralytic was, as an event in the world, an act of God? This oddity, like others in Bultmann's thought, is to be explained only if we go back to his regulative concept of human freedom. By some fancy conceptual footwork in his article "The Problem of Wonder"[17] he attempts to establish that the real meaning of 'miracle' (which he designates as *'Wunder'*, in distinction from *'Mirakel'*—the world event of mythological thinking) is that of an act of God which is *contra naturam* in the sense that it frees the individual from all understanding of himself in terms of his accomplishments past and future; that is, it frees him from a worldly self-understanding.

> Now every such existentiell[18] encounter takes place in a concrete situation, and so it is natural, or, for him who is encountered, one might even say self-evident, to attribute this situation to God's action. And this is perfectly legitimate, if only the origin in God's will is not confused with a causality accessible to objectifying sight. Here to speak of a *Wunder* — not of a *Mirakel*!—is justified.[19]

That is, the situation is objective, but there is nothing peculiar in this situation itself. What makes it an encounter with God is the act of faith in which it becomes an ambiguous accompaniment to the "miracle"—which is nothing other than the momentary eschatological event of self-understanding.

So it is clear enough why Bultmann feels compelled to say that "in no sense whatever is *Wunder* as *Wunder* an observable event in the world, not in any place nor at any time."[20] Observable events must never have decisive significance for my self-understanding. If I depend on the belief that Jesus was raised from the dead, then I am tied down to something past and something within the world; I have failed to find my security by casting away all particular securities, and have thus denied my authentic self as decision-maker. Likewise if that paralytic lived the rest of his life seeing himself primarily as the one upon whom God in Jesus had bestowed the grace of healing, if whenever he was cast down by a sad thought about himself he reflected on

---

[17] Cf. *FU*, pp. 254ff.

[18] Rather than multiply confusions by translating the German words *'existential'* and *'existentiell'* into English, I shall just take them over and use them as English words, modifying also any quoted passages from translations to conform with this policy. For an explanation of how Bultmann uses these words, see the beginning of chapter six.

[19] *GV*, IV, p. 135.

[20] *FU*, p. 252.

the deed which Jesus did that day, if whenever despair threatened to grip his soul he turned it around in hope of a time when healing would extend not only to those limbs once stiff but also to the present hardness of his heart—if that paralytic understood himself thus, then he forfeited his freedom in capitulation to the world.

III. Psychic interference

Modern thought, according to Bultmann, considers that *"man is essentially a unity.* He bears the sole responsibility for his own feeling, thinking, and willing." Modern man's view of himself is contradicted by the New Testament's view, according to which his nature exposes him "to the interference of powers outside himself."[21] As evidence for attributing this anthropology to the New Testament, Bultmann cites what it has to say about the Holy Spirit and the sacraments. The Holy Spirit is a power which grasps man from without, and controls his action and thought. Likewise belief in the efficacy of the Eucharist involves believing in spiritual influence through the physical means of bread and wine. In both cases the closed autonomy of man's spirit, its radical distinction from physical and worldly powers, is contravened, and modern man, who cannot think of himself in any other way, finds what the New Testament says of Spirit and sacraments "completely unintelligible."

Now it seems to me that this unintelligibility might be corrected by loosening such a modern man's attachment to existentialist anthropology, on the one hand, and by encouraging him to read the New Testament a little more carefully on the other. For in order to be able to cast St. Paul's teaching under the rubric of "the interference of powers outside of man," Bultmann interprets this teaching (in accordance with a tendency we have already noted) in the crudest and most magical way, as though when Paul talked about the Spirit dwelling in the Christian believer there was lurking behind this talk the theory of a kind of quasi-physical ether pervading the believer's body and guiding his thoughts and actions almost, as it were, against his will. But this theory is clearly a speculative construction which Bultmann

---

[21] *KM*, p. 6.

has placed upon the passages in which Paul speaks of the Holy Spirit, and not one which can be drawn directly from them. Likewise he takes Paul's remarks that unworthy reception of the Eucharist was the reason for the illness and death of some of the Corinthians as the clue to Paul's theory of the sacraments, and concludes from this that Paul believed the efficacy of the sacrament was dependent on a causal relation between this physical food and the believer's spiritual and physical condition. But this interpretation is tendentious in two ways. First it attributes to Paul a rather explicit theory of the sacraments on the basis of what looks like a casual remark. And second it takes that casual remark in the most magical way, when another reading is possible. For one can interpret Paul's remark as meaning that God *punished* the Corinthians for a misuse of the sacrament by bringing illness upon some of them; it is not at all necessary to regard the passage as supposing that the food and drink are themselves poisonous to one who receives them unworthily. And the Christian belief that human suffering is sometimes attributable to God's wrath is certainly not dependent on any magical theory.

If we discount Bultmann's tendentious exegesis, his complaint against St. Paul's teachings about the Spirit and the sacraments seems to come down to this: Paul was not a Kantian, and thus it did not occur to him that mind or spirit (the realm of freedom, of practical reason, of existential decision) is a radically different sphere from the world (the realm of things and influences, causes and effects, theoretical reason). On the other hand, Bultmann's notion that modern man *is* a Kantian, for whom "nature" and "spirit" never overlap,[22] is a very convenient belief for one who thinks of faith as a decisive spiritual act by which an individual comes to understand himself as in no way identified by his relation to the world.

IV. Eschatology

Bultmann opens his lectures entitled *Jesus Christ and Mythology* by saying that the New Testament is fundamentally eschatological. By that he seems to mean that any interpretation which does not preserve the New Testament's affirmation that the world is coming to an end will not preserve its message either.

---

[22] Cf. *KM,* p. 6.

Unfortunately, what it meant by saying that the world was coming to an end was that the public world itself (and thus public history) would soon end cataclysmically, and another aeon would begin. Since this has not occurred, and nearly 2000 years have elapsed since the time when the end was expected imminently, we can say with confidence that the New Testament writers were wrong in this belief. But if the message is to continue to be a message for us, occasioning faith, we must be careful, thinks Bultmann, not to eliminate this eschatological element. What shall we do, since the New Testament has proven wrong on this point? Bultmann's answer is that we must "re-interpret" it in the following way: we must take 'history' to mean not public history, but the past of each individual, in dependence on which he inauthentically lives his life; and we must take the 'world' not to be the public world of space and time, but all those roles, institutions, and events by reference to which the individual has heretofore inauthentically understood himself. Then the 'end of the world' preached in the gospel means not a public event, but the decision by which the individual comes to understand himself apart from the world and his past, and according to his being as decision-maker. In this way Bultmann thinks he has retained the "eschatology" of the New Testament, without having to accept its unacceptable belief. We may wonder whether this interpretation is anything more than a piece of verbal sleight-of-hand turning on words like *history, eschatology,* and *world*. This is surely not so much interpretation as invention based on remote analogies.

Shifts of belief are to be found in the Bible too, and more in conformity with those shifts than this inventive "re-interpretation" might be a revision of the New Testament eschatology. It might be legitimate to say that what was most important about the biblical eschatology was not the ending of the world, but the having of hope—something which is notably missing from Bultmann's so-called eschatology. And the having of hope might be retained by adjusting the New Testament's eschatology in one of two ways, both of which are suggested in the New Testament. We might simply admit that the early church was wrong in expecting the parousia and transformation of this world in the imminent future, while not giving up the idea that it will one day happen, perhaps in a very distant future. Surely for St. Paul *that* it would happen was much more certain, on the basis of Jesus' resurrection from the dead, than *when* it would happen. And it seems a bit arbitrary for Bultmann to make so much of the early church's mistake about the precise time. Or, a bit more radically, we might sit loose to the New Testament's idea that it is this order which will be transformed, and speculate (though not without biblical warrant) that the resurrection of the dead takes place (or will take place) in another order. Both of these revisions of the New Testament eschatology have the virtue, unlike Bultmann's, of retaining the possibility of Christian hope. Bultmann, however, precludes any such adjustment as this (insuring thus the necessity of a radical re-interpretation, and the possibility of an existential one) by assigning any eschatological hope, as "objectivizing," to a today-impossible "mythological world-view."

V. Conclusion

Bultmann uses the concept of mythological world-view as a device for explaining why the beliefs presented in the New Testament were held, and this mode of explanation serves as a way of denying their truth. Although, as we have seen, Bultmann's notion of the mythological world-view is fraught with confusions, it is, of course, sometimes true that a person's beliefs are to be explained in part by reference to the intellectual atmosphere in which he flourished. But as far as Bultmann is concerned, it seems that only ancient man was capable of being duped by his age, whereas modern man can give himself over to the spirit of his age without the least danger. Here we might proffer a modest little suggestion that Bultmann's unwavering and enthusiastic faith in naturalistic metaphysics is also perhaps an instance of a man's being the unfortunate child of his age. Emile Zola is supposed to have declared that he wouldn't believe a miracle even if he saw it happen. If Zola had seen one, and had in fact maintained, against all the evidence of his own two eyes, that he had not seen a miracle, one could imagine a Christian (whose Christianity might in this respect *save* him from being too unhesitating in accepting the beliefs of his age) explaining Zola's disbelief by saying, "Oh, he disbelieved because he has accepted the idea of the closed causal continuum of the world process"—that is, Zola disbelieved because he was a child of his age.

It may be that in our preaching and teaching we will be at a loss to know what to do with some of the things affirmed in the New Testament. It is the function of concepts like "New Testament cosmology" and "modern scientific world-view" to tell us that it is not legitimate to use our heads to pick and choose among the beliefs presented us there. If we buy Bultmann's notion of the world-views, then we commit ourselves to a wholesale rejection of the New Testament beliefs and correspondingly to slogans like "Don't eliminate; interpret!" (which interpreted means "Eliminate everything, insofar as it is a *belief!*"). So one of the upshots of this chapter's dissolution of the two world-view theory has been to show that the beliefs of the New Testament fit together or fail to fit together in a variety of ways with the results and methods of modern science and that therefore the *only* intelligent approach to the New Testament is piecemeal. It is Bultmann's wholesale approach which is obscurantist. We have also seen that Bultmann's eagerness to treat the beliefs of the New Testament in a "radical" way rests ultimately neither on a reading of the New Testament nor on an assessment of modern man, but rather on a peculiar notion of what it is for a man to be free, derived neither from the New Testament nor from modern scientific anthropology, but rather from the philosophy of existentialism.

5

Language
and Meaning (I)

In chapter one we saw how a division of reality into 'world' and
'existence' lay at the basis of Bultmann's conception of freedom,
and began to see how his theological reflection consists in a
systematic reduction of the substance of Christian theology to
freedom thus characterized. His view of language and meaning,
as we might expect, is the mirror image of this division of reality.
Just as there are two kinds of reality there are two kinds of
language. "Objectifying" language represents worldly objects
such as those of nature and of history in the sense of past events.
Its way of meaning is that of referring, describing, picturing. The
most perfect example of this kind of language is that of natural
science; scientific historical writing, it seems, approximates as
nearly as possible to this ideal, against the disadvantages under
which it inherently works. Religious language, which belongs to
the language of existence, is of two kinds, both in the service of
human freedom. Theological language expresses the freedom
from worldly existence which is the self-understanding of faith.
Kerygmatic language provides the phenomenon in face of which
freedom from worldly existence arises. It seems that, unlike objectifying language, neither theology nor the kerygma means by
referring or describing; that is, though they may refer to and
describe things, their essentially theological or kerygmatic meaning is not to be found in this referring or describing function.
Theology has meaning when it is expressing the self-under-

157

standing of faith; kerygma has meaning when it is taken as direct address, that is, when it is treated as the object in face of which this new self-understanding is grasped in decision, or when it is rejected in a scandalized decision for the old inauthentic self-understanding.

I should perhaps say a few words about the status of my claims in this chapter and the next. Bultmann does not have an explicit, systematic statement of how language works; indeed, it is my claim that if he worked out the implications of some of the things he says in this regard, he would not say them. Inasmuch as my discussion of his views attempts to look at these in a somewhat systematic and theoretical manner, it has very much the character of an *interpretation*. As will be seen from my exposition, his views about language have to be gleaned from a variety of remote places in his literature, in many of which language is discussed only in an indirect or secondary manner, or where the point which I pick up for discussion was not the main issue for Bultmann. And yet it is my hope to be able to show that many of the things he says here and there about language, meaning, interpretation, preaching, and other things, commit him to some beliefs about language which, if they were brought together and made explicit, would constitute something like a theory of language, however inadequate it may be, and however little Bultmann himself may be conscious of his dependence on it. So I am not saying that Bultmann *says* everything I attribute to him; but if anyone wants to dispute my claims, he will have to show that our theologian does not *imply* the theoretical beliefs I discern in the structure of his thought.

The objection has been raised against my treatment of Bultmann's views on language that it is unfair to demand of him the kind of rigor I do. He is, it is said, primarily a religious writer whose validity or invalidity lies in his religious sentiments and insights, so that when he makes remarks about language, meaning, interpretation, and related matters we should not hold him strictly accountable in a theoretical way, but should see these rather as (admittedly imprecise) ways of expressing his religious insights. It seems to me that this is a thorough misunderstanding of what Bultmann is about. The whole of his intellectual activity revolves around technical hermeneutical questions—questions about understanding, meaning, translation, and interpretation. His entire career has been devoted to the problem of translating the meaning of the New Testament into the thought forms of the modern age. If he is involved in fundamental imprecisions or confusions about these matters, then it may be no peripheral or localized difficulty with which we are confronted, but one which calls into question the validity of everything that he has done as a theologian. Here, if anywhere, we are warranted in demanding rigor of him.

I. Theological language and meaning

In an early essay, Bultmann broaches the question of what it is for theological language to be meaningful:

> If 'speaking of God' is understood as *'speaking about God'*, then such speaking has no meaning whatever, for its subject, God, is lost in the very moment it takes place. Whenever the idea, God, comes to mind, it connotes that God is the Almighty; in other words, God is the reality determining all else. But this idea is not recognized at all when I speak *about* God, i.e. when I regard God as an object of thought, about which I can inform myself if I take a standpoint where I can be neutral on the question of God and can formulate propositions dealing with the reality and nature of God, which I can reject or, if they are enlightening, accept.[1]

Whether talk in which the word *God* appears has meaning is dependent on what happens in "the very moment" this speaking "takes place." If in the moment of speaking "its subject . . . is lost," then the speaking "has no meaning whatever." Conversely we can presume that if in the moment of speech the subject is retained or grasped, then the speaking is meaningful. The meaningfulness of the utterance hangs on whether the correlate of the word *God* is retained or lost in the moment of speaking. Bultmann tells us later in the article that the only way the loss of the subject in speaking of God is avoided is when the moment of speech is characterized by the act of obedient response to God's word which addresses us in such a way that we have no control over whether it confronts us or not. In other words, the existentiell stance which retains the meaningfulness of the word *God*

---

[1] *FU,* p. 53.

is that of the momentary act of faith. Contrariwise, what happens in the moment when *God* is uttered in the mode of referential speech (language "about" God, with its correlate thinking "about" God) is that God's almightiness is necessarily contravened by the stance of the speaker, the act of faith is absent, and the language is meaningless. The reason for this failure of meaning seems to be that to speak about God is to objectify him, and to treat him as an object is effectively to deny his omnipotence. So Bultmann seems to be making two claims about language and meaning: first, that to lose the "subject" (I shall refer to this latter with the general and antiseptic term 'phenomenon') is to lose the meaning; and second, that to speak about God involves losing the subject of the speech. Let us examine each of these claims, beginning with the second.

Where does Bultmann get the idea that to make God an object is to deny his omnipotence? Surely simply thinking about him or talking about him is not to question his authority,[2] or view him with the cool eye of neutral observation,[3] or to put him at our "disposal."[4] There are certainly ways of thinking about him or referring to him which violate the logic of the concept of God; but there are other ways of thinking about him which give him the glory (even if we never perfectly attain to them). To say "His steadfast love endures forever," or "God was in Christ reconciling the world to himself," is to speak about God, and yet spoken by the right person these are utterances which are used to praise and magnify him—indeed precisely to express our belief in his almightiness. Surely the aboutness does not in itself constitute a violation. Where does Bultmann get this idea?

One answer is that he believes that

> every 'speaking *about*' presupposes a standpoint external to that which is being talked about. But there cannot be any standpoint which is external to God. Therefore it is not legitimate to speak about God in general statements, in universal truths which are valid without references to the concrete, existentiell position of the speaker.[5]

---

[2] *FU*, p. 54.
[3] *Ibid.*, p. 60.
[4] *Ibid.*
[5] *Ibid.*, p. 53.

What he seems to mean by this is that as soon as we start talking or thinking about God we step outside our faithful acts of surrender and trust, and adopt toward him the neutral attitude which is appropriate to science alone, and is the antithesis of faith, which must always be personally interested and involved. In a similarly neutral and worldly manner, our statements using the word *God* become general statements[6] or universal truths, and lose all reference to our own personal existence. With a little charity for Bultmann, one might allow him the idea that to shift to the "about" mood in one's use of the word *faith* is to take up a standpoint of neutral observation, and thus not to be using the word in the prosecution of the faithful life (although even here it is only a certain way of speaking and thinking about faith which is to be eschewed, for there is much in St. Paul's writings which would count as faithful speaking about faith). But to say that talking about God involves stepping outside faith and taking up a neutral attitude seems to be clearly false, since much of our talking about God is done in precisely the context of faith—of witnessing to his deeds and attributes, of exhorting ourselves and others to love him, of concerning ourselves with our eternal destiny, and so on. Why does Bultmann say these things?

I think we may become clearer about this matter if we take a careful look at an analogy upon which Bultman draws to explain his views on speaking of God.

> It is as impossible to speak meaningfully about God as it is about *love*. Actually, one cannot speak *about* love at all unless the speaking about it is itself an act of love. Any other talk about love does not speak about *love,* for it stands outside love. Therefore a psychology of love would in every case treat of something other than love. Love is not something external in respect of which it is possible either to act and speak or to refrain from acting and speaking. Love exists only as a determining element of love itself. Love *is* there only when I love or am loved; it has no existence alongside me or behind me.[7]

There are two, and possibly three ideas here. The first is that

---

[6] See the next section of this chapter for a discussion of Bultmann's use of the notion of a general truth.

[7] *FU*, pp. 53f.

as soon as we start to talk *about* love, we lose the phenomenon of love. "Objectification" is essentially incongruous with the phenomenon of love. The second is that to lose the phenomenon of love is to fail to use the word meaningfully. The third can be derived only by a little speculation on what Bultmann is assuming here. It is natural to assume that the meaning of a word is what it represents, and it is possible that this is how Bultmann is here thinking about the meaning of the word *love*. He is saying that the only cases in which the word *love* is used meaningfully are those in which the utterance is itself an *act* of love. It is very tempting to think that Bultmann is here equating the act of love with the meaning of the word *love*. That would be why, when the act is absent, the meaning is absent as well. That would be why, in the context of the question of meaning, Bultmann is preoccupied with the question of the "how" of love's existence: "Love exists only. . . . Love *is* there only. . . . it has no existence alongside. . . ." If Bultmann is assuming that the meaning of a word is the phenomenon, or subject, or object, or whatever, with which it is correlated, this would explain too why he thinks that if "God is lost" in the moment of speaking, the utterance is meaningless, and why at the end of the article he says that "if God is not, [the lecture] is meaningless."[8]

First, let us look at the claim that to speak about love always fails, because in any speaking in the "about" mood this phenomenon is lost. When Bultmann says that one "cannot speak *about* love at all unless the speaking about it is itself an act of love," he seems to have in mind noun-instances of the word used in performing an act of love. Thus the husband, in the right circumstances, says, "My love for you knows no bounds, my dear." He speaks about his love, but in such a way that the speaking is also an act of affection. Now in denying that any other use of the word would be about love at all, he perhaps has in mind the case where the husband talks about love all the time (maybe he's a minister) but in all his talk never shows forth any love. And a certain popular usage has it that such a man's talk is "meaningless," even if the sentences he speaks are in another sense correct. We say, "Oh, he *talks* about love all the time, but it doesn't mean a thing." But Bultmann would

---

[8] *FU*, p. 65.

clearly not be content with such a casual construing of his assertions: "Any other talk about love does not speak about *love,*
for it stands outside love." Although a saying like this catches our
hearts in a certain way, it will not stand up to scrutiny.

Imagine an observer standing outside a relationship of love
(that is, the observer is not one of the lovers presently in question) and making the observation, "She showed her love for him
in sticking by him even after he betrayed her." It is a highly paradoxical remark to say that this sentence "is not *about* love at all."
By any of the normal criteria we should judge this sentence to
be fully as much about love as a sentence about a brick is about
a brick. Or take another kind of sentence which Bultmann considers to be literally meaningless as language about love, namely
the general statement, the abstract proposition, the universal
truth. One could imagine such a sentence occurring in a "psychology of love": "Sometimes love between spouses or brothers
or friends becomes so deep and compelling a motive that it leads
one person to sacrifice his whole welfare for another." Is it
correct to say that this sentence is not about love at all? In trying to be "objective," a certain kind of positivistic "science" does
sometimes fail to refer when it speaks of spiritual things. We can
imagine somebody writing a "psychology of love" in which he
states that "Love is purely glandular." And here it is surely correct to say that what he is speaking about is not what most of us
refer to by using the word *love.* Yet it is not the generality of this
statement that makes it fail, but rather that what, in particular, it
says about love is erroneous. For it is no more general than the
meaningful and true sentence about sacrifice. It is worth noting
that its failure (which can be construed as a failure to refer)
is not in the mode of meaninglessness (for we have ways of
deciding what it means) but in the mode of falsity.

Second, let us look at the claim that the existentiell absence
of the phenomenon of love implies the meaninglessness of the
word *love* in that situation. Behind this claim may lie the correct
insight that the meaning of a word is tied up with what people do
with it. Thus one might be led to believe that what one does with
love is perform acts of love, and that if the doing is absent so is
the meaning. But this belief is erroneous for two reasons. First,
performing acts of love is only one of many things one can do
with the word *love.* One can also describe behavior, evaluate
persons, condemn an individual, praise someone, exhort some-

one, call forth sentiments from people, and so on and on. There are many things one can do with the word *love,* and it is simply arbitrary to say that the only meaningful use of it is to express a present phenomenon, the absence of which therefore involves its meaninglessness. The second reason the belief is erroneous is that although a word would be meaningless if nobody ever did anything with it, it does not become meaningless if on a given occasion an individual fails to do something with it. Although words and expressions depend for their meaning on their having some use, they do not become meaningless if on a given occasion they are used wrongly. The use upon which meaning is dependent resides in a community of language-users, and not in any individual. We might say that meaning depends on usefulness, rather than on instances of use.

Third, let us look at the view that the meaning of a word is the phenomenon it represents, since it seems likely that Bultmann holds it. Usually when we ask, "What is the meaning of the word_____?" the forthcoming answer is of the form, "The word means_____" and in the blank are more words. Where people share the same language and have some familiarity with the context in which these words do their work, such a response is accepted as an instance of giving the meaning. But philosophers find such an account unsatisfying because, they think, what we are after is not more *words.* After all, the same question can be asked about *them.* The interesting question is, "What is the meaning itself?" Occasionally, especially with words for physical objects, we can show someone what a word means by showing him what it names. Here the philosopher begins to feel a little happier. We asked what the meaning of the word was, and were shown something, something which was not a word. That looks like progress. But have we, by being shown what we can use the word to refer to, been shown its meaning?

There are three things to note here. One is that meaning always has to be something known or having been known by people. Physical objects may be what they are whether or not anybody knows about them, but the meaning of a word is always tied to people's employment of it. So the question of the meaning of a word is always located among human beings who can (at least potentially) use that word. Thus, perhaps a better way of approaching the question of meaning is to ask what it is to know the meaning of a word, or to learn it, rather than to ask the perhaps oddly inappropriate question, what the meaning of a word itself is. The second thing to note is that correlating a word with a phenomenon (usually called ostensive definition) only works against the background of some mastery of words. Somebody's showing me a shovel counts as giving me the meaning of *shovel* only if I have some concept of an implement, know what it is to be shown something, can understand the other words which may be used in the showing, and the like. And surely this necessary background of linguistic and practical mastery is also part of what it is for me to know the meaning of *shovel*. The third thing to note is that not all words are such that their meaning can be given by pointing to a phenomenon. Words like *is*, *that* (conjunction), *beside*, and countless others clearly have meaning, and yet there is no phenomenon which they either refer to or express. Even in the case of love there is no one thing that could be pointed to as an instance of love, no single act, or feeling, or piece of behavior. Just as learning the meaning of *shovel* involves a tremendous mastery of thing-language, so knowing the meaning of *love* involves the mastery of what we might call soul-language—concepts like good and evil, hate, kindness, happiness, hurt, and many others. So knowing the meaning of *love* is not a matter of correlating an utterance of a word with a momentary existentiell act, but involves almost everything essential to being an adult human person.

Rather than answer too quickly the question, "What is the meaning of *love*?" by saying that it is obviously the phenomenon of love, it would perhaps be better to ask a different but related question, namely, "What is it to *know* the meaning of *love*?" And the answer to this question would be that it is the capacity to recognize a wide variety of actions, feelings, thoughts, and expressions as instances of love or its contraries. It is a peculiar capacity to distinguish human actions and characters from one another. It is a capacity to evaluate people, behavior, feelings, thoughts, and utterances. It is, indeed, a specific part of the human ability to be "objective" about oneself and other people. And it is, among all these other things, also the capacity to perform verbal acts of love—to say "I love you" in the appropriate circumstances. When a man exercises any of the capacities engendered in him by a knowledge of the meaning of the word, then he is using the word meaningfully. If we see the philosophical question about the word's meaning in the light of this question, then the restriction of meaningfulness to only those uses of the word in which love is actually expressed begins to look simply arbitrary.

If he means to point to the fact that the sentences of a psychology of love are not necessarily themselves expressions of love, this is certainly a true observation, but not one which warrants saying either that they are meaningless or that they are not about love. But we have to add the qualification "not necessarily," because a book on the psychology of love *could* be an expression of love—or of hate, or of the desire to become famous, or of anxiety about one's job, or any of a great number of things. What the book expresses depends upon the circumstances in which it was written, and the character and purposes of the writer—as much, perhaps, as upon what the book says. If the maiden aunt says "There's a mouse in the kitchen," the sentence may express anxiety; if the matron of the house says it, it may express embarrassment; if the eight-year-old boy, then perhaps delight. In all these cases the sentence *means* the same thing, namely that there is a mouse in the kitchen. In none is what the sentence expresses the same as what it means, though if one did not know at least what it means, one would probably be unable to discern what in a given circumstance was being expressed by it. A sentence cannot express anything about the speaker unless it already, and independently, has meaning. What it means is rarely, if ever, what it expresses. And often perfectly meaningful sentences don't express anything. But if meaning is not dependent on expression, but expression on meaning, then a sentence's failure to express love or faith does not imply its failure to be meaningful or to be about love or faith.

Now it might be objected that the expression-theory by itself is not quite enough to warrant Bultmann's claim that all general and non-involved language about love is meaningless. For is it not possible that the phenomenon which was (possibly) *expressed* originally by a speaker might subsequently be *referred* to by someone else or in a general proposition? The answer is that this might be possible on the basis of our more ordinary thinking about love, according to which we allow worldly criteria (notably behavior that can be described and referred to) as relevant to questions about love; but that on the basis of the existentialist metaphysic it is not possible. In accordance with the radical separation which Bultmann makes between existence and world, he also thinks that the existential meaning of language such as that of the New Testament (dependent on, and perhaps even constituted by acts and decisions in their existentiell purity) can be distilled out of all essential relation to worldly objects without changing it. This is the aim of demythologizing, and it is why the demythologized interpretation of the gospel message will include no essential reference to or description of any worldly thing or event.

The New Testament remains a somewhat strange world to most of us, rendered still more strange by the technical flourishes of the scholars, and consequently with respect to it the proposal of such a separation and such an interpretation may succeed in leading many down the garden path. But the oddness of this proposal begins to strike us when we examine critically its application to something with which we are more at home.

> The love of another is an encounter whose essential character depends upon its being an event. For it cannot be apprehended as love by objective observation, but only by myself who am encountered by it. Looked at from the outside, it is certainly not visible as love in the real sense of the word, but only as a phenomenon of spiritual or psychic history which is open to various interpretations.[9]

Does Bultmann mean to say that an objective observer watching a man sacrifice his time, his pleasure, his career, and his energy for a hopelessly invalid wife, could not perceive this with certainty as love? Does he really mean that worldly phenomena such as his sitting by her bedside hour after hour, his waiting on her, his solicitude with the doctors, cannot directly count as evidence of this man's love, but are only phenomena "open to various interpretations"? If he means by "objective" an observation made from totally outside the human situation and consequently in independence of all concepts of human affection, then it is clear that this observation would not apprehend what human beings know as love; but in that case we are also talking about something totally different from what human beings know as observation. Our speaking of love, like our speaking of other things, depends on our observing things that happen, things people do

---

[9] *KM,* p. 200.

and say, ways people feel, and so on, all of which are "worldly" phenomena in Bultmann's sense of the word. The language of love, *as* language of existence, is also *necessarily* language about the world.

Were it deprived of all reference to things that happen in the world, as Bultmann threatens to do to the language of faith, it would simply cease to be the language of love as we know it. In failing to describe the world, it would also fail to describe and express existence. And such, we might fear, is what has happened to the language of our faith in Bultmann's hands.

And now we can ask our question again: where does Bultmann get the idea that to make God an object is to deny his omnipotence? That is, why does speaking about God make faith impossible? And the only answer is the one to which we find ourselves constantly returning to explain the oddities in Bultmann: it has been established *a priori* by the existentialist metaphysic—the strict division of all reality into world (*objects* of possible reference) and existence (the purely personal reality of "acts" which can only be expressed)—that any "God" whom we can think about, or refer to, or describe, any God who is an object or a being (even if he is conceived as the source of everything that is), cannot be God. According to the existentialist metaphysic such a God can only be an idol, since he falls on the worldly side of the dividing line, and thus faith in him can only be inauthenticity and a degradation of the purity of existence.

I need to mention one more difficulty in Bultmann's discussion of the meaning of *God*. Even if we were to draw, as he does, a strong distinction between the language of love and the language about love, it would surely be improper to analogize between this and the language about God. For surely the analogy with the language about God would be the language about the *beloved,* not about love. The analogy with the language about love, on the other hand, would be the language about *faith*, not about God. If we found someone who talked a great deal about love but never had anything good to say about his beloved, we might become suspicious—not that his language was meaningless, but that he wasn't taking it very much to heart. For here we might say that this person talked about love, but in failing to talk in certain ways about the *beloved,* he failed to speak the language *of* love. Likewise if a person talked a lot about faith, but never had any occasion in his life for speaking about God in a faithful way, we might be suspicious that what he understood about faith did not play in his life the role which we could hope for it. But the important thing to see here is that, contrary to Bultmann's belief, there is nothing wrong with speaking about God. Indeed, language about God is one of the forms of language of faith. What is to be eschewed (though probably not because it is meaningless) is the language about God which is very remote from the language of faith. But even here it is probably right to say that the border between the language about God which is, and that which is not, the language of faith, is a gray line, dependent more than anything else on the character of the man in whose mouth it is found.

II. General truths, theology, and kerygma

Bultmann seems to think that if a sentence has its proper locus in the prosecution of the faithful life, it therefore cannot be a general truth. It can be said to be true only on specific occasions of existentiell decision. On other occasions the sentence is not true (though it is better to say that it is untrue because it is meaningless, than because it is false).

> The propositions of faith are not abstract truths. Those who have endured the hardships of a Russian prison camp know better than anyone else that you cannot say *"Terra ubique Domini"* as an explicit dogma: it is something which can be uttered only on specific occasions in existentiell decision.[10]

But do we really want to say that "All the earth is the Lord's" is not meaningful except when uttered in conjunction with an existentiell decision on the part of the utterer? It is certainly right to say that the proper use of the sentence is in the context of a life in which God is praised and loved and trusted and thanked regardless of the location in time, space, and circumstances of the believer concerned. And thus if we found a person using the sentence not for these purposes but rather as an argument against private property, we should perhaps say that he did not understand the meaning of the sentence. The problem would not be that the *sentence* was untrue, but rather that the *man* did not

---

[10] *KM*, p. 198. See also *JCM*, pp. 66ff.

understand its meaning. And we could make this judgment about the man's individual and occasional use of the sentence only because it had meaning *independent* of this or that occasional use (though of course it would not have meaning independent of *any* use). That is, it is only because we know what the *sentence* means, that we can judge particular instances of its use to be proper or improper. To make its meaning totally dependent on a feature of individual instances of its employment is to render all judgment about its *right* use impossible.

Imagine someone saying "All the earth is the Lord's" while talking about his plight with a fellow inmate of a Russian camp. This utterance was on the occasion of his decisively grasping the insight that no matter what happened to him, his integrity as a person could not be violated. His interlocutor might then ask him whether he really thought it was true that God was caring for the whole earth, thinking particularly of his mother back in Germany whom he hadn't heard from for months. If the utterer had read a little of Bultmann's theorizing about religious language, he might respond that he couldn't say anything about whether God was caring for this man's mother, because the sentence he had uttered was not a general truth, but was true only when uttered on the occasion of existentiell decision. And surely his interlocutor would then be justified in concluding that the man was not talking about God at all, but was only using a very strange mode of expression for saying something about a courageous decision and insight. The sentence certainly has the *form* of a truth independent of any individual's self-understanding, and if someone found he did not believe it to be true in that sense, we might suggest that the best move would be not to develop a theory about how it doesn't really mean what it seems to (that's such a messy procedure, because you're forever having to explain yourself), but rather simply to give up using it and find a more apt mode of expression.

To say that the sentence expresses a belief about what is generally true is not to deny (as Bultmann thinks it is) that there are proper and improper ways of asserting this truth which have reference to the comportment of a man's individual existence. If a person went around repeating "Terra ubique Domini," and yet was anxious about his life and hated his neighbor, we would say that this assertion was not playing in his life the role which its logic demands. We would not say that the sentence is meaningless, but that he does not understand or exhibit its meaning. But Bultmann is also wrong in thinking that the only way to exhibit its meaning is by an existentiell decision. Dispositions such as trust and love and joy, as well as sustained perceptual capacities connected with the right use of the language of faith, are fully as important as decisions. To make decision alone the warrant for the right use of faith's language is to render the life of faith hopelessly punctiliar and unfairly to make the vast majority of instances of Christian talk inauthentic. We will have more to say about the relations between decision and faith in chapter eleven.

What our theologian says about the relation between general truths and theological language is paralleled by some things he has to say about their relation to the kerygma, a topic which he discusses in an article called "General Truths and Christian Proclamation."[11] He begins the article by remembering the policy which certain pastors at the beginning of this century had of preaching sermons on poetic texts by Schiller and Goethe. Of these he remarks, "Such sermons did not have the character of proclamation, but rather they developed general truths."[12] Proclamation, by way of contrast, must be *address*. However, he acknowledges that often in Christian proclamation and indeed in the preaching of Jesus himself there appear a multitude of sentences which have the form of general truths. But if preaching of general truths is not proclamation, and yet sentences of this form appear in true proclamation, the question forces itself upon him: what is the relationship between these general truths (e.g., "No man can serve two masters") and the proclamation itself which cannot be anything other than address?[13]

His answer to this question is twofold: first, general truths can receive the address-character of Christian proclamation if at a given moment in a concrete situation they lose the character of general truths by qualifying the Now of one who is addressed, that is, by becoming for him no longer general truth but now a word of judgment or humiliation, of comfort or encouragement, which calls him to decision about the way he is to

---

[11] *GV*, **III**.
[12] *Ibid.*, p. 166.
[13] *Ibid.*, p. 170.

understand himself.[14] The second part of his answer has to do
with the relation in Christian theology between law and gospel.
Here he identifies law with general truths. "It belongs to the being of man to stand under the law; or, as we can now also say: to
live in the domain of general truths."[15] To live in the domain of
general truths is to stand under an imperative which only *demands*. The gospel, on the other hand, which has not the character of general truth but that of address, is concrete and spoken
in a particular situation at a particular moment (unlike the law,
which is general); it is in the indicative (unlike the law, which
is in the imperative); and it bestows freedom (unlike the law,
which only demands it). What happens when grace is preached
and accepted is that the same thing which was demanded to be
achieved by the efforts of the individual himself "in the domain
of general truths" is now received as a free gift: the content of
the law or imperative (which is here identified with general
truth) is transformed while remaining the same—transformed in
that it is now an indicative rather than an imperative, a gift rather
than a demand, something concrete and in the moment rather
than general and timeless; the same in that nothing other than the
very freedom which the law demanded is what is now bestowed
in the gospel. That is, Bultmann's second answer to his question
amounts to the same thing as the first: in entering into the
Christian proclamation, the sentences in question lose the character of general truths. (Though in some unexplained way they retain the "content" of those truths.)

From a logical point of view this is such a tangle that one
hardly knows where to start sorting it out. But let us begin with
Bultmann's identification of the imperative with general truths.
If he means to claim that all general truths are imperatives and/
or that all imperatives are general truths, this is clearly an error,
because truths cannot be imperatives at all. Sentences can be true
or false only if they assert something, and imperatives don't
assert anything. "No man can serve two masters" is a general
truth because it asserts something about the way a man is in his
relation to God. When it is correctly understood, it *implies* an
imperative something to this effect: "You shall have no other

---

[14] *GV*, III, pp. 170ff.
[15] *Ibid.*, p. 174.

gods before the Lord your God." The latter sentence is a genuine imperative, and as such asserts nothing and is neither true nor false. Imperatives and assertions are interrelated in complex ways in the language of faith, and are mutually dependent and mutually implying within that language; but imperatives are not themselves truths, nor truths imperatives.

But if imperatives are not truths, can we not at least say that they are *general?* The question whether imperatives are general is not to be answered by looking to see whether they have particular application. For surely to be an imperative at all, a sentence has to be capable of demanding something *of somebody.* The use to which "You shall have no other gods" is put when it is rightly understood is that each man should look to his own life seeing to it that he is not committing idolatry. If this imperative did not have application in particular situations and for particular individuals, it is hard to see how it could be an imperative at all. But the sentence is certainly a general imperative in that it is not tailored or tied to any particular situation. By way of contrast, "You ought to take your wife out to dinner more often" is a highly particular imperative; it is tailored to a specific kind of set of circumstances. "You shall have no other gods" can appropriately be addressed to anyone; to take one's wife out to dinner more often can only be demanded of married males. But as far as the logical property of being an imperative goes, the latter is as much an imperative as the first commandment. Thus it seems that imperatives are not general truths, not only because none of them are truths, but also because not all of them are general.

Bultmann's correlation of address with the indicative is similarly confused. Not all address is in the indicative, nor are all indicatives used as address. Practically anything can be put in the form of address, if we mean by that speaking to somebody in a concrete situation. When in the appropriate circumstances the doctor says "Your wife has just given birth to a seven-pound boy," what is addressed to the husband is an indicative, non-general truth. If in the appropriate circumstances the physics teacher tells his pupils, "Water boils at 212°F.," what he addresses them with is a general truth in the indicative. But it is quite obvious that a person can also be addressed with imperatives, either particular or general: "Quit beating your wife" could be a case of the former; "You shall not steal," of the latter.

Bultmann contrasts general truths with address, as though when sentences in the form of general truths are taken up into the address, they must cease to have the character of general truths. However, the contrary of a general truth is not an addressed truth, but a particular truth. "All men are mortal" is a general truth; "George Washington is dead" is a particular one. We can conceive speaking either of these truths in the form of address. "All have sinned and fallen short of the glory of God" is a general truth; "Mrs. Robinson committed adultery" is a particular truth. Either can appear in the form of address; and there is no reason to think that when the former does, it somehow ceases to be a general truth—it merely becomes now a general truth which is being spoken in the mode of address. Of course the point of saying "All have sinned" is usually such that the proper response of the hearer is to acknowledge that *he* is a sinner. But the fact that the hearer makes a particular application of the truth in question does not mean that the sentence ceases to be a general truth.

Now there are certain non-general truths which are at the heart of the Christian gospel: for example, "Jesus is the Messiah," "Jesus died for the sins of the world." These are not general truths, and we say so for reasons of the same sort as we would give for denying that "Washington was the first U.S. president" and "The Declaration of Independence was signed in 1776" are general truths: they identify particular individuals and refer to particular occurrences. These non-general truths of the gospel are such that it is appropriate that men be addressed with them in a way that we have little concern to address men with the truths about Washington and the Declaration of Independence. (Though we can conceive using the latter truths in the context of patriotic exhortations.) But these would not become general truths if we were to leave them in the history books and never address anybody with them; they would still remain particular truths. Likewise, the truths of the gospel would not become general if preaching were to cease; for whether or not they are couched in the mode of address has nothing to do with their generality or particularity. *Address* denotes only a way in which the sentences are used.

And this brings us to what Bultmann seems to be getting

at through all this messy logic. He sees that there is a proper and an improper way of taking the sentences of the New Testament. If I take a sentence like "No man can serve two masters" in such a way that it has no bearing on my own attempts to serve both God and mammon, but rather in a disinterested manner (perhaps to solve some theological problem for a paper I'm writing), then I am misusing this truth. Bultmann wants to guard against such misuse by saying that this changes the sentence: it becomes a "general truth"; it has ceased to be "address." But this is a very confusing way of speaking. The sentence above just is a general truth, regardless of how in any particular instance it is used. The use or misuse to which it is put is something completely different from its status of generality or particularity. This comes out clearly in the case of those non-general truths about Jesus which are central to the gospel. "Jesus is the Son of God" is a particular truth (because about a particular man) which is misused if employed in vain speculations about his two natures, but rightly used when employed in the prosecution of the life devoted to him. According to Bultmann's notion, the sentence would become a general truth, if I misused it in speculation. But if it actually became a general truth, then it couldn't be the sentence it is. Again, the proper use (which may include address) is something independent of the particularity or generality of the sentences of the language of Christian faith.

There is in principle no reason why preaching upon texts of Schiller and Goethe could not have the character of address, whether the truths contained in the poems were particular or general. They might even have the character of words of judgment or comfort, calling the individual to a decision about his understanding of himself and God and the world. The reason that such preaching is not Christian proclamation is not that it cannot have the character of address, but rather that it is not a proclamation of those particular truths about Jesus Christ which are at the center of the Christian gospel.

6

Language
and Meaning (II)

I. Theology and objectivity

The distinction between general truths and the language of existence is paralleled by a distinction to which Bultmann attaches great importance, which he designates with the words *existential* and *existentiell*. The word *existential* is used to describe certain technical and reflective activities such as interpretation and analysis, along with their products. For example, Heidegger's analysis of human being in his book *Being and Time* is existential analysis. Likewise, the activity in which Bultmann engages in his *Theology of the New Testament,* of discerning in a scientific way "the understanding of human existence which finds expression in the Scriptures,"[1] is an example of existential interpretation. The person who engages in these kinds of reflection gains a conceptualized and explicit understanding in consequence of it, which is called an existential understanding. This is the particular understanding of the philosopher or scientific theologian, and is something quite different from the (existentiell) understanding which any individual may have of his own existence.[2]

Philosophy

does not pose the problem of existence as an existentiell ques-

---

[1] *Essays,* p. 258.
[2] Cf. *KM,* p. 203.

tion, but asks in existential analysis about the meaning of existence in the abstract: for it is aware that the existentiell problem can be answered only in existence itself.[3]

The kind of knowledge gained from existential analysis always has the character of general truth. These truths, however, are not just any general truths, but to be existential have to be general truths about existence.

The word *existentiell,* on the other hand, can never be used to describe interpretation or analysis. Indeed, an existentiell analysis is a contradiction in terms, for this word is used to describe the non-thematic, non-scientific kind of understanding of existence which comes along with simply being involved in existence. Heidegger's analysis of existence analyzes everyday existence, and consequently also the understanding of existence which is necessarily a part of it; in this way the existential analysis is dependent on the existentiell understanding of existence. Likewise Bultmann's existential analysis of the self-understanding of faith in the New Testament is an analysis of an existentiell understanding, and thus obviously dependent on it.

With respect to Bultmann's typical division of language into worldly language and language of existence, that of existential analysis seems to be an odd hybrid. In being descriptive and scientific it shares characteristics of worldly language; and yet what it is about is precisely that which is utterly different from every worldly thing: existence. It is quite clear that in having the character of general truths about human existence, the language of existential analysis does not have meaning in the manner that the language of existence normally does for Bultmann; that is, it does not have its meaning by expressing the momentary act of existing of its speaker, but rather by describing in general what such a momentary act might be. Thus it seems that Bultmann is committed to a distinction between two kinds of theological utterances: on the one hand there are those which express the decisive act in which the individual comes to understand his existence in an authentic way. An example would be, "I count everything as loss because of the surpassing worth of knowing Christ Jesus my Lord" (Phil. 3:8), when spoken sincerely on one's own behalf. On the other hand, there are those

---

[3] *KM,* p. 193.

analytical utterances which attempt to describe this act. An example would be one like the following from the *TNT:*

> Faith's obedient submission to God's "grace," the acceptance of the cross of Christ, is the surrender of man's old understanding of himself, in which he lives "unto himself," tries to achieve life by his own strength, and by that very fact falls victim to the powers of sin and death and loses himself.[4]

Here a difficulty arises. If what Bultmann said about the failure of every "psychology" of love to treat of love itself can be applied here too, it would seem that the existential analysis of existence, as a "scientific" description of the existentiell understanding, would likewise always describe something other than that act of existence. On the basis of the view we have found in Bultmann, it seems we could say that as language of existence, the language of existential analysis is literally meaningless. I can see no reason why we should not generalize from love to existence, and quote him to this effect:

> Actually, one cannot speak *about* existence at all unless the speaking about it is itself an act of existence. Any other talk about existence does not speak about *existence,* for it stands outside existence.[5]

Bultmann himself sometimes draws this kind of conclusion:

> Thus we find ourselves led to the conclusion that our own existence, since it depends on our free act, can never be known by us. Is this existence illusion? Unreality? Certainly it is nothing about which we have knowledge, about which we can speak.[6]

Thus he makes for existential analysis only the extremely modest claim of having discerned that existence can be understood only by being involved in existence: as regards the understanding of love which can be gained from it, Bultmann says,

> Existential analysis can only make clear to me that each con-

---

[4] *TNT,* I, pp. 330ff.
[5] Cf. above, p. 161.
[6] *FU,* p. 63.

crete instance of love can only be understood in an existentiell manner.[7]

But if existential analysis does no more than make this simple remark about what it is to understand the phenomena of existence, then it is hard to see why anyone should preoccupy himself with it for very long, or why it should go on for volumes the length of Heidegger's and Bultmann's books. In fact, however, Bultmann's existential analysis does claim to be telling us more about faith than simply that you can't understand it unless you have it, as a cursory reading of the *TNT* will show. The trouble with this claim is that if what Bultmann says elsewhere about language is right, it cannot be true.

Bultmann hints at an attempted resolution of this difficulty when he makes a distinction between talking about existence itself and talking about the *concept* of existence. At the end of an article in which he has manifestly been trying to talk about existence, and in which one of the main points he makes about it is that one cannot talk about it, he says,

> Hopefully it has become clear that there can be thought and speech about existence only in the sense that the concept of existence is explicated — as I have tried to do in the foregoing discussion. Its upshot is that the meaning of existence is that it is always my existence, *about* which I cannot speak, but only *from* which I can speak.[8]

The meaning of existence is that existence is always only my own—that much we can evidently tell by an objectifying look at the *concept* of existence. On the other hand, we can neither talk nor think about existence *itself,* nor even know about it. Thinking, talking, and knowing about something *an sich* is a characteristic of objectifying, worldly language, the language of science alone,[9] and this evidently is one of the traits which the hybrid called existential analysis does not receive from its father science. There is no way to talk about existence *an sich* in the way in which it is possible to talk about the objects of nature and

---

[7] *KM,* p. 195.
[8] *GV,* III, p. 120.
[9] *Ibid.,* p. 107.

history (in the sense of past events), so the only way of talking objectifyingly and in general truths about it is to talk about the *concept* of it. The closest one can ever get to the *an sich* of existence is the expressing of it in the existentiell language of the moment, but since it is always only the vanishing momentary act which when seized by objectifying sight immediately and by logical necessity ceases to be what it is, there is in principle no reflective access to it. Where existence is concerned, the concept is all we ever have to look at, not the thing itself.

But is it possible to make sense of a claim to analyze the concept of something in independence of any access to the thing itself? "Linguistic" philosophers have sometimes been zealous to distinguish between the truths to which philosophy is the means of access and "empirical" truths, and have thus bordered on thinking it possible to analyze just concepts, independently of any empirical consideration of the concepts' referents. It is one of the salutary effects of Wittgenstein's thought to teach us that concepts are what they are only in their interlocking with the activities and practices of human life, so that to analyze a concept *is* to analyze some facet of human life—and presumably to analyze some facet of human life involves knowing about it, and at least in principle being able to talk about it. The ability to analyze the concept of love is possessed only by the person who knows what love is (in itself). The idea of knowing the concept of love without being able to talk objectively without love— to recognize instances of it—is one to which I, at least, can attach no meaning. If existential analysis has any value or truth at all, it has to be about human existence *in* being about the concept of existence. It cannot be objective about the concept without being objective about existence too.

But Bultmann thinks it impossible to be directly objective about existence, and thus also about faith, and love, and God. The language of existential analysis is not about existence itself at all, and thus with respect to existence is literally meaningless. This is a conclusion which strikes us as very odd if we read some of the analysis of Bultmann or Heidegger: wrong here and there it may be, but meaningless, or not about existence at all? By now it will be clear enough why Bultmann is forced to such an odd conclusion. For he has limited existence to moments of pure existentiell decision, which can have no *essential* relationship to anything worldly—to behavior, to past events, to roles

and institutions, in fact to anything that can be talked "about."
Even the word *act* which is such a favorite of his he uses in a
specialized sense according to which every objectively discernible
piece of behavior, of speech, every confirmed character-trait or
role-identity of the person doing the act, is inessential.[10] What
people discernibly do and say, and who they are in terms of
the relations constituted by their social and historical connections and by the confirmed dispositions of their lives are not a
part of existence or truly human life for Bultmann, but all fall
on the side of world. And these are, of course, precisely the
aspects of human life which make it possible to talk *about* it. If
human existence is really constituted only by purely non-
objective and non-public acts of existentiell encounter, then it is
true that we cannot talk about it at all; but it is then also true
that Heidegger's and Bultmann's existential analysis in a strong
and literal sense does not tell us *anything at all* about it.

However, it seems to me clear that Heidegger's analysis
does tell us true things about human life, for example that existence is, in a fundamental way, characterized by concern for
things and people. (He calls it, rather abstractly, *Sorge,* or
'care.') That is, when they are alive and kicking, human beings
are characterized by, for example, their susceptibility to worry.

Now where does Heidegger get the ability to make this
kind of observation? Does he know it by an analysis of the pure
concept of existence, independent of all direct and objective
observation of human lives? It seems to me the obvious answer
is that he knows that human beings are characterized by care
and concern and solicitude because he has observed people—
their behavior, their emotions, their talk, in short, their total
comportment as people—as a participant, as it were. But for
Bultmann this kind of observation cannot be the basis for an
analysis of existence, because everything that is here observable
is world. That is why he is forced to draw the paradoxical conclusion that existential analysis is not about existence at all.

---

[10] "For the free act which is truly the expression of our existence (in
the proper sense we exist only in such action and not otherwise and such
action is really nothing other than our existence itself), the truly free act
can never be known in the sense of being objectively proven. . . . A free
act can only be *done* and in so far as we *speak* of such doing, the possibility of it can only be believed" (*FU*, p. 63).

II. Theology and dogma

Bultmann often expresses his dislike for orthodox theology by setting a holding of fixed doctrines or dogmas in contrast with true faith, which is the momentary decision to be free from everything which is fixed and past and thus worldly.[11] In his interpretation of a passage from the Gospel of John, Bultmann concludes that it is impossible to give a definitive dogmatic statement of the Christian proclamation.

At the end of the story of Jesus and the Samaritan woman (John 4:7–42), the Samaritans whom the woman has told about Jesus come to him to hear Jesus' own words, and the passage ends with the Samaritans saying to the woman, "It is no longer because of your words (*lalia*) that we believe, for we have heard for ourselves, and we know that this is indeed the Savior of the world" (v. 42). Bultmann takes this story as symbolic of the relationship between human words of witness to Jesus and faith in him. The woman

> symbolizes mediatory proclamation which brings its hearers to Jesus. This idea is strongly emphasized. For if the woman's witness was for the people the necessary condition of their faith, in itself it is of no importance; rather its importance lies in the fact that it brings people to Jesus, so that faith becomes faith *dia ton logon autou,* while human witness appears by contrast as *lalia,* as mere words which in themselves do not contain that to which witness is borne. That is to say, the believer may not base his faith on the authority of others, but must himself find the object of faith; he must perceive, through the proclaimed word, the word of the Revealer himself. Thus we are faced with the strange paradox that the proclamation, without which no man can be brought to Jesus, is itself insignificant, in that the hearer who enjoys the knowledge of faith is freed from its tutelage, is free, that is, to criticise the proclamation which brought him himself to faith. That is why it is impossible ever to give a definitive dogmatic statement of the proclamation, because every fixed form of words, in that they are human words, becomes *lalia.* The eschatological word becomes a phenomenon within the history of ideas.[2]

---

[11] Cf. *Religion and Culture: Essays in Honor of Paul Tillich,* ed. Walter Leibrecht (New York: Harper & Row, 1959), pp. 241ff.; *EF,* pp. 70, 85f; *FU,* p. 316.

[12] *GJC,* p. 201.

An aspect of Bultmann's view of language on which his whole hermeneutical theory and practice turn comes out very clearly in this passage. This is his belief that the object of faith is essentially independent of the language of faith. No particular propositions are either adequate or necessary to faith. It is, he admits, true that a man would not come to faith initially if it were not for the words which someone spoke to him; but the words are dispensable in that they are only the vehicle for his arriving at the kerygma itself, the *Sache* which the merely human words of proclamation can express but not "contain," the "word of the Revealer himself." The words which men actually speak are all always only interpretations of this mysterious thing itself which is the object of faith. Thus the knowledge of this object frees the man of faith from the language of faith, giving him an independent (non-linguistic) access to this object, and consequently also enabling him to stand in judgment on any particular formation of the language of faith. In this latter idea we can sense the demythologizing project crouched in waiting.

But where would we be if it were really "impossible ever to give a definitive dogmatic statement of the proclamation"? If there are not, for example, some descriptions of Jesus which stand fast for me, which I take to be true yesterday, today, and forever, how can I be said to have any access to "Jesus" at all? I take it that the following would qualify as a dogmatic statement: Jesus gave his life for the sins of many and God raised him from the dead. Now what this sentence and others like it do, is to tell us *who Jesus is;* that is, by telling what he did and underwent they describe for us the object of Christian faith. Since the same description can be given in different sentences, the one above is dispensable for the following reasons: (1) the same proposition can be expressed in French, Italian, and, I take it, any human language; (2) even within one language, there are alternative ways of expressing the same proposition (one could say that Jesus died for the sins of the world, and God resurrected him, instead of the sentence above); (3) a different set of propositions can amount to the same, or a similar, description—the Gospel of Luke and the Gospel of John, while having no sentence in common and much diversity of vocabulary, are manifestly similar descriptions of a single person. For these reasons, particular formulations of the language of faith are dispensable. But the above sentence is a definitive dogmatic statement of the proclamation in the following sense: any other particular sentences in which it was expressed would have to yield the same or a similar description of Jesus, and thus also the same or similar concepts of sin and grace and God and salvation, as the propositions which form a possible network with this one. If alternative propositions amounted to a different description of Jesus, then by a change in its object Christian faith would lose the particular definiteness it has. Certainly the particular sentences, even of the New Testament, are not indispensable; for the same description of the man might have been yielded in a million different ways. But the description which those particular sentences of the New Testament do in fact yield is indispensable, for it is only through the description of Jesus that we have access to him, and if the description is substantially changed, faith itself becomes something different from what is known by that name in the church of Jesus Christ.

It is true that when a man has grown many long years into faith, he gains a conceptual suppleness which may allow him to talk about Christian faith in original ways, that is, in a kind of freedom from quoting texts from the Scripture and remarks of theologians. There is no practical limit to the ways a man may express himself without transgressing the Christian concepts. Someone who was brought to the Lord in a revival camp meeting and subsequently grew into a Christian maturity which was beyond that of the people who had originally proclaimed the gospel to him, might, through the maturity of his faith, gain the freedom to "criticise the proclamation which brought him himself to faith." But this would be possible only as long as the concepts in which he expressed himself and which constituted the criteria by which he makes his criticisms are the *Christian* concepts. If someone thought, by virtue of his faith, to have an adequate criterion for denying that Jesus could have atoned, by his death, for the sins of many,[13] then we would be right to deny the validity of this judgment, since the faith which is supposedly the criterion is here out of conformity with the Christian concepts, that is, does not have the definiteness belonging to *Christian* faith, whose object is, and must be defined as, the man who died for the sins of many. Since faith gets its definiteness from

---

[13] Cf. *KM*, p. 7.

the concepts, and the concepts are not what they are except as the words appear in the propositions of the language of faith (here above all in the story of Jesus of Nazareth), it is simply erroneous to think that faith provides non-propositional criteria for judging the language of faith in any sense that would promote demythologizing.

Bultmann believes that human words (at least when they figure in religious language) do not in themselves "contain that to which witness is borne." He concludes from this that the object of faith is encountered only "through" the words of proclamation. It is difficult to see what precisely is being denied in denying that the words themselves contain Jesus, for it is hard to know what would be meant by asserting that any words at all "contain" what they refer to. The words of the proclamation obviously do not contain Jesus, in themselves or otherwise. But they do refer to him, and here the qualification "in themselves" is instructive. Words do not refer in themselves; people use words to refer. And there are a variety of ways of referring to Jesus, some appropriate and some inappropriate, the criteria of appropriateness being yielded by the descriptions of Jesus given in the language of faith. If Jesus is the Savior of the world, then it is appropriate that he be referred to lovingly and gratefully and hopefully, rather than despitefully or disinterestedly. And there is a sense in which a person who referred to him despitefully or disinterestedly would not "find Jesus," even though he used some of the New Testament descriptions of him. But here it is not a fault of the words being human words (what other kind is there?) but rather of those human words being used by a *person* in one way or another; it is a matter of how the words by which Jesus can be referred to fit together with the rest of the speaker's or hearer's life — with his attitudes and behavior, his understanding of himself and his neighbor and his world. If the words of Christian proclamation become "mere words" or a mere phenomenon within the history of ideas, it is not because they are human, or because they have a fixed form (even the form of the proposition), but rather because those people for whom they could be the access to the Savior of the world and to new life through him do not use them to that happy end.

III. Theology as thoroughly interpretive

We have begun to touch on another main aspect of Bultmann's view of religious language: that its nature involves an
inherent failure to represent completely or adequately the phenomena in question. The two phenomena upon which depends
the meaning of religious discourse, according to Bultmann, are
faith's decisive act of self-understanding, on the one hand, and
the kerygma, which is the phenomenon in face of which this
self-understanding is decisively grasped (faith's object), on the
other. But there is a certain incommensurability between these
realities and the words in which they are expressed — hence,
the sentences of language can in principle never be anything
more than "interpretations" of them.

> For both the kerygma and faith's self-understanding always ap-
> pear in the texts, so far as they are expressed in words and
> sentences, already interpreted in some particular way — i.e. in
> theological thoughts.[4]

And this is not a limitation characteristic only of the New
Testament. It is one under which the theologian labors, too,
since he too has only language to work with. Putting the self-
understanding of faith into words is not a task which admits of
being accomplished once for all. "There can be no normative
Christian dogmatics," for the task is one which "permits only
ever-repeated solutions, or attempts at solution."[15] Like faith's
self-understanding, the kerygma too can never be stated in
any other than the interpretive mode:

> But the kerygma is just what theology can never seize in defini-
> tive form; it can always take hold of it only as something con-
> ceptually stated, and that means as something already theologi-
> cally interpreted.[16]

And,

> Although there are single statements in the New Testament

---

[14] *TNT,* II, p. 239.
[15] *Ibid.,* p. 237.
[16] *Ibid.,* p. 240.

which can be designated as specifically kerygmatic, even they are always formulated in a particular theological terminology — take, for instance, that simplest sentence, "Jesus, Lord" (II Cor. 4.5), for it presupposes a particular understanding of the term "Lord."[17]

Bultmann's thought here seems to be that kerygma and faith are two concept-independent realities, one which meets men as forgiveness and demand, the other the spiritual reality which arises out of this meeting which we, in order to communicate about them at all, must unfortunately force into the unreceptive mold of particular words and concepts. It is almost as though faith formed by and thus necessarily expressed in *particular* concepts could not really be faith; nor could a kerygma which was tied to particular words (e.g., *Jesus*?), which could not be expressed without these particular words, be the phenomenon in face of which such a pure existential reality as faith arises. And since the existential nature of the kerygma and faith makes it impossible that they should be essentially dependent on particular, historically bound concepts, all language in which they are couched has the character of interpretation.

But let us reflect for a moment on what it would be for *all* the language of faith to be only interpretation. If a person says "Jesus Christ is my Lord," we are presumably warranted, on the basis of the theory, to conclude that this expression is only an interpretation of the man's self-understanding. He may actually believe that there is a person in heaven named Jesus who has such authority that he is rightly called "Lord"; but this does not directly count as what he means by the expression, for it too is only interpretation. And so we ask, "What are the characteristics of what is being interpreted in this language?" And Bultmann has an answer ready: what the man is expressing by saying that Jesus is his Lord is the decisive act of self-understanding by which he has given up all particular securities within the world and has paradoxically found a new life of security in this total letting-go.

"And now, Mr. Bultmann, is this last sentence an interpretation, or not?"

---

[17] *TNT*, II, p. 239.

"It is an interpretation, for in this sphere there can only be interpretations."

"And what is it an interpretation *of,* Mr. Bultmann?"

"Of the act of faith."

"But what is the act of faith itself, Mr. Bultmann?"

"That I cannot tell you, because it cannot be described in language."

"Then how do you know that your interpretation, and that of the man who says Jesus is his Lord, are interpretations of *that,* rather than of something else?"

"It is a private affair, and each man can know it only for himself."

What is the criterion for saying that the "event" which takes place at the preaching of the demythologized kerygma and which is expressed in the sentences of demythologized theology is the same one which took place in the old days? The criterion is clearly not a linguistic or conceptual one, for Bultmann claims to have an access to the content (*Sache*) of Paul's language which will enable him to say better than Paul what Paul really meant, and thus to understand Paul "better than he understood himself!"[18] That is, Paul's words, or even his concepts, are not the last resort in adjudicating what Paul meant, and thus in adjudicating whether the meaning of our religious language is the same as that of his. Nor (to say something very similar) is the criterion for the sameness of meaning something "objective." That is, we do not, as we might in traditional Christianity, adjudicate the question by asking whether the alternative expressions can be used to refer to the same object. (The reason this is to say something very similar to the first alternative is that our only access to such objects as God and Jesus, as Luther pointed out, is through "these words.") Nor can the criterion be *tout simple* to look at the life or "existence" which is governed by the two alternative languages to see whether it is the same in both cases. For the attitude, to take an example, toward the future which corresponds to Paul's language about the resurrection is not the "radical openness" expressed in demythologized theology, but rather a somewhat specific *hope.* Nor does Paul's language about Jesus involve casting off all worldly secu-

---

[18] *FU,* p. 93.

rities in Bultmann's sense of 'worldly'; for in Paul's thinking, being a Christian is trusting, and finding security in, the man Jesus, and casting off all other securities than that one. And these are "existential" differences — differences of attitude, of decision, of self-understanding. But if the sameness of meaning which Bultmann claims for his demythologizing interpretation is neither a conceptual, nor an objective, nor an existential sameness, what *is* the criterion by which he judges the meaning to be the same in the two cases? The answer seems to be that, on the basis of his belief in the radical separability of existence and world, he simply does not think that in adjudicating existential sameness he has to take into consideration anything objective or worldly which might be thought (by, e.g., St. Paul) essentially to qualify existence. So it doesn't bother him particularly that Paul hoped for the resurrection of the dead and trusted Jesus, for on the basis of his existential metaphysic he knows better than Paul what Paul means. Since existence in its pure form (and that is surely what Christianity must be) cannot involve a worldly object such as a future resurrection or a man, Paul's meaning must have been that Christian life is radical openness to the future and the casting off of all particular securities. Thus for Bultmann, the existentialist metaphysic is the court of last appeal, by which he confidently decides what the real meaning of the New Testament is.[19]

Bultmann's predisposition against particular words and concepts, and above all against particular propositions as characterizing faith and the object of faith, is of special utility to him in his demythologizing project. For it stifles one of the cries which most often forces itself to our lips when we read his demythologizing "interpretations": "That isn't what the text says!" When *everything* is interpretation, then the sentences in the New Testament are every bit as much an interpretation as those of Bultmann's essays, and when the criterion (the reality itself) is

---

[19] Thus, with the help of the refining fire of the existentialist division of reality, Bultmann can tell us that having a future hope, as in the Bible, "is only one among other possible conceptions of man's relation to the unworldly" (*KM,* p. 113). What this hope conceptualizes, on the other hand, is provided only by existentialist philosophy; for in the New Testament nothing so pure as this is to be found, but only "possible conceptions" of such things.

something to which we have no conceptually direct access but is in the moment of decision, then it is as though *anything* goes. On the basis of Bultmann's theory of language his interpretation of Christian faith is absolutely protected against criticism, though, we might add, with the dubious result that every other interpretation is also so protected.

In his expression theory about the language of faith, and in his notion that all of it is interpretation, the relation between faith and its language is that faith comes first, and then any of an indefinite variety of concepts are found to express it. His existentialist metaphysic keeps him from being very impressed with all the evidence to the contrary which would be available to anyone who actually looked to see the genetic relations between faith and its language. For surely in non-existentialist Christianity the language of faith is not only expressive of faith, but also formative of it. The peculiarities of the affective, perceptual, and behavioral aspects of the life of faith arise in conformity with the rules governing the language of faith. To take an example, the defining characteristics of the peculiar *concept* of hope as it appears in Christian discourse begin to define the *affection* of Christian hope in the individual as he grows in faith. Without the prior availability of the Christian concept the education of the soul in hope could never begin to take place. And why, if this is the way things are among us, should we assume that things were radically different for the early Christians? It is only when faith is assumed to have no *object* which would have to be described and referred to in what Bultmann deplores as "objectifying" language, that one can maintain the strict primacy of faith over language as Bultmann does. If faith's object is essential to it and describable, then it may well be that certain elements in the language of faith both precede faith logically and temporally, and have a once-and-for-all character—the character of a "normative Christian dogmatics," if one wishes so to speak. And it may be that not only *can* the theological task be accomplished once for all, but that it *has been* so accomplished, in its essentials at least—by the writers of the New Testament.

IV. Preaching and its referent

The biblical understanding of preaching is that it is a report in which is mentioned the life, death, and resurrection of Jesus as the event in which God's salvation has been worked for mankind. It is by my believing the report to be true (and thus coming to have a variety of affective, actional, and perceptual consequences in my personal life) that this salvation becomes mine. The act of God can be *referred to* in the address by which it is hoped that I will grasp this good news as my own, because the address is not identical with the act of God. Bultmann refuses to make the distinction between the act of God and the address in which it is reported to me, and likewise the distinction between salvation and that salvation's becoming my own. He holds that the object of faith is not what the preaching refers to, but is the preaching itself, which is to be taken as the direct address of God, offering his forgiveness to the person addressed. Thus it is in encountering the direct address of God that the new self-understanding called "faith" arises.

Now a worthy scholar of Bultmann's writings has objected to me on this point that it is possible that the kerygma is *both* direct address and a report of the grace of God. But I think that a little reflection on the logic of the matter will show us that this is not possible.

If my mother says "I love you," that may, in the appropriate circumstances, be an act of love on my mother's part. But it would be strange to say that the utterance also reports on or refers to an act of love, namely the act of saying "I love you." If my father says "Your mother loves you," that may be both a report and an act of love on my father's part, but not on my mother's; and as report it reports not her act, but her *disposition* (a more or less general truth about my mother). If my father says, "Your mother told me to tell you she loves you," this is a report of my mother's act of love, but my mother's act is not identical with the pronouncement. It is antecedent to the pronouncement, and only as such can the pronouncement be a report of it.

What tempts us to say that "You are accepted by God" (which is pretty much the essence of the Bultmannian kerygma) is both an instance of God's acceptance and a report of it, is that the pronouncement is made by a third party on God's behalf. God uses the mouths of preachers to speak his words of direct address; and most preachers confuse the issue further by not adopting the style of the Hebrew prophets: "Thus saith the Lord, 'I accept you.'" Now if the preacher says, "The Lord says that he accepts you," then the preacher refers to God's words (and thus to his act of pronouncement). But insofar as the preacher refers to God's words, the words are not direct address, for the reference is the preacher's. On the other hand, if we are to understand the open mouth of the preacher as simply a vehicle through which the Lord himself speaks, then we have a case of direct address by God (and this is how Bultmann seems to want to conceive the matter), but we no longer have any reference to or report of God's act, for the word-act does not mention itself any more than my mother's "I love you" mentions her act of saying "I love you."

The liturgical language of the church has the character of direct address "when it is a call to repentance, an exhortation, a proclamation of the forgiveness of sin, etc.," that is, when the use of the language is such that "as it is proclaimed and heard repentance results or impenitence becomes an actuality."[20] Now we might expect, on the basis of the relation between faith and worldly things in Bultmann's thought, that this would be all there is to direct address: we would not expect it to impart any information. But Bultmann goes on to say that

> such examples do not, however, fully define the content of the church's kerygma, for it also includes (linked always with the content already described) the *communication of facts.*[21]

But what does Bultmann mean by "facts" here? In the mouth of other theologians, or of the writers of the New Testament, we might expect this word to refer to the death and resurrection of Jesus, that is, to ostensible data of world history which are the kerygmatic "facts" *par excellence.* But it is clear that it is not to these facts that Bultmann refers; the ones communicated in the kerygma are rather "eschatological facts. . . . And as such they are undiscoverable by any investigation of the world."[22] In contrast, the crucifixion even Bultmann believes to be discoverable through the investigation of the New Testament. And he interprets I Corinthians 15:3–7 as though Paul there took the resurrection of Jesus to be a historically discoverable fact.[23]

---

20 *FU,* p. 189.
21 *Ibid.*
22 *Ibid.*
23 Cf. *Ibid.,* pp. 66ff.

(For this reason, characteristically, Bultmann denies this passage to be an instance of kerygma.)

What, then, are these eschatological facts which must be mentioned in the kerygma? What Bultmann means by saying that these facts are undiscoverable by any investigation is not that the situation or event in question cannot be described, but that the description of the situation or event in question says absolutely nothing about the eschatological significance of the fact, which is superimposed upon it by way of interpretation by the act of faith. Thus, worldly facts become eschatological facts, not through any characteristics they themselves have (and which would thus have to be describable), but entirely by what they are seen as through the eyes of faith. So actual worldly facts are referred to in the kerygma (facts in the ordinary sense of happenings and situations describable in objective language); but his denial that the description of these facts has anything to do with their significance for faith seems to imply that it is totally indifferent *which* worldly facts get mentioned. If their eschatologicality is entirely interpretive and entirely supplied by faith, and has nothing to do with anything that a non-believer might notice about them, then surely one fact is as good as another as a backdrop upon which to superimpose the eschatological interpretation. Bultmann thinks that "Jesus was crucified" is a worldly fact, so it could, presumably, along with an indefinite number of other happenings and situations, be mentioned in the kerygma, and could become an eschatological fact, if it became the occasion for hearing the direct address of forgiveness which enables the decision in favor of authentic existence.[24] And indeed, since on Bultmann's view the death of Jesus was the first occasion in the history of the world for the apprehension of an (the) eschatological fact, it might, through this historical accident, get mentioned in subsequent kerygmatic pronouncements more than any other fact. My contention that in the normal sense of 'fact' there are no particular facts which must be mentioned in the kerygma in order that it be kerygma for Bultmann, is borne out in the discussion which immediately follows the passages quoted above. There he continues to talk in general about the relation between address and reference to facts, and, in contradistinction

---

[24] Cf. *FU,* p. 209.

from the New Testament where the preaching addresses the hearer with the saving facts about Jesus our Lord, the facts become not the object addressed to the hearer, but a mode of addressing something else to him.

> But there is clearly nothing anomalous in the fact that information can be communicated, not for the purpose of increasing knowledge and enlarging understanding of the world, but to bring about commitment; in other words, to disclose to me a new possibility of my existence. Indeed when the direct address specifies something that I ought to do, it always does so on the basis of some fact which is kept in view. . . . The communication of the fact can then acquire the character of address; it can be *indirect* summons.[25]

The essential thing, indeed the event of salvation, is that I be addressed with a word which summons me to cast off all worldly securities; the reference to and description of the worldly fact of Jesus' crucifixion can be a *mode* (albeit an indirect one) in which this summons comes to me. But the eschatological fact remains this, and no more than this: *that* I am so summoned.

Now Bultmann's making the talk about the history of Jesus just an indirect mode in which people can be addressed with the direct address of forgiveness and demand is a reversal of the logic of the New Testament. There we might say that the history of Jesus is such that it simply *is* forgiveness and demand, so that to couch it in any other mode is to falsify it, to make it something other than what it objectively is. It is not to be denied that to communicate to someone the fact that Jesus has died for his sins is indirectly to summon him to repentance and rejoicing. If he does not repent and rejoice, then we may conclude that he has either not understood or not believed what we have told him, or that somehow we have not told him the right story. But the communication of the fact is not simply a way of summoning him to repentance and rejoicing. The facts that are communicated in preaching are not indirect summons in the sense that the same summons might in principle be occasioned by other worldly facts. Salvation (repentance and rejoicing and much else besides) becomes loving him whose identity is for us determined by what

---

[25] *FU*, pp. 189f.

he did and said and underwent in this world. The rejoicing and the repentance gain their specific character in the context of a remembrance that he who was who he was did what he did for our sakes. And thus the kerygma, when rightly preached, refers to specific facts and recounts a specific story again and again, ever anew setting the hearers in relation to those facts and into the context of that story. Thus, reference to the facts is not so much an oblique way of summoning men to repentance and joy, as the repentance and the joy constitute the correct mode in which to refer to those facts and to tell that story.

As we have seen, Bultmann's crude distinction between human existence and the world—the division of reality which controls every aspect of his theology—controls also his theory of language. The consequence of the division's empire in this sphere is that all directly referential language is relegated to "objectification"—description of facts and objects and events in the world. When it is operating correctly, this is the language of science; when it falsely arises in the religious sphere (existence) it is castigated as mythology, that is, as an extremely misleading way of expressing human self-understanding. He does not deny that the language of faith can legitimately refer to worldly events and objects, but holds that insofar as they are worldly, that is, describable and neutrally observable, they cannot be the object of faith, the "saving act" or "eschatological event." The reference to them must remain "ambiguous" with respect to the question whether a saving event can be seen "in" them, in order to protect religious language from being directly descriptive and thus providing a worldly object for faith. Accordingly, Bultmann says,

> The saving act is not something objectively present, nor is it perceived by scientific observation as objective entities or events which occur or have occurred in the world are perceived. As the cross of Christ, it is certainly *also* a fact of the world — that is exactly what constitutes its ambiguity.[26]

But it is only because Bultmann's metaphysical distinction demands that faith not have a directly describable object that he believes that the "worldliness" of the death of Christ makes it ambiguous as a saving event. If our thinking is not dominated

---

[26] *FU,* p. 209.

by this crude division of reality, as the New Testament's is not, then it may be that the worldly character of the death of Christ, far from being the source of its *ambiguity* as a saving event, is a necessary condition for our apprehension of it as a saving event. If there were nothing observable and discussable about this death warranting our distinguishing it from other deaths and other events as the saving act of God, then reference to it and description of it would indeed be no description of the saving act, but only an incidental element in a linguistic usage which essentially bore a totally different relation to the so-called "event." Bultmann's view is that the saving event is "expressed" but not described in pieces of language which also refer to and describe the death of Jesus. But this is to do extreme violence to the New Testament's use of language about Jesus' death. There the saving act of God can be described in public language, and it is only because this death has features which are thus worldly and in the broadest sense observable, that we ever come at all to apprehend it as a saving event. There to talk about Jesus' death is not a way of *expressing* the saving event (though it may be a way of expressing one's joy and thankfulness that the saving event has occurred), but a way of *referring* to it. And thus it is that the kerygma is not direct address (except in the trivial sense that in actual preaching the preacher—not God— always addresses somebody in particular), but *report*. One can, of course, in a somewhat metaphorical way, say that through the report about what God has done for us in Jesus Christ, God himself "speaks" to us. But this seems to be only another way of saying that these words are significant for our own individual relation to God. It is in fact the preacher who literally addresses us; and what he addresses us with is a story about Jesus.

Now the worldly features of the death of Jesus which enable us to call it the saving act of God are mostly not features of that event in the narrower sense: that he was condemned unjustly, that it was a criminal execution, the role of the Jews and the role of the Romans, that he died by crucifixion, are certainly not enough to warrant a belief that this was the saving act of God. That he died at the hands of sinners rather than quietly in his bed at a ripe old age is important, but only in conjunction with those public features which, broadly speaking, constitute the *identity* of the one who died. It is because of who he was that his death was the salvation of the world; and who he was is not given by a narrow description of the events surrounding his death alone, but by a description of what preceded—and also eminently what followed—this event. It is because Jesus was publicly identifiable—as the one who healed the sick, cast out demons, forgave sins as God, ate with tax collectors and sinners, taught with authority, and after his death appeared alive to his disciples—that his death could be apprehended as God's act of salvation on behalf of men. All this informational, publicly accessible, worldly, factual content determines the concepts of Lord, Messiah, Savior, and the like, by which he is identified, by which he is referred to in the preaching of the church, and by which he becomes the object of the individual's faith.

Bultmann's division of reality into world and existence, and his consequent division of meaning into reference and expression, serve to obscure the complex relationships between concepts and objects, and the similarities which exist between religious and other discourse. Bultmann seems to think that the language of science, which is the epitome of worldly language, is, at least ideally, pure description and reference unadulterated by any tie to human interests and needs and purposes, and is thus the vehicle of a completely neutral perception. What is said in scientific discourse is one hundred percent warranted by the objects considered only on the basis of their characteristics in themselves. Religious language, by contrast, is in its essence completely nonreferential, so that when it does refer to the same objects which might be described in science, it must be completely *interpretation*,[27] since the object considered in itself (that is, from a scientific standpoint) is *ambiguous* with respect to what is "meant" in the language.

But this is a caricature of both scientific and religious language. Scientific language is highly selective, purposive, inter-

---

[27] We have already observed the thoroughgoing way in which he hypothesizes that the christologically significant material in the Gospels is the production of the early church—an interpretive cloak wrapped (albeit unfortunately for the scientific historian very tightly) around the unsuspecting apocalyptic preacher from Galilee. But when we combine the observation about how utterly speculative this hypothesis is with the observation about how neatly it accommodates his philosophical theory concerning how religious language has its meaning, we find that our inclination to take these so-called scholarly results seriously has seriously abated.

pretive, "interested," and its concepts arise fully as much from this side as they do from the way the world is. It is as true in science as elsewhere that, as Wittgenstein says, "Concepts lead us to make investigations; are the expression of our interests, and direct our interests."[28] Conversely, some of the concepts of religion arise fully as much from what is the case and what has happened as they express our understanding of ourselves: for example, the concepts of Messiah, Lord, and Savior are logically tied to what Jesus of Nazareth said and did and underwent. The concepts by which he is identified determine the possibility of his death being, and being apprehended as, the event of salvation; but these concepts are in turn dependent on worldly facts, many of which are of the same sort investigated in so-called "scientific" history.

When I say that these facts are publicly accessible, I do not mean that their apprehension is concept-independent and independent of all predisposition by human interests (for the idea of such neutral observation is a fantasy). Bultmann often speaks as though there is no middle ground between the total ambiguity of the worldly with respect to faith and the situation in which what is publicly accessible forces belief. But this is clearly an artificial and tendentious "either/or." When I say that an understanding of the relevant facts is publicly accessible, I mean that, though the language for construing the facts may be local to Judaism or Christianity, it is a language which can be learned by any normal human being. To take only one example, to appreciate the significance of Jesus' forgiving the paralytic's sins, those who witnessed this fact had to have a grasp of the concept of sin and thus also of the concept of God. A person unacquainted with these concepts would not be able to see what claim was being made. But to perceive the claim the person would only have to have a fairly rich acquaintance with the concepts; he would not necessarily have to *believe* in God, much less believe that Jesus had the right to perform this act of forgiveness. So when I say that facts of this sort about Jesus are publicly accessible I do not mean that just anyone can see their import; but within the specific context of Jewish piety Jesus' act

---

[28] *Philosophical Investigations,* tr. G. E. M. Anscombe (New York: The Macmillan Company, 1953), Part I, 570.

of forgiveness and the significance of the claim he thereby made about his identity is neither opaque nor even ambiguous—it is capable of being clear to all, whether they believe or not.

Though the difference between belief and unbelief is not the difference between understanding and failing to understand the fact and its significance, there is certainly a difference in how the fact is apprehended. For in the story cited, believing meant rejoicing and trusting and perhaps even seeing God's mercy for the first time; and disbelieving meant becoming angry and fearful and threatened. And belief can also be the causal ground for a deepened understanding. For the happy emotions attendant on believing may, psychologically-religiously, predispose an individual to behavior which will eventually prove to enrich his understanding of Jesus, God, the world, and himself; whereas the disbelief of the Scribes may mean that they effectively cut themselves off from growth in understanding—perhaps even to the extent that eventually there comes to be quite a gulf between what the one, and what the others, understand.

7

Understanding

I. Pre-understanding

The problem which Meno set for Socrates was this: how can a man come to know something which he does not know—for if he does not know it at all, how can he even know what he is inquiring after; or how will he know, when he learns it, that what he has learned is what he wanted to know (*Meno*, 80d–e)? Socrates' solution was to appeal to the phenomenon of forgetfulness: to have forgotten is to be ignorant of it, yet not ignorant in the same way as not knowing it at all. Thus the answer is that when we learn something, we already know it (having learned it in a previous existence) but in such a way that the knowledge is not yet explicit. What we call learning, which is really a form of remembering, makes it explicit.

Bultmann's notion of pre-understanding answers a difficulty similar to the one which Socrates' theory of the pre-existence of the soul was designed to alleviate. Stated in its most general way, Bultmann's problem is this: How can we come to understand something which is unfamiliar to us? And his answer is that if it is totally unfamiliar to us, then we cannot understand it; every actual instance of understanding is founded upon a pre-understanding of the matter in question.[1] Bultmann's own in-

---

[1] This needs to be qualified. Bultmann seems to believe that the knowledge gained through natural science does not place this demand

terest, of course, is in the question of how it is that a person comes to an understanding of the Christian message. And since that message is mediated to us through texts, the problem can be couched in terms of the understanding of those texts. The pre-

---

on the knower. In one passage he contrasts the gaining of historical knowledge with acquiring a knowledge of nature: ". . . history precisely in its objective content can only be understood by a subject who is *existentiell* moved and alive. . . . for historical understanding, the schema of subject and object that has validity for natural science is invalid. . . . the phenomena of history are not facts that can be neutrally observed, but rather open themselves in their meaning only to one who approaches them alive with questions" (*EF*, p. 294). In the inquiry of natural science, this being "alive with questions" is deliberately eliminated in favor of pure, disinterested receptivity: "In *science* objectifying thought is developed consistently and methodically. When the phenomenon is made into an object, the influence it may exert upon me or any significance it may have for me is eliminated. For the object must be seen as it is in itself (*an sich*), and the discourse must not be about me, the subject. In the relation to the object which is characteristic of science, my receptivity is purely passive, that is to say, purely receptive, disinterested *seeing,* in distinction from a *hearing* of that which the object has to say for my personal life. The conduct of scientific activity consists precisely in the accomplishment of a disinterested seeing—disinterested in the sense that all personal interest is eliminated" (*GV,* III, p. 108). Now this seems to me to be patently inaccurate as an account of the way scientists go about their business. Scientists are highly "interested" in the objects of their inquiry in at least three ways. They always approach their inquiry with some kind of expectation and hope about the results of it. They always proceed "alive with questions," and these questions are often highly specific ones which predispose beforehand the kind of answers they will get or the kinds of descriptions which will be counted acceptable. Also, scientists often argue as long as possible for their own favorite hypotheses. As William James has said, "science would be far less advanced than she is if the passionate desires of individuals to get their own faiths confirmed had been kept out of the game" (*The Will to Believe* [New York, Dover Publications, Inc., 1956], p. 21). It is not disinterested seeing which gives rise to the objectivity and certainty of scientific results, but rather the fact that hypotheses are thrown into the refining fire of public scientific discussion and experiment, where only the best ones last. As for the scientist who has absolutely no personal interest in the objects of his inquiry, it is difficult to see not only how such a passive, dispassionate, and questionless pure eyeball could manage to roll out of bed in the morning, but indeed what reason he would have for doing one thing rather than another once he got to the lab. In any case, Bultmann seems to think that natural scientific understanding, unlike that of history, does not require any pre-understanding, since in pure receptivity it simply lets the phenomena shine forth as they are in themselves.

understanding which we have and must have to understand the New Testament is, Bultmann thinks, a pre-understanding of the *subject-matter* with which the New Testament deals.

> . . . every interpretation incorporates a particular prior understanding, namely, that which arises out of the context of living experience to which the subject belongs.
>
> The fact can be clearly illustrated by consideration of *the process of translating from a foreign language,* that at the back of every interpretation there lies a relationship in life to the subject about which the investigation of the text is concerned. . . . Knowledge of a foreign language can only be acquired afresh (assuming texts in several languages are not available) when the objects (things, relations, etc.) designated by the words are familiar — familiar from use and wont.[2]
>
> Interpretation, therefore, always presupposes a *living relationship to the subjects* which are directly or indirectly expressed in the text.[3]

What this means is that if the Bible is about God's action and we are able to understand it, we must already have a prior understanding of God and of his action:

> . . . *the comprehension of records about events as the action of God* presupposes a prior understanding of what may in my case be termed the action of God — let us say, as distinct from man's action, or from natural events. . . . In human existence an *existentiell* knowledge about God is alive in the form of the inquiry about 'happiness', 'salvation', the meaning of the world and of history; and in the inquiry into the real nature of each person's particular 'being'. If the right to designate such inquiries as the inquiry about God can be attained only from belief in the revelation of God, the phenomenon as such is the essential relation to the revelation.[4]

The reader (interpreter) of the text must have already both a prior understanding of the subject-matter of the text, and his own particular way of asking the pertinent questions of the text:

> The demand that the interpreter must silence his subjectivity

---

[2] *Essays,* pp. 241ff.
[3] *Ibid.,* p. 242.
[4] *Ibid.,* pp. 257f.

and extinguish his individuality, in order to attain to an objective knowledge is, therefore, the most absurd one that can be imagined.[5]

Now all this looks innocent enough, and even plausible. Who will deny that when we read a text, even the New Testament, we come to it with concerns, interests, questions, and the like, which are particular and our own, and that if we came to it with nothing at all of this sort, we would not even begin to understand it? Or who can deny that what it speaks of has to be something with which we have some rapport or other; for if it spoke of something utterly foreign to everything within our acquaintance and our own life, we would surely not be able to understand it. If Bultmann were only remarking that to understand a text requires (1) that the reader have some interest in what the text is saying and (2) that the text bear some relation to the reader's life, then we might admit that what he says about pre-understanding is true, while passing it off as a little trivial.

But we might suspect that the paradox which the concept of pre-understanding is to resolve is something more peculiar to Bultmann's thinking, and something more urgently in need of resolution for him, than the general problem about how we can understand something unfamiliar to us (which is, after all, a highly artificial paradox). And from what we have seen of Bultmann's views on language, we can with some confidence say that if he does not feel a little anxiety about finding a way out of the corner he has got himself into, it is at least not to his credit that he does not. Since all descriptive language is "ambiguous" with respect to the object of faith, that is, since there is no public or objectifying language which will tell us that *this* and not *that* is the object of faith, understanding this object to be what it is is coterminous with believing in it. This involves us in holding that the act of belief (or of offended disbelief) is performed with respect to an object which it has not yet understood; but it is of course absurd to talk of believing in something when one does not know what it is. Therefore it is plausible to think that it is because Bultmann wants to hold that understanding is in this way private to faith that he has to posit another kind of understanding, which is at the same time understanding (so that the

[5] *Essays*, p. 255.

paradox doesn't arise) and not understanding (so that all objectifying language remains ambiguous with respect to the object of faith). This understanding which is not understanding, this knowing which is in the mode of not-knowing, he calls "pre-understanding."

A similar paradox is generated by Bultmann's doctrine of the momentary character of existentiell understanding. Only in the moment of decision is there really understanding of the act of God which is expressed and proclaimed in the words of Scripture. Now, granted that it is also good Bultmannian doctrine that the individual does not work himself up to that moment, that the word addresses him as it were out of nowhere and without any preparation on his part, yet it would seem just too paradoxical to assert that that momentary, existentiell, believing understanding occurs in total independence of the time-continuum in which the individual is reading or hearing the sermon. Otherwise it would not matter at all whether it was a sermon or a newspaper or a hoot on the beach which happened (in the time-continuum) to correspond to the moment of "understanding." There must be something about the time preceding the moment of decision which could be characterized as understanding, for if the individual understood nothing in the time preceding the moment, it is very difficult to see why we should call what happens in the moment understanding at all, much less understanding of the text or sermon which in the preceding moment was being read or heard. It is not difficult to see how the concept of pre-understanding is tailored (if somewhat grossly) to this difficulty. If the pre-understanding of existence is something that can be laid out in existential interpretation, then it has to do with those general features of our existence which, though foundational for any momentary act of existentiell understanding, are not to be identified with any such act. Thus, pre-understanding can play something like the role of the temporal glue which holds together the discrete moments of existentiell understanding and makes them characterizable both as understanding and as understanding *of* the text, the sermon, or the like.

My characterization of these last two uses of the concept of pre-understanding is a piece of speculation, since Bultmann does not, to my knowledge, deal with the paradoxes which might call them forth. The use which I mention now is much more clearly in his mind, though it is interesting that he does not, when talking about pre-understanding, explicitly draw the inference which is undoubtedly present. Why he does not do so will be clear enough when I show what the connection is.

The primary way the concept of pre-understanding functions in Bultmann's thought is to provide a justification for letting a question formulated by existentialist philosophy and shaped by its concepts and beliefs be the guide for the theological exegesis of the New Testament. Stated in its most explicit way, the argument would run something like this:

> A necessary condition for understanding a text is a preunderstanding which takes the form of *specific* questions arising out of the interpreter's own *existence*. The philosophy of Heidegger provides a specific question arising out of human existence. Therefore we must let this question guide our interpretation of the New Testament.

In chapter one we saw that this question is "How can I become free?" where the concept of freedom is shaped by the existence/world dichotomy; and in chapter two we saw that this dichotomy, and thus this concept of freedom, fit New Testament thought very ill.

The argument is clearly invalid. None will deny that an interpreter must come to a text alive with questions and concerns nor that the kind of questions requisite for understanding the Bible are those "about 'happiness', 'salvation', the meaning of the world and history." But there is no such one thing as *the* question about happiness, for happiness can be conceived in various ways; and particular questions about salvation may be more or less adequate, more or less distorting, as a means of access to the answers of the New Testament. For example, if somebody thought of salvation as the annihilation of all desires, and then came to the New Testament with the question "How can I be saved?" he would end up either frustrated or with the meaning of his question changed by the answer provided there. To draw from the observation that questions of a certain *type* (e.g., about happiness) are appropriate and necessary, the conclusion that some *particular* question of this type must be trustworthy as a guiding principle of our interpretation, is bad logic. Each question has to be examined in its specificity to see whether it is an opening into the meaning of the Scriptures; it avails nothing to keep appealing, as Bultmann does, to the general observation that questions are important. Questioning, in order to guard against distorting interpretations, must be flexible enough to allow of modification through its reading of the New Testament's answers. So if somebody came with the existentialist question, and found that by its standards the conceptions of freedom in the Scriptures were worldly and inauthentic, then he should concede that it does not answer his question, and either abandon it or start asking the question it does answer.

Bultmann says that our pre-understanding (which for him amounts to an explicit or implicit knowledge that our life is inauthentic in Heidegger's sense) is a pre-understanding of, variously, God, God's act (cf. above), the Christian proclamation,[6] or "revelation."[7] He believes that one can call it a question about God ("die existentielle Frage nach Gott")

> regardless of the form that this question actually takes in [the exegete's] consciousness (say, for example, as the question concerning 'salvation', or escape from death, or certainty in the face of a constantly shifting destiny, or truth in the midst of a world that is a riddle to him).[8]

But what warrant is there for saying that this "question" and this pre-understanding are, in their diverse forms, about God, revelation, the Christian proclamation, and so on? Is the question "How can I escape death?" really a question about God? In what sense is the question "How can I be saved?" really a pre-understanding of the Christian revelation? Bultmann illustrates and argues his point by the analogies of light and friendship.

> Even the blind man knows what light is. And I can know what love and friendship are even if I have not found love and have not met any friend. Thus I know what revelation is without having found revelation — and yet I do not *really* know it. For the blind man also only really knows what light is when he sees, and the person who is friendless and unloved only really knows what friendship and love are when he finds a friend and is given love.[9]

---

[6] E.g., *FU*, p. 315.
[7] *EF*, p. 62.
[8] *Ibid.*, p. 296.
[9] *Ibid.*, p. 62.

Let us examine the analogies here offered.

It is true that blind people usually know what light is, and that what they know in knowing this is different from what people know who can see. But what *do* they know? A person blind from birth who lives among sighted people will know that in the daytime there is natural light and at night there is little or none; he will know that sighted people depend on light for telling where they are and for ambulating; he will probably know that light is associated with heat—that when, outdoors, he feels an intense heat on his skin, it is because the sun is shining on him, and that when an electric lightbulb is hot it is probably giving off light. But what if a person blind from birth lived exclusively in a society of people also blind from birth? Such a person would surely have no idea what light is. He would have no way of knowing that the difference between day and night is characterized by a difference of light (though he might have a parallel distinction based on temperatures). He would have no idea about being dependent on light for spatial calculation and ambulation, nor would it occur to him that this could be arranged any other way than by feel and hearing. Nor would the idea of heat be correlated with that of light, as it is for those who live among the seeing. What then does the blind person living among the sighted know about light? What we can say is that he has a mastery of the concepts connected with light—and this he has learned not through any native pre-understanding of light, but by sharing a language and way of life with those who can see. Without this language he would not have any knowledge—not even a "not-knowing kind of knowledge," whatever that might be—of light.

Knowledge or understanding can be distinguished from what we might call an ontological predisposition. Blind people, like sighted ones, have to get around in a spatial world, and inasmuch as this is the case, are the kind of beings for whom it would be good to be able to make use of light. So light and sight, if they are restored to a blind person, find a place in his life. There is a distinction, which Bultmann seems to neglect entirely, between knowing about something and being the kind of being into whose life such a knowledge can in principle fit. He seems to infer in a Socratic manner that wherever there is an ontological predisposition to knowledge, there must be knowledge (though perhaps in a not-knowing mode).

In contrast with the case of light, no human being very far beyond the dawn of consciousness can have escaped an acquaintance with human affection. Even in the extreme case in which the individual has received very little affection himself (and such cases would surely be found mostly in the mental hospitals) he will have seen people behave in a friendly manner with one another. Human beings of some age do not have a *pre*-understanding of friendship, but simply an understanding of it *per se*. This is not to deny that there is a vast difference between the mature person who has been friends with someone faithful through hardships and temptations as well as good times, and the immature person who has perhaps never had a firm and fruitful friendship. But the difference here is not at all like the difference between the blind and the sighted person with respect to an acquaintance with light. There is a qualitative difference of knowledge in the case of light; but in the understanding of what it is to be a friend, all kinds of subtle *gradation*s and *types* of understanding are attributable to individual cases. Here it is not a qualitative difference between one who has a merely linguistic mastery but not any direct acquaintance, and one who has direct acquaintance. Rather, even in the deepest understanding of friendship there is room for deepening; and even in the case of the teenager who never had a real friend, it is hardly appropriate, except as hyperbole, to say that he does not know what friendship itself is.

The case of revelation is different still, if we mean by that the message of the Christian proclamation. It is unlike the case of friendship in that it is not a phenomenon pervasive and fundamental to the tissue of human life as such, but like other historical accounts must be learned in specific by a linguistic communication. It is unlike the case of light in that there is not simply a qualitative distinction to be made between knowing it by acquaintance and knowing it conceptually; for in a certain sense to know it conceptually is to know it by acquaintance, and yet there is in this knowledge an almost infinite gradation of understanding possible, dependent mostly on the degree to which the individual's religious life is developed. I have distinguished between something's being a possible part of human life and thus fitting or appropriate to it, and a person's having a knowledge of it. Bultmann seems to confuse these two things when he says that *"We know about revelation because it belongs to our life."*[10] The fact that we can understand the gospel when it is preached to us certainly indicates that it "belongs to our life" in the sense that it is the sort of thing which fits into our life—it is something appropriate to human beings, something that speaks to our condition, something that can be incorporated into human consciousness. But it is either illicit or a very confusing way of speaking to conclude therefrom that we already know about the revelation, or that we have a pre-*understanding* of *it*. It would be clearer to say simply that human beings are capable of understanding it. Then one could enumerate what sorts of features of human life make it susceptible to the revelation, and in such an enumeration would no doubt have to be included some things which people may understand—that they are guilty, that they are going to die, that they want to be happy, and so on (though it is possible they may need to be taught even some of these things).

II. Professional hermeneutics and the common man

We have already discussed the distinction Bultmann draws between *existential* and *existentiell,* and have noted some internal difficulties which it causes in his thought. He applies this distinction also to pre-understanding, so that we come out with two kinds, one required by the common reader of Scripture, the other required by the "scientific" interpreter. A non-explicit pre-understanding of the text, the sort every man has in virtue of being a man, is enough, avers Bultmann, for "paying simple heed to what the New Testament says," but for the scientific interpreter it is necessary to have an explicit description of what is understood in his pre-understanding:

> Now at least for scientific exegesis, it is decisively a question of the relevant interpretation of the inquiry, and that means, at the same time, the *relevant interpretation of human existence.* To work this out is a matter for human reflection — concretely, the task of philosophical, or existential analysis of human being. It is axiomatic that such work is not the prerequisite for paying simple heed to what the New Testament says — which is directed directly towards an *existentiell* understanding of the self,

---

[10] *EF*, p. 62.

and not towards an existential knowledge. The case is different, however, when it is a question of scientific interpretation of Scripture. It takes its orientation from the inquiry into the understanding of human existence which finds expression in the Scriptures. Hence it has to concern itself with the relevant concepts in which human existence may be spoken of. These lie in the life relationship of the exegete to the subject expressed in Scripture, and they include a prior understanding of the subject. It is a mistake to think we can understand a word of the New Testament without such a prior understanding and the concepts which emanate from it, if it is to be understood as the Word of God. The interpreter requires critical reflection on the relevant concepts if he does not seek to read the biblical writings as a compendium of dogmatic pronouncements, or as 'sources' for the reconstruction of a section of past history, or to study a religious phenomenon or the nature of religion in general, or to know the psychological course and theoretical objectivization of religious experiences; and if, on the contrary, he wishes to make Scripture itself speak as a power which has something to say to the present, to present-day existence.[11]

This is clearly a defense of Bultmann's use of the existential analysis of Martin Heidegger as the conceptualization of pre-understanding required for any understanding of Scripture. As he says in another essay,

> the work of existential philosophy, which I came to know through my discussion with Martin Heidegger, has become of decisive significance for me. I found in it the conceptuality in which it is possible to speak adequately of human existence and therefore also of the existence of the believer.[12]

But look at the claims that are being made for this philosophical analysis! Without it "it is a mistake to think that we can understand a word of the New Testament"; without it, the Scripture will have nothing "to say to the present," but will be treated as a "compendium of dogmatic pronouncements," as "sources" for mere historical work or the phenomenology of religion or religious psychology.

But how can this be true, if the common reader is able

---

[11] *Essays*, pp. 258f.
[12] *EF*, p. 288.

to pay simple heed to what the New Testament says without the help of Heidegger? If he can do it, why cannot the professional exegete?

This question leads us to an even more basic one: What is the difference between a scientific understanding of Scripture and an ordinary one, and what are the relations holding between the two? When Bultmann speaks here of a scientific understanding, he is not referring to a knowledge of nice historical details of which the layman might be ignorant; he is speaking of a religious or existential understanding, that is, an understanding of the import that the text's "subject matter" has for present-day existence. A religious-scientific understanding seems to mean for Bultmann an understanding of the ontological and abstract features of the understanding of existence which lie behind the particular beliefs of the writers.

The common reader may read the New Testament with the same kind of naivete with which the ancient writer wrote the sentence, and thus may share his existentiell self-understanding; and just as through existential analysis Bultmann can know better than St. Paul what Paul meant, so he can tell the modern-day individual which features of his existentiell understanding are really Christian-authentic, and which are merely accidental. Thus one of the relations which Bultmann would want to see between an ordinary and a scientific understanding of Scripture would be that the exegete can tell the layman which features of his existentiell understanding are essential and which accidental, and can thus free him from superstition, *sacrificium intellectus,* or a simple rejection of the New Testament message. But why can the professional exegete not read the Bible as the word of God unless he has made explicit the ontological structure of human existence through existential analysis? The answer seems to be a simple one (however unbelievable): existential analysis tells us what the meaning of the Scripture is in telling us how to interpret it, and in telling us beforehand what is essential to it and what is historically accidental. The reason the non-professional can be said to understand it without Heidegger's help is that in the end only existential analysis gives us the key to what he can be said to have really understood. What *he* might say he had understood will thus, like the New Testament itself, undergo "interpretation." And this real meaning yielded by existential analysis simply *is* for Bultmann the meaning of Scripture as the word of

God. How this works will become clearer in the next chapter, where I examine a particular instance of Bultmann's "translating" exegesis.

But seeing how arbitrary Bultmann's peculiar notion of being exegetically "scientific" is need not lead us to deny that there is such a thing as a scientific understanding of the Scriptures, or to hold that one man's understanding is as good as another's. It may be that a scientific understanding is simply one which is careful, which is the fruit of much study and discussion, and of the wisdom of years and of the heart's purity. If we conceived the matter in this way, then scientific exegesis would mostly differ in *degree* from non-scientific, and would depend more on the man who was doing it than on its relation to an explicit theory about what it is to be human, or having the right hermeneutical method. It would be sufficient simply to make explicit for ourselves in a fresh way what the Scriptures say and how they bear upon our life. Sometimes the best exegetes have been without very much explicit general theory about the nature of man, using as their knowledge of man only what they get from Scripture itself and from the kind of wisdom which accrues to a life lived in its light. I think of Luther as an example. On the other hand the exegetes who have learned (and retained explicitly) most from the philosophers have often been among the worst. Origen comes to mind.

Nor is the idea of pre-understanding in itself wrong. It is not enough that we be merely ontologically predisposed for the gospel message. If we are to receive it in such a way that it can become *for us* salvation, we must certainly understand it, and that will involve understanding other things about ourselves and the world. I should think that the more perfectly a man comes to grips with the fact that he is going to die, the better he is prepared to see the point which the gospel message might have for his existence. This could be called a pre-understanding, though it would be wrong to say that it is, as such, a pre-understanding of God, or revelation, or the gospel message. Since understanding one's mortality is important to any individual's understanding of the evangel, it should be a concern of pastors to see that their people have plenty of opportunity to develop an awareness of death, and it should be the responsibility of every individual to see that he deepens his own awareness of it. It is surely also true that the capacity to feel moral pain and pleasure, to grieve at guilt and wrong and to rejoice in the presence of what is right and good, is a prerequisite for understanding the Christian message. If a person had little or no moral sensitivity, it is hard to see how he could resonate to what is proclaimed in the New Testament. This is not to say that to understand guilt and goodness is to understand Christianity, for the consciousness of God's existence and holiness and of the fact that his Son has died for our sins transforms moral capacities into something quite other. And yet there is an undeniable kinship.

Human beings have more or less specific emotional needs which, when rendered conscious, can play the part of a preparatory understanding. For example, however pleasant and perfect present circumstances may be, if a man has nothing to look forward to, he cannot be called happy. The gospel casts a specific kind of hope into a specific framework of beliefs. So not every felt need for hope is a felt need for *this* hope. And yet the hope which the gospel offers has enough affinities with the different hopes which men set themselves to be capable of replacing or qualifying these others. Because of the general need for hope, a person can learn to find in the Christian hope the basis of his happiness. When a person becomes aware of this need, he has understood something which makes him more capable of comprehending the Christian proclamation. The same could be said about peace. Even those who have a taste for strife need some foundation, as it were, of rest and harmony. The gospel proclaims reconciliation with God and an end to the strife and enmity constituted by sin—a kind of peace which surely does not occur to men apart from a specific hearing of the Christian story, and one which will strike as odd most who are searching for their various kinds of peace. And yet, since the gospel is capable of giving a person peace when all the other sources of it have failed, since it is capable in an odd way of being a substitute for all those other objects of search, it is not wrong to say that the searching, and the understanding involved in it, were preparatory to an understanding of the message of Jesus Christ. So there is nothing wrong with the idea of pre-understanding in itself, as long as we do not think that it is somehow mysteriously a pre-understanding *of the gospel,* and as long as the idea is not used as an argument for pushing off on us some particular controlling principle for the interpretation of Holy Scripture.

Bultmann's doctrine of pre-understanding is tailored for a

view according to which understanding itself is momentary and qualitatively distinct from non-understanding. The kind of self-understanding which characterizes faith and is the only authentic understanding of the New Testament occurs for Bultmann only in the moment of decision to exist in independence from every worldly conception, and such understanding is held onto only insofar as this decision is repeated ever anew in every new moment. Thus Bultmann's notion of understanding is conceived according to the model of flash insight: in the decision to live in independence of every worldly thing and conception, suddenly one sees what life is all about—one sees oneself really as not belonging to the world. Outside of this decision, which occurs only in the moment, this only true understanding of the New Testament is qualitatively absent.

The question is whether an understanding which occurs only in the moment can be called understanding at all. If a person claims to have had a flash insight into a philosophical argument, then we wait to see whether he actually works out the argument before we pass judgment on whether or not that moment constituted coming to an understanding. Likewise, I should think, if it were a question whether a person had in a flash insight really understood the statement that no man can serve two masters, the way to adjudicate the question would be to see what followed in the man's life. It seems that in making the moment everything constituting understanding, Bultmann has effectively deprived us of every criterion for determining whether an alleged instance of understanding was truly such.[13]

---

[13] For a fuller discussion of Bultmann's belief that understanding is a momentary act, see chapter eleven.

8

"Translating" Exegesis

I. Introductory remarks

Bultmann believes that, for modern man at least, there is something fundamentally inadequate about the New Testament as it stands. It has a meaning, but because of the faulty way in which it expresses it, the meaning does not come through. Its mode of expression may have been adequate to communicate its message to men who understood that mode of expression, but to modern men it serves only to hide the true meaning. If we give our children books in German when the only language they know is English, we can hardly expect them to understand the meaning, even if there is no doubt the books themselves have meaning. To make the books understandable what is needed is to change the mode of expression, while retaining the same meaning as was in the original; what is needed is a *translation*. And so it is, according to Bultmann, with the New Testament: unless it is "translated" into modern terms, unless it is "restated" in a modern conceptuality, unless it is "interpreted," it cannot be understood by modern men.

Bultmann thinks of "mythology" as a *language*. Thus the objective claims of the New Testament are no more essential to the meaning which is expressed in them than German is essential to Bultmann's essays. Just as the latter can be translated into English, so the former can be translated into the language of existentialist philosophy. Just as little utility as German has for those who speak only English, so little use have we modern men for "the language of mythology." Thus Bultmann can, referring to the New Testament story, propose substituting "an intelligible language for an unintelligible imagery."[1] Speaking of the objective descriptive terms in which the New Testament speaks of the cross of Jesus Christ (e.g., his bearing vicariously the sin of the world, his enduring punishment for sin on our behalf that we might be freed from death) Bultmann says, "they fail to do justice to what the New Testament is trying to say."[2] Fortunately, however, such aspects of the New Testament are only "language":

> We are compelled to ask whether all this mythological language is not simply an attempt to express the meaning of the historical figure of Jesus and the events of his life; in other words, significance of these as a figure and event of salvation. If that be so, we can dispense with the objective form in which they are cast.[3]

The true intention of the New Testament, which is almost completely obscured by the way it expresses itself, must, through a demythologizing translation, be again brought to light.

> Mythological thought, however, naively objectifies the Beyond, transposing it into this world, in that, contrary to its real intention, it represents the transcendent as extended in space and its power as only quantitatively greater than human capabilities. Demythologizing on the other hand desires to make manifest the real intention of myth, namely the intention to speak of authentic human reality. . . . But the decisive thing is that such images and symbols actually hide a meaning, and it is the task of philosophical and theological reflection to make this meaning clear. But this is why this meaning must not, in turn, be expressed in mythological language; for then the meaning of *that* language would have to be clarified — and so on *ad infinitum*.[4]

Moreover, without such a translation the true meaning of the New Testament cannot be understood:

---

[1] *KM*, p. 122.
[2] *Ibid*., pp. 35f.
[3] *Ibid*.
[4] *GV*, IV, pp. 134f.

I am bound to say that to speak of faith in the living God and
in his presence in Christ . . . is pure myth unless these things are
given an existential interpretation. . . . True, freedom, in the
New Testament sense of the word, means *facultas standi extra
se coram deo,* freedom from condemnation, freedom from the
bondage of the law, etc. But all this requires interpretation;
these things must be shown to be real experiences in human
life. . . . Otherwise all this is simply unintelligible mythology.
I am seeking to elucidate this freedom by interpreting it as the
freedom of man from himself and his past for himself and his
future. . . . Apart from such an interpretation the New Testament message of freedom remains utterly unintelligible.[5]

If the biblical writings are ever to be understood as affirmations
of faith and proclamation,

they must first of all be interpreted historically, inasmuch as
they speak in a strange language in concepts of a faraway time,
of a world-picture that is alien to us. Put quite simply, they
must be *translated,* and translation is the task of historical
science.[6]

It is clear what Bultmann means to suggest by calling his
hermeneutical procedure "translation." It is to claim that, for
example, the words "Jesus died for our sins" are not so much
something *said* as a *way* of saying something. Their real meaning
(as opposed to their mythological) intends not to say anything
about Jesus; rather they are an inadequate way of expressing
that the utterer has been freed from every worldly attachment.
And since they are only a way of saying something, the same
thing which they are a way of saying may be said in another (and
perhaps more adequate) way. So "Jesus died for our sins" and "I
have been freed from every worldly attachment" are merely
two ways of saying the same thing: the latter being understandable while the former is (at least without the latter) "utterly unintelligible."

Bultmann's belief in the need for demythologizing seems to
be based on reasoning which I might clarify something like this:
True Christian understanding is a momentary act, which is identi-

[5] *KM,* pp. 105f.
[6] *EF,* p. 292.

cal with the act of faith. I shall call understanding in this sense "understanding₁." The act of understanding₁, however, is impeded by what we might call the "hermeneutical problem." The truth of the matter is that the New Testament and Christian sermons are calling men to perform the act of understanding₁, but they cannot do so because they do not understand what is being called for. This second kind of understanding, failure of which prevents understanding₁, I shall call "understanding₂." Understanding₂ is achieved only when the *real* meaning of the New Testament (as opposed to its apparent meaning) is laid out. This real existential meaning is veiled by the fact that the New Testament seems to be talking about a Savior who is God's Son, a visible future kingdom of God, a bodily resurrection, a reportable and describable crucifixion which was at the same time the atonement for the sins of the world, and the like, whereas the real meaning of all this talk is an eschatological self-understanding (in Bultmann's peculiarly Heidegger-flavored sense of "eschatology"). This real meaning is not essentially tied to the above descriptions and references, and can be effectively distilled off from them by an existential interpretation. For the enabling of understanding₂ this interpretation which lays out the meaning in its existential purity of everything worldly is *necessary* and evidently also *adequate*. When the interpretation has made clear what the real meaning of the New Testament is, then understanding₂ must follow without further ado, and since the individual is thus brought face to face with the offered and demanding grace, all that remains is for the decision for or against it, which constitutes understanding₁, to be consummated.

II. A case study

Related to the interpretation- and expression-views of religious language (see chapters five and six) is Bultmann's assumption that there is something which might be called the existential meaning which has no essential dependence on any particular worldly referent, and which can thus be strained off from any such referents which might happen to figure in the language in which this meaning is expressed. Such a worldly referent occurs, for example, in the doctrine of creation when it is affirmed that God has made things in the past, or that there was an event "in the beginning" in which God made out of nothing everything that is. (It will be remembered that past events are, as such, worldly and cannot be the object of an encounter in which authentic self-understanding arises.) Thus Bultmann thinks of the reference to the past in the doctrine of creation as only a way of speaking; its real meaning is the self-understanding which is expressed in the doctrine, and this self-understanding or existential meaning can be preserved in independence of any beliefs about the past origin of things.

In an article called "The Meaning of Christian Faith in Creation,"[7] Bultmann gives what I take to be a demythologizing of the doctrine of creation. Let us examine it as an example of Bultmannian "translation."

He starts out by giving the existential meaning, not just of the story of creation found in Genesis, but of "creation myths" in general. This meaning is threefold. First, man's belief that he is created arises from a sense of wonder in face of the uncanniness of the world, and expresses that he is not the source of his own being, nor his own master. Second, it expresses an understanding which is essentially applicable only to his present situation: "It tells him how he is to understand himself *now;* and the reference to the past is only for the purpose of teaching him to understand his situation in the present."[8] Third, belief in creation expresses that man understands himself as discontinuous with the world in which he lives; it is at his disposal and a different kind of being from himself, from which he stands off at a kind of distance.

Thus, if the source of man's being and of the world's is understood as rational mind (*à la* Greek and idealistic science) the idea of creation is surrendered, because man, as participating in that source via his rationality, is thought of as the source of his own being. Or if he is understood as simply another part of the world, coming under universal laws of nature, the idea of creation is likewise surrendered, because man is not characterized as having the distance from the world required by that idea.

But denying man's creatureliness does not require a *theory* which raises him to the status of being his own creator. For by trying to secure himself by means of worldly things, position, in-

[7] *EF,* pp. 206ff.
[8] *Ibid.,* pp. 207f.

stitutions, roles, and achievements (as all men in fact do), man
has already attempted to make himself into his own creator while
at the same time identifying himself in worldly terms, rather than
affirming his distance from the world. The consequence of man's
thus understanding himself as his own master and in identification with the world is that the world becomes "uncanny" for him.
Where he tries to be secure, he finds that he is beset with anxiety
about his life; the world which ought to be his home becomes
instead a threat to him—and not one threat among others, like
some particular danger that he might arrange to avoid; but the
whole of life, existence in the world as such, becomes a threat to
him. Nothing that he can grasp within the world is truly an
answer to this anxiety, because the anxiety is the product precisely of grasping for one's *own* security in terms of things *within*
the world. The only truly appropriate answer is that man come
to understand himself in a radically new way, truly in accordance with his being as one who is not his own creator and who
is discontinuous with everything worldly. Only by making the
decision in which he gives up the attempt to be his own master
and to secure his life by worldly means will he gain the freedom
from anxiety and the uncanniness of the world to which that
attempt was misguidedly directed.

Bultmann defines the goodness and the wrath of God in
terms of these alternative possibilities of man's self-understanding:

> God's goodness is precisely that man should be himself and
> receive his selfhood from God his Creator as a creature. . . .
> The uncanniness that enters the world through sin and persis-
> tently encompasses man is, as the New Testament expresses it,
> *the wrath of God.*[9]

Thus, when he says

> that the world is uncanny for man shows that he is God's crea-
> ture and that his being a creature continues to determine him
> whether he knows it or not,[10]

this is not to be taken as an inference from the uncanniness of

---

[9] *EF,* p. 219.
[10] *Ibid.*

the world that God exists and has made the world. It is to be taken rather as a definition of 'God the creator.' That is, to assert that God is creator amounts to asserting that man is not his own master and not continuous with the world and that when he tries to live understanding himself as self-master and as worldly he becomes anxious and the world looks uncanny. Faith in God the creator is equivalent to an existentiell understanding of one-self as not one's own master and as utterly distinct from everything worldly. It is by decisively facing one's anxiety and the uncanniness of the world, by making the decision in which one honestly grasps and affirms the insecurity of life in the world, that is, in "genuine submission to God's wrath," that one finds a new paradoxical release from anxiety, a new paradoxical at-homeness in the world, a new paradoxical security, which is "faith in God the Creator." That is, faith in God the creator is equivalent to freedom in the sense in which we explored it in chapter one. Needless to say, Bultmann believes that such "faith in creation" can be actually achieved only in response to the kerygma.

At the end of his essay he adds a couple of other associations which seem to be contained in the doctrine of creation. One is that the world stands at man's disposal: though he is not lord of his own life, which can be referred only to God, he is lord of the world, which he makes use of and dwells in. The second is that man is a historical being, so that the nature of himself and the world and his neighbor is seen not to lie in their subsumability under general and timeless laws, but in their concrete character. Thus a man's world is always this particular world at this particular time; his neighbor is always this or that particular man or woman; he himself is always someone in particular: "a man or a woman, . . . old or young, strong or weak, clever or untalented, well or ill, German or French, etc."[11]

In this "translation" of the doctrine of creation, Bultmann has attempted to give us the existential meaning without the objectifying meaning, which he would take to be mythology and primitive science, and a mere husk in which the existential meaning is enshrined. He has tried to strain off the self-understanding involved in a belief in creation and to preserve it in indepen-

---

[11] *EF,* p. 223.

dence of any objectifying assertions about God and the world. Now in a translation what we have is the *same meaning* as was in the original text, but in a *different language*. In a good translation, something is always lost, namely the old language; what must be preserved the same is the meaning. What is lost in Bultmann's "translation"? A. H. Strong expresses succinctly that element of the belief in creation which Bultmann takes to be merely the antiquated and eliminable "language" or mode of speech for conveying an understanding of existence.

> By creation we mean that free act of the triune God by which in the beginning for his own glory he made, without the use of pre-existing materials, the whole visible and invisible universe.[12]

As Bultmann says,

> Faith in creation . . . is not a theory about the past. It does not have its meaning by relating what took place at some earlier time and no longer concerns man in the present, but rather speaks precisely about man's *present* situation. It tells him how he is to understand himself *now;* and the reference to the past is only for the purpose of teaching him to understand his situation in the present, i.e., to understand that he is not permitted to raise questions about the "why," to make claims, but rather is abandoned to a higher will.[13]

Now to be fair to Strong we should say that he does not imply that the belief in creation has the character of a scientific hypothesis, and indeed expressly denies that this is the purpose of the Scriptural account of creation: "it is foreign to the purpose of revelation to teach science."[14] Nor would Strong think that it follows from the fact that God's act of creation is a past event that it "no longer concerns man in the present." Strong would certainly affirm that a belief in creation has consequences for how a man understands himself *now*. But the point I want to make is that the element of the belief in creation which Strong emphasizes in his definition is for Bultmann no more essential

---

[12] *Systematic Theology* (Old Tappan, N.J.: Fleming H. Revell Company, 1907), p. 371.

[13] *EF,* pp. 207f.

[14] Strong, *op. cit.*, p. 395.

to the meaning of the doctrine than German is to a proposition which happens to be expressed in that language. For Bultmann the whole meaning of the doctrine can be reduced to its significance in any individual believer's present moment; in this essay he thinks of the reference to the past as an incidental teaching device; later, in the essay on demythologizing, he will think of this kind of element as language or conceptuality for expressing an understanding of human existence, which is not only dispensable, but must be lost in a translation into a modern conceptuality.

We should remark that the language of faith in creation, in Bultmann's proposed translation, does not aim simply to eliminate all reference to non-existential realities like the physical world and history.

> Faith speaks of God's action not only as miracle but also as his creatorhood and lordship in nature and history; and it must speak thus. For if man knows himself in his existence to be called and led into life through God's omnipotence, he knows also therewith that nature and history, within which his life runs its course, are also ruled by God's action. But this knowledge can be expressed only as a confession, and never as a general truth as in the theories of natural science or the philosophy of history. Otherwise God's action would be objectivized into a worldly occurrence. The proposition about God's creatorhood and lordship has its legitimate basis only in the existentiell self-understanding of man.[15]

So we have here the picture of someone confessing that this very concrete sticks-and-stones-and-flesh-and-water world is the creation of God, but in such a way that he does not utter a general truth. I take it that one of the characteristics of a general truth, whether it is found in science or in the philosophy of history or just in everyday discourse, is that inferences about particulars can be drawn from it. Thus if the general truth is that all mammals nurse their young, its generality involves the possibility of inferring of any particular mammal that it belongs to a class of which the females nurse their young. Similarly it would seem that ordinary, non-existentialist believers in creation would agree

---

[15] *GV*, IV, p. 135.

that it is part of the logic of "God created the world" that one can infer from it that God created the brown trout that I caught near Gunnison, Colorado, in July of 1956. We do not usually make such inferences, but reflecting on the legitimacy of doing so seems to me to bring out one of the ways in which assertions about creation are *about* the world. Bultmann seems to want to deny, through his translation, that sentences about creation have to be able to be about the world in this way. He seems to think that one could assert that God is the creator of the world, while at the same time denying the legitimacy of drawing such inferences. But surely to say, in a believing way, that God created the world, is to say something whose significance goes beyond the expression of my present, momentary, existentiell self-understanding. A man who uttered the confession, but then when asked about the significance of his utterance, denied that he meant any more than to express his existentiell freedom from every worldly encumbrance, might well be thought not to believe that God created the world at all. The utterance then really *would* amount to a (very oblique) manner of speaking; it would be a kind of code for expressing one's existentiell acts.

What Bultmann seems to be contending, then, is that one can have the existentiell self-understanding which is involved in a right holding of the Christian doctrine of creation, without believing that God actually made everything that is. But is it true that a man's self-understanding remains the same if he ceases to have a use for these descriptive elements of the doctrine? If elements of this objective and worldly sort are entirely eliminated from the use that is made of the sentences about God's creating, is it really possible to claim that we have retained the essential meaning of the biblical or creedal language? Can there really be any such thing as a purely existential meaning distilled off without loss from the objective "what" which is believed? Does not *what* is believed determine, to a great extent, what the shape of the Christian life will be, in such a way that a language of faith deprived of its worldly elements would not even have the same existential meaning? Is it not possible to object to demythologizing translation not just that the objects of faith are lost, but that even as existential it is not a *restatement* of Christian existence, but a *transformation* of it into something very different?

Bultmann quotes the following passage from Luther:

This is without doubt the supreme article of faith of which we speak: I believe in God the Father almighty, Maker of heaven and earth. And whoever honestly believes this is already helped and is once again brought back to the place whence Adam fell. But few are they who go so far as to believe fully that he is the God who makes and creates all things. For such a man must be dead to everything, to good and bad, to death and life, to hell and to heaven, and must confess in his heart that he is able to do nothing by his own power.

Then Bultmann comments:

This kind of faith in creation is not a theory about some past occurrence such as might be depicted in mythological tales or cosmological speculation and natural scientific research; rather it is faith in man's present determination by God.[16]

This latter interpretive sentence I take to be a typical example of the move which Bultmann calls translation: the effect is to tell us that those aspects of the doctrine which speak of a past occurrence are mere language, a manner of speaking, and that the meaning of the doctrine is quite independent of them. Note what happens: Luther clarifies the attitudinal import that a belief that God is creator should rightly have in a man's life. And this is precisely what the preacher ought to do, for to believe that God is creator has logically different characteristics from the belief, for example, that Thomas Edison invented the light-bulb, and the differences are rightly pointed up by referring to the attitudes, the behavior, the passions and emotions which are involved in a belief that God is creator of all that is. Really to hold this belief is to have one's whole perception of the world transformed, and surely one of the purposes of preaching is to make this clear, so that people do not hold the belief in the wrong mode and thus miss the blessings of faith. But look now at what Bultmann does with it, something different from what Luther did and in the end (as I am trying to show) not even possible on logical grounds: Bultmann would have us believe that the whole meaning of the sentence "I believe in God the Father almighty, Maker of heaven and earth" is that import which it has in the individual's present. That is, since it has im-

---

[16] *EF,* p. 220.

port for the present, it cannot be about the past (for that, Bultmann implies, would have to make it a mere theory, or mythology, or natural science). Thus we are confronted with the typical Bultmannian either/or which follows the schema existence/world: *either* it is about the past and must be a form of science or primitive science or mere theory *or* it is a possibility of authentic self-understanding in which case it can only be about the present. That is, belief in creation is for Bultmann not really a *belief* at all, once it has been interpreted, once the existential meaning has been siphoned off from the mythological (worldly) dregs. It is not the belief that God made the heavens and earth, and that (in a perhaps different sense) he continues to make and sustain them. To believe that would be inauthentic and worldly, because it would be to understand oneself in terms of a past event (or past process, or whatever it is).

So what Bultmann wants to do is to take the personal import of believing that God made the heavens and the earth, which Luther so well lays out, and to call that by itself "the meaning of Christian belief in creation," while throwing out the belief. But is it really possible to take the "existential" meaning in independence of the belief? Does Bultmann's translation really preserve what Luther meant? Is not the belief that God "makes and creates all things" inextricably bound up with the existence of the believer, in such a way that when he ceases to believe that God actually made this earth, these trees, those little girls playing in the sand, and himself, he also ceases to understand himself in the ways that a believer does? Surely the man who confesses "in his heart that he is able to do nothing of his own power" *in connection with* the belief that God made the world, sees the world and himself differently from the man who holds no belief about where rocks and earth and trees and stars and little girls came from, but has somehow come to the momentary insight that he can do nothing of his own power.

A pertinent case would be table prayers. When Christians give thanks before eating, they do so in the belief that this very food, these very physical and worldly objects steaming in all their particularity before them on the table, have been provided by the Lord for their use. It is part of the logic of thanksgiving that there be a connection between the objects for which thanks are given and the one to whom thanks are given, and in Christianity this connection is established for each individual in his believing that this food came from the Lord. If this connection is lost, the whole of thanksgiving becomes fatuous. (It is of course possible to conceive of people who got together and agreed that whenever they bowed their heads and said "We thank thee Lord for these gifts" what they really meant was to express their acknowledgment of the fact that they are not able to live by their own power. But we would have the right to say that their meaning is eccentric, that it is not what those words convey ordinarily among speakers of English, and that it would perhaps be less confusing if they found another way of expressing it.)

By reducing the whole Christian life to a single decisive act of self-understanding, Bultmann neglects much of the richness of Christian existence. To enjoy a mountain or a sunset or a child as something that God has made is a peculiar kind of enjoyment of mountain or sunset or child, and one which depends on believing that God made them. To feel guilty about the burning of a forest as the destruction of something God has made is not the same as a guilt about its loss which does not so connect it with him. To grieve about the corruption of a person as of a creature is a peculiar grief, and one inextricably tied to believing that God made him. Surely such perceptions as these are a part of Christian existence, and they are ones which would be lost if we were to eliminate all objective and worldly reference from the doctrine of creation, as though it were nothing more than a way of speaking about our self-understanding. For to eliminate such reference from the language of faith is to change precisely that which Bultmann's translation so devoutly desires to isolate and preserve—the Christian self-understanding. By allowing the existentialist metaphysic to be regulative for his work, Bultmann has been led to the belief that there is something called the existential meaning, which can be freed up from all objectifying reference. In this he is surely wrong; for it is precisely Christian *existence* which is dependent on many of the things which he counts as worldly and thus eliminable, and thus treatable as merely language. When the Christian says that God made the world, this is not simply a way of expressing his decision to live as though he can do nothing of himself (although it may be that too); it is, as a way of expressing specifically Christian attitudes, perceptions, and emotions, also necessarily an assertion about the world.

Bultmann prejudices the account by denying that faith in creation is a theory or a mythological tale or a sentence from natural science. For those who believe that the things presently in the world were created by God in the past do not hold this belief as a theory, that is, they do not do the same things with it as one does with a theory. The passage from Luther shows nicely what role the belief ought to play in the believer's life, but this role does not make it any the less an objectifying belief.

The idea of an existential meaning allows Bultmann effectively to deny that what the text *says* is an adequate criterion for what it *means*. But if what is said is not an adequate guide to what is meant, the question arises, "How can you tell when you have the meaning?" Thus, if the meaning of talk about a coming kingdom of God is not necessarily that a kingdom is coming, but rather perhaps that those who thus talk are radically open to the future, how can we tell that this is the meaning, rather than, for example, that all men should work hard to establish the perfect society upon earth? Interpreting sin as attachment to one's past and forgiveness as being set free from it, by associations Bultmann can get to the notion that the meaning of the hope for a future kingdom of God is radical openness to the future. But if we were to start from a different system than the existentialist one (especially its notions of freedom and time), making different associations and applying again the assumption that what the text says is no adequate criterion of what it means, we could conceivably, without too much difficulty, come up with a totally different "meaning" for the texts which refer to a coming kingdom of God.

What does translation really amount to in Bultmann's work? Judging from what he promises in some passages, we might expect to find that traditional words such as *God, grace, forgiveness* and *salvation* would no longer appear in the translation (just as German words no longer appear in an English translation of a German text), and that they would be replaced by other words taken from the philosophy of existentialism. But when we look at Bultmann's pages this is not at all what we find. Rather we meet with the same old words, for the most part, interspersed with *explanations* of what they mean. The explanations very often make use of the language of existentialist philosophy, but there seems to be no literary product which could be called "the translation," couched in this latter-day terminology. What the literary output of Bultmann seems to do is to tell us the meaning of the texts, so that when we hear the texts themselves we will know what they mean, and be able to make the decision of faith or offense.

Bultmann sometimes talks as though demythologizing is the activity of translating the meaning of the texts out of the *conceptuality* of mythology into the *conceptuality* of modern philosophy. Now it is a little bit unclear what a conceptuality amounts to, but the idea seems to be that different concepts can be used to convey the same meaning. If this is what is meant, the idea is confused. A little thought experiment will demonstrate this. Suppose someone proposed the following: Where the New Testament uses the word *salvation,* we will now use the word *authenticity,* and where it uses *faith* we will now use *resolve.* Now authenticity and resolve are clearly not the same concepts as salvation and faith, so in order to make the new speaking into a real translation (rather than just talk about something else) one would have to stipulate that *authenticity* and *resolve* be used in the same way as *salvation* and *faith* were in the old one. But of course this would be worse than no improvement at all, since to understand the translation one would not only have to understand already the original language, he would also have to keep constantly in mind that the words of the new language were being used in an eccentric way. What this little thought experiment shows is that a translation from concept to concept is a contradiction. This is because the idea of expressing the same meaning in different concepts is a contradiction. *Words* can be different and the meaning the same, but this can be so only on the condition that they express the *same concepts.* If the concepts are really different, then the meaning is different too, and the word *translation* is wholly inappropriate. For a translation is precisely a different set of words which carry the same meaning. There is no such thing as a different set of concepts which carry the same meaning, and thus no translation from conceptuality to conceptuality.

III. Christian education

We have seen that for Bultmann the project of translation is a response to the problem of understanding. We have seen also that he sees essentially only two barriers to understanding. There is, of course, always the possible barrier constituted by the individual's refusal, in the face of the kerygma, to perform the required existentiell act. This is a barrier to which no hermeneutical procedure can minister; each individual must either make the called for decision or not. But the barrier Bultmann calls the "hermeneutical problem" arises from the New Testament's expressing itself in an "inadequate way" and thus his method of removing it can be to translate the meaning of the New Testament out of the conceptuality of mythology into the conceptuality of existentialism.

Now the one thing notably lacking from this way of construing Christian understanding is any reference to education. Neither of the barriers to understanding which Bultmann sees is to be corrected by the education of the individual's mind or heart. The hermeneutical problem gets solved in the theologian's study or behind his lectern or in learned monographs; and once it has been solved everything else is decided in the momentary decision of the individual's response. Totally irrelevant is any such thing as what Kierkegaard called "Christian upbringing" or "training in Christianity" or even the kind of striving in which the individual grows into holiness and thus also into a deeper understanding. This is consistent with Bultmann's predisposition against confirmed character-traits as inauthentic. Since Christian education involves the development of such dispositions as the individual's interests and passions (e.g., a love for Jesus, an interest in an eternal happiness), his capacity for feeling and emotion (e.g., grief over his sin, and joy in the Lord), and his ability to perceive himself and his neighbor and the world in peculiar ways determined by the Christian concepts (e.g., as the creation of God, as people for whom Christ died), it must be anathema to an existentialist for whom all dispositions and confirmed character-traits are worldly and a temptation to inauthenticity. And consequently, the kind of understanding which is ingredient in such interests, attitudes, passions, feelings, emotions, and perceptual capacities is likely to be ignored or thought inessential to true Christian understanding.

Bultmann explicitly denies that there can be such a thing as Christian education or training

> provided that we understand education and training in their original sense as the methodical development of human capaci-

ties and characteristics. Christian faith does not have its basis
in reason and cannot be the result of methodical development.[17]

The only basis of Christian faith is the word of God itself, says
he, and the real problem is making that word available in such
a manner that it can be understood.

> That can happen in various ways, corresponding to the differ-
> ences between individual human beings and in their concrete
> situations. However, there are two things which are always the
> same in this regard. The first is this: man must reach the point
> that he reflects concerning himself, that he asks himself what is
> human, what his being is. He must learn to understand which
> questions are authentic for him, to become aware of what he
> authentically requires, what truth, reality, and genuine existence
> denote. And then it must be pointed out to him what the mean-
> ing of Christian faith is, what is intended when Christian faith
> speaks of God, of sin, and of grace; and how Christian faith
> understands the situation of man in the world. What is needed
> for this purpose is not "education," but rather "instruction in
> the Christian religion."[18]

He acknowledges that in rendering the word of God understandable the Christian teacher has to take into account differences between individual men and their concrete situations. But he
is clearly not talking here about *fostering* differences which would
adapt individuals to grasp the peculiarities of the Christian message. That, evidently, would be "education." Individual differences are no more than the occasion for differences in hermeneutical *strategy:* there may be different methods required for
jockeying the individual into the position of asking the question
about his own being (but it will have to be this universal question, which Heidegger has so well laid bare for us); and there
may also be different strategies (though all characterized as
"translation" of one form or another) for getting him to see the
real meaning of talk about God, sin, and grace. The peculiar
development of the individual thus has nothing to do with
whether he comes to Christian faith, nor with the understanding which is peculiar and necessary to it.

---

[17] *GV,* IV, p. 53.
[18] *Ibid.,* p. 54.

Bultmann's actual argument against education's having a constitutive role in the rise of Christian faith, namely, that it is merely "the methodical development of human capacities and characteristics," seems to be confused. It is hard to know what is to be contrasted with "human capacities and characteristics." When a man has a love for Jesus Christ, this is surely no less a human capacity or characteristic than other loves and passions. Bultmann will no doubt reply that the gospel comes to us from beyond ourselves, from beyond everything human. In a certain sense that is true, and yet surely our appropriation of it, the effects it has on our existence, which we call "faith," is a characteristic of human beings. People who advocate Christian education or "training in Christianity" do not deny that God has first loved us, or think of such training as a mere development of man's reason. They think of it rather as the development of emotions, passions, perceptual abilities, and behavior dispositions through the learning of the Christian concepts which arise out of the story of Jesus Christ and are communicated only by repeating that story, and which thus come from "beyond" ourselves. Bultmann encourages us to think of education as methodical, and thus draws our attention to such things as the systematic textbooks full of daily exercises from which we learned arithmetic and algebra as children. But this is only one kind of education. A person's development of moral sensitivities is no less education because there is no set method or exercises for gaining them. Growing up in a home characterized by restraint and purity and integrity and love is surely an education of the soul. It is simply tendentious for Bultmann to fix our attention on the former kind of education in order to convince us that education is foreign to Christian faith.

Bultmann's real reason for eschewing education seems to be his existentialist predisposition against everything that smacks of temporality in the normal sense of the word, in particular, dispositions which are more or less fixed and settled and thus continue through time. According to the existentialist concept of freedom, for an individual to understand himself in terms of such character-traits is inauthentic. Everything which is continuous through time is "worldly," and authentic existence is to be found only in the moment. Thus Bultmann denies that the light which is Jesus Christ can become a part of the character of Christian individuals:

For the eternal light never becomes a light that belongs to this world. That is, it can never become our possession, a quality of our nature, a property of our character. Always it can only be received — and only be received again and again — as a gift.[19]

Note here the connection between the notion of a disposition ("a quality of our nature, a property of our character") and that of world, mediated, as usual, by the ambiguous and evocative word *possession*. To possess something is to hold it through time, but we are no doubt also supposed to think here of things like possessive mothers and misers, clinging dependently and selfishly to what they have. But of course, a property of our character, for example an abiding and characteristic love for Jesus Christ, is not something about which one would have to be "possessive" in this sense. Indeed this property of character would seem to be at odds with being possessive in this way. And one could certainly view one's love for Jesus Christ as being a gift from God without its ceasing to be a possession in the sense of something one's own which abides through time. The contrary of gift is not possession; rather to give someone a gift is precisely to give it into his possession—otherwise we say that it has strings attached and is a second-rate gift, if a gift at all. One violates one's relation to the giver not by possessing the gift, but by being ungrateful for it.

At any rate, it seems to be this existentialist inclination against abidingness and in favor of spontaneity and immediacy, rather than the artificial reason he gives, which induces Bultmann to deny the significance of "capacities and characteristics" and "development," and to assert rather that "Christian faith is an act of the will, a resolve, or, more precisely: a decision."[20] And for this reason, too, translation plays the central role in his hermeneutical activity it does. It is instructive here to compare Bultmann's strategy with that of Søren Kierkegaard. Kierkegaard never made any suggestions about how Christian teachings might be re-interpreted or translated into a modern conceptuality in order to make them understandable to men. He too acknowledged that there was a barrier to understanding, and he too devoted his literary talents to breaking down this barrier. But

---

[19] *EF*, p. 281.
[20] *GV*, IV, p. 53.

he thought that the difficulty lay not in the way the New Testament expressed itself, but with the men who proposed to understand it. He thought that the passions of most men, the degree of development of their capacities of moral insight, their loves, their interests, their desires, were so incongruent with the demands of understanding that the New Testament lays upon a man, that for this reason they did not understand it. The solution, if there was to be one, was to change not the New Testament but the men, and it was to this task that Kierkegaard's literary output was devoted. By way of contrast, Bultmann's project of translation assumes that the difficulty lies in the New Testament's mode of expression, and that as soon as the hermeneutician's task has been accomplished (given, perhaps, strategy differences for different individuals) every man, regardless of his character, cannot but understand the New Testament's meaning and thus stand confronted with the necessity to make a decision for or against it.

Speaking of the free act of faith, which for him constitutes religious understanding in the eminent sense, Bultmann says,

> A greater or lesser degree of enthusiasm has as little to do with a free act as has greater or lesser resistance, greater or lesser self-mastery, which may make an act appear to be a greater or lesser sacrifice in human eyes.[21]

But this is to neglect totally the fact that understanding is something which accrues with years, that a man grows in understanding, that one individual, because of his development, understands differently from another. It is to neglect the fact that what a man loves and desires and what interests him determine, especially in matters religious, what he will see and understand. It is to neglect the fact that wisdom, which is certainly a name for a set of dispositions to perceive and understand, is also connected with firmness of moral and religious character (indeed, with "greater or lesser resistance, greater or lesser self-mastery"). It is to neglect the fact that interpretation will not provide understanding to one who does not already possess the capacity to understand, and that such a capacity depends on how one's past has been lived. It is to neglect the fact that what one comes to un-

---

[21] *FU*, p. 62.

derstand through one's decisions is both dependent on prior capacities and productive of further ones. As I shall argue in the final chapter of this work, understanding is not an act, but a capacity, not a momentary flash, but a perduring personal trait. For if it is claimed that a person understands or has come to understand something, we expect him to have certain constituting abilities: abilities to perceive, to feel, to discuss, to act, and the like.

IV. Conclusion

Is there really a hermeneutical problem at all? If we mean hereby to ask whether difficulties of understanding the Bible and the Christian faith ever arise, then the answer is obviously Yes. There will always be people who do not understand this or that; and where the failure bears on their access to the blessings of faith, this constitutes a worthy problem for the church. But what the problem amounts to in different cases may be quite different, and the way the problem is to be solved will accordingly differ greatly too. If a child does not understand the word *resurrection,* then a simple explanation of the word's meaning will probably help him along. If an adult does not see why belief in the resurrection would contribute to a person's happiness (even though he has a good grasp of the teachings here involved), then it may be that nothing short of a revision of his whole way of looking at the world and weighting his desires will constitute progress in understanding. If we do not understand what Paul referred to by talking about "principalities" and "powers," then we may be aided in a certain way by looking at some of the more astute scholarly guesses about the matter. These cases and similarly diverse ones might be gathered under the label "problems of hermeneutics." But in none of these cases would there be a single science or method which could be applied to all the failures of understanding to remedy them. In the one case, explanation of how a word is used is appropriate; in another, Christian education in a deeper sense is requisite; in still another, recourse to scholarship is the only road to success.

Every good preacher engages in a family of activities which might be called, metaphorically, "translating." He puts the thoughts of Paul and John, as nearly as he can, into the vernacular of his congregation. He gives examples of sin, of righteousness, of joy and peace. He tells stories which illuminate the Christian concepts by setting them in contrast with something other, or by embodying them in very concrete depictions of the human heart. Where the biblical writer speaks in high generality about sin, the preacher perhaps translates by way of describing the complex and concrete perversions to which the soul is susceptible. The preacher does more than read the words of the Bible to his congregation. In a thousand ways he circumscribes, he juxtaposes, he illustrates and distinguishes, in order to head off misunderstandings and confusions and to nudge his congregation along the way of understanding the gospel's blessings and demands. And thus, something like a translator, he mediates between those strange yet overfamiliar words of Jesus and Luke and Paul and the religious-conceptual life of his people.

If, however, we mean by "hermeneutical problem" a single difficulty which goes through the whole of the New Testament in its relation to modern man, and to which a single method or principle could be applied, then there simply is no hermeneutical problem at all; it is a fiction invented by some philosophically minded interpreters. There are only problems with equally various methods of solution. If we agree that the New Testament presents problems of understanding, then Bultmann's mistake is not that he set out upon a remedy, but that he thought it necessary to give a single, gross diagnosis of the difficulty, and then to use in service of the cure some correspondingly blunt instruments. His approach to the Bible with concepts like "mythology," "modern scientific world-view," "existential meaning," "demythologizing," and even "kerygma" (an otherwise good enough word), reminds one of a surgeon trying to perform a brain operation with a dull axe. The result we have seen is one we might have predicted—we could hardly expect the patient to live through such a cure.

We have now completed our excursion through that family of pivotal issues in Bultmann's thought called "hermeneutics," and have seen that his setting of the problem and the various aspects of his solution to it are sufficiently confused as to fail to perform the function they seem to be assigned: to mediate the contradiction between the existence/world dichotomy and the thought of the New Testament. In the process of this discussion

we have already touched on several substantive theological issues. In the third part of this essay we must now turn our attention explicitly to some issues of Christian theology which we
have so far only touched upon. We must examine critically and
in detail Bultmann's conceptions of God, Christian ethics, and
faith.

Part III

Some
Theological
Details

9

God

I. God as geschehende Transzendenz

One of the primary features of the revolt waged against liberal theology by the "dialectical" theologians (Barth, Bultmann, Brunner, Gogarten, *et al.*) was a dissatisfaction with the previous generation's understanding of God. Along with their new appreciation of the role of eschatology in the New Testament, and of the consequent discontinuity of New Testament faith with natural human attitudes, practices, and institutions, these theologians also came to speak of God as the "Wholly Other." They so insisted on God's otherness that to believe in him was *eo ipso* to break completely (though, to be sure, in a "dialectical" manner) with one's previous life in the world. What had been lost in liberalism was the bite of eternity, the disrupting, the shattering, and thus the renewing, character of the gospel of Jesus Christ. God, if he had not yet quite emerged as an Englishman, was certainly well on the way to becoming a respected member of the German bourgeoisie. To these theologians it seemed an unworthy fate for the lordly Judge of the Old and New Testaments that he should be retained and put to good use as the inspiration for the highest and noblest in moral European culture. Thus Barth could say in 1921,

> if I have a system, it is limited to a recognition of what Kierkegaard called the 'infinite qualitative distinction' between time

and eternity, and to my regarding this as possessing negative as well as positive significance: 'God is in heaven, and thou art on earth'.[1]

Since the early days of dialectical theology, Barth's ideas about the nature of God have undergone considerable transformation. But almost half a century later Bultmann was still valiantly bearing the old banner against "religiosity"—that comfortable, practical, "inspiring" bourgeois religion:

> Religiosity abandons precisely that — at least according to the Christian faith — upon which genuine religion is based: the relation of man to the transcendent God as that which stands over against.[2]

Throughout Bultmann's writings, God's otherness, his being "beyond," his utter difference from all worldly being—or, as he usually expresses it, his "transcendence"—is the fundamental determining feature of his concept of God.

Indeed, God is so transcendent that he cannot be made into an object of thought,[3] nor is he a being, nor does his "revelation" have the form of discursive (propositional, doctrinal) knowledge, nor is he to be regarded as an existent entity. For Protestant theology, says Bultmann, a theology based on the knowledge of God derived from rational arguments by the light of natural reason is impossible. But this impossibility does not lie where it has traditionally been thought to:

> not only, nor even primarily, because philosophical criticism has shown the impossibility of giving a proof of God, but especially because this view of natural theology ignores the truth that the only possible access to God is faith. Catholic theology must understand revelation primarily as the communication of doctrines which are superior to the natural knowledge of reason, not in kind but only in degree. God is regarded as an existent entity, of the same kind as the world, an entity which like the phenomena of the world can be an object of knowledge.[4]

---

[1] *The Epistle to the Romans,* tr. E. C. Hoskyns (London: Oxford University Press, 1933).

[2] *Journal for Theology and Church,* 2, 1965, p. 85.

[3] Cf. *FU,* pp. 53ff.

[4] *Ibid.,* p. 313.

But what can he mean by accusing Catholic theology of regarding God "as an existent entity, *of the same kind as the world*"? Surely he is aware that Roman theology has not, in the ordinary sense of *same kind,* regarded God as being an entity of the same kind as the world.[5] God is differentiated from trees and gophers and people and galaxies by, for example, his having created them. And the knowledge of God differs from knowledge of the world in that it is knowledge of *God*—that is, the knowledge is different because its object is different. (Even the doctrine of analogy does not say that since our descriptions of God employ vocabulary suited to finite objects, our knowledge of God is nothing more than our knowledge of those objects.)[6] What then can Bultmann mean by this accusation? It seems that he can only be denying that God is an existent entity at all, and thus that anything can be known about him at all. He confirms this deduction:

> *God is not a given entity.* The question . . . of the adequacy of our knowledge of God, must be rejected completely. For that question conceives of God as a given entity of which direct knowledge is possible, as an object which we can recognize in more or less the same way as other objects. Such knowledge could be a possession and could produce effects within our life. It could progress and grow like other segments of knowledge. But it could still not take us to God, who can never be something given, something which is, so to speak, crystallized in knowledge.[7]

And if we have any doubt about what he means by "given" or "existent" in these passages, he himself can clear it up for us:

> If one speaks of God's existence, he lays himself open to the suspicion that he understands 'existence' in the old pre-kierke-

---

[5] Aquinas, for example, says, "God is not a measure that is proportionate to what is measured; so it does not follow that he and his creatures belong to the same order" (*Summa Theologica, Prima Pars,* Qu. 13, Art. 5).

[6] Aquinas holds that we do perceive God's essence, but that we do not do so through any created "likeness." Cf. *Prima Pars,* Qu. 12, Art. 2.

[7] *FU,* p. 45.

gaardian sense, namely as real presence (*Vorhandensein*) in distinction from 'essence'.[8]

In that old pre-Kierkegaardian sense a unicorn has essence, but not existence: we can describe unicorns just as well as we can alligators; but unlike the alligators, there aren't any unicorns. To say that God exists is to say that there is one; and in a certain sense, Bultmann wants to deny that God exists, or to deny that it is proper or true to say that God exists. How does this position differ from atheism? Is it not precisely atheism to say, "Yes, you can describe God all day, but there isn't one"?

Bultmann distinguishes two kinds of atheism, which he designates as "methodical atheism" and "real atheism." Speaking of the former he says,

> If God is conceived as a being who belongs to the world of beings, even as the highest being, then the science whose object of research is precisely this world is of necessity atheistic. For its research takes account solely of phenomena that are objectifiable and at the disposal of its kind of thinking, and a God who could be disposed of by objectifying thinking would not be God.[9]

This kind of atheism is also spread abroad in a secularized culture, though, of course, then it is not necessarily always held consciously or "methodically." Everyone who lives the life of modern man shares in this kind of atheism.[10] But science does not in itself deny the reality of God altogether.[11] The real God is not a being at all, so science actually performs a useful service for religion by clearing away that misconception: "it forces theology to speak of the reality of God as a reality beyond that of beings."[12] But there is another kind of atheism, which is a positive evil:

> the only atheism relevant to theology is a real atheism, that is,

---

[8] *GV*, IV, p. 105.

[9] "Protestant Theology and Atheism," *The Journal of Religion*, vol. 52, 1972, p. 331.

[10] Cf. *FU*, p. 59.

[11] Cf. *ibid.*, p. 54.

[12] "Protestant Theology and Atheism," *The Journal of Religion*, vol. 52, 1972, p. 331.

one which denies the being of God as a reality beyond the world of beings, and thus as a transcendent reality.[13]

But if God is not a being, not even the highest being, if he does not exist in the sense of being really present (*vorhanden*), if his very being implies that nothing statable in dogmatics can be known about him, what is that transcendent reality which real atheism denies? What kind of reality does it have?

For Bultmann, God has his reality in relation to man. God's being the beyond is constituted by his setting the limit to man's being as not-beyond, as limited. In an almost poetic mood, he expresses the matter thus:

> *It is God who makes man finite,* who makes a comedy of man's care, who allows his longing to miscarry, who casts him into solitude, who sets a terminus to his knowing and doing, who calls him to duty, and who gives the guilty over to torment. And yet at the same time it is God who forces man into life and drives him into care; who puts longing and the desire for love in his heart; who gives him thoughts and strength for his work, and who places him in the eternal struggle between self-assertion and duty. God is the enigmatic power beyond time, yet master of the temporal; beyond being, yet working in it.[14]

If we came across this passage in isolation from its context in Bultmann's writings, we would be tempted to think that the writer was talking about an objectively real being. For he designates God as a "Power," and uses active verbs, as though in the absence of this power things would not happen to man which do happen to him: God "makes," "allows," "casts," "calls," "forces," "drives," man, and so on. But knowing what we know of Bultmann's thought, we might suspect that all this is only a rather misleading way of saying that man is finite, that his longing does miscarry, that there is a terminus to his knowing and doing, that he is tormented by guilt, that he does care. We might suspect that *God* does not designate a "power" at all, but is only an elliptical expression for the limitation of man's life. Is the "reality" of God as transcendent precisely equivalent (as, so to

---

[13] *Ibid.*
[14] *Essays,* p. 5.

speak, the other side of the same coin) to the reality of man
as finite?

In a somewhat less poetic passage, Bultmann seems to bear
out this interpretation:

> God represents the total annulment of man, his negation, call-
> ing him in question, indeed judging him. Whether God is
> known adequately or inadequately, whether or not God is to
> be spoken of in anthropomorphic terms is irrelevant. The one
> essential question is: What does God represent for men? And
> wherever the idea of God is really grasped, the result is the
> radical calling of man in question.[15]

And in the article in which he describes God as a "power," he
himself goes on immediately to deny that his description is adequate to the idea of God:

> But what we have just said is not adequate as a description of
> the Christian idea of God, or indeed of the idea of God at all.
> For why do we call this mysterious power '*God*'? Why give the
> enigma, the mystery which drives us this way and that and
> hedges us in, any other name than simply 'the enigma', or
> 'fate'?[16]

True, our lives are hemmed in by death, failure, and guilt,
and these aspects of our finitude determine the shape and character of our existence. But the fact that our life is so limited is
surely not equivalent to the positive reality of God. To believe in
God is surely the end of anxiety and despair; to believe in our
finitude is quite compatible with nihilism. But if belief in God
is not a belief that he exists and thus actually forgives and sus-
tains our life and overcomes our failures, what is it that belief
opposes to man's finitude?

> Is it not to the point, in face of the enigma and the mystery, to
> insist on the purposefulness of life with a cry of 'nevertheless!'?
> However that may be, this cry is in any event the point of belief
> in God. It is the courage to designate that mysterious, sovereign
> power as God, and as my God. It is the courage to assert that

---

[15] *FU*, p. 46.
[16] *Essays,* p. 6.

in the knowledge of this power every being acquires its meaning, that in knowing this power I also realize I belong to it, and that the limit which fences my being is, in my mind, removed. This will, of course, happen when I give up my claim to make my own way — when I submit to this power as that which brought me into existence — when I can acknowledge it.[17]

To believe in God is to cry "Nevertheless!" in the face of my death, failure and guilt. It is to be decisively reconciled to my finitude. This happens when I make the decision to be what I truly am—to be limited. Most of our lives are spent in the desperate attempt to be what we are not, to secure our lives, by our own efforts, against death, failure, and guilt. That is, instead of acknowledging our finitude (which is the same as acknowledging transcendence), we fight it and attempt to be what, by our very nature, we are not. Only by submitting to our finitude (that is, to transcendence as that which we are not) do we become what we are. It is in this act of submission that the "enigma," which might otherwise be called "the devil," becomes "God." So far, then, the "reality" of God seems to amount to this: God is equivalent to man's finitude insofar as man does not resist it, but submits to it, and thus finds positive meaning in it.

Bultmann is quite aware that up to this point his account does not give God any objective reality at all.

> How far is such a belief belief in *God?* Is it not simply *belief in man?* Are we not using the word God here to gloss over a fatal self-deception? Is this 'nevertheless!' not simply a cry of defiance, of the courage bred by despair? In fact, belief as it has been described need not be anything but belief in man — that is, fundamentally not a belief in something standing over against man, but a human attitude, a disposition of the soul, which in overcoming despair and resignation, stupidity and thoughtlessness, takes stock of the reality in which it exists, acknowledging it in awe and gratitude, in pride and humility at one and the same time — refusing to be discomfited, but on the contrary, going on its way composedly and courageously.[18]

What is required for this humanistic courage to be transformed

[17] *Essays,* p. 6.
[18] *Ibid.,* p. 10.

into a real belief in God, a belief "in something standing over against man"? Bultmann's answer is that belief becomes something more than a merely human attitude when the submission to transcendence is thought of as taking place in an encounter in the concrete here and now. An encounter is after all not merely something going on in the enclosed interior of the soul, but is rather an event in which the relation to what is encountered is essential. Christian faith renders God objective by insisting that faith takes place only in encounter with God's concrete word (the kerygma):

> *Christian belief* has its peculiar character in speaking of an *event* that gives [the right to speak of God], in saying that it hears a *Word* which demands that it should recognize God as standing over against man. For Christianity belief in God is not belief and trust in God as a general principle, but belief in a definite Word proclaimed to the believer.[19]

In chapter three we considered at some length and with critical reservations Bultmann's thoughts about the kerygma; I will not reiterate my criticisms now, though some of them might be pertinent. The essential point to see here is that he is willing to let the entire objectivity of God be constituted by what he considers to be the formal structure of Christian faith—namely that faith is an encounter with an "event." So we can define the reality of Bultmann's God, finally, as this: God is equivalent to man's finitude insofar as man submits to it as he encounters the event of Christian preaching. "Real atheism" could, it seems, be achieved by operation on any one of these three elements: by denying one's finitude (trying to secure one's own existence), by a nihilism in which one recognizes one's finitude but despairs (does not submit to it), or by a humanistic courage in which one attempts to find happiness out of the transcendent (and thus in submission to one's finitude) but apart from an encounter with the Christian word of grace.

II. Criticism

Bultmann's denial that God is an object seems to be

---

[19] *Essays,* p. 11.

founded on conceptual confusion. Two senses of the word *object* are relevant here, and his case seems to depend on shifting between them.

In one use, *object* is a formal concept. Here, anything that can be talked about at all is an object. In this sense, to call something an object is not to say anything about *what* is being designated, but only to indicate *that* it is being designated. If someone speaks about a piston rod, it is an object; similarly if one speaks about a friend, or about love or the square root of 45, the person, the emotion, and the number are objects. To say that *object* is a formal concept is to say that to treat something as an object is not to treat it in any particular way, but only to treat it in some way. Thus in this sense to make God an object is not to treat him in one way or another, but only to have something to do with him. One makes God an object equally in cursing him, researching him, and praising him.

But there is a non-formal sense of *object* in which we do indicate something about what is being designated, and also about how it is being treated. Here the word is used, roughly, to distinguish things which are persons (and thus ought to be treated as persons) from things which are not persons. Thus, when the girl complains that her boyfriend treats her like an object, she means that his behavior assimilates her to his truck and his shotgun, or at best to his hound. Bultmann trades on this non-formal sense when he implies that to treat God as an object is to put him at our disposal, or treat him with the kind of neutrality with which we approach the objects of scientific research. That this use of the word guides and aids his case is indicated also by what we saw in chapter five: for Bultmann it is not just God, but also human "existence" which cannot be made into an object. This notion involved him in the extremely counter-intuitive denial that we know anything about ourselves or others, that a third party can observe the phenomenon of love, and the like, and in theoretical embarrassment about the status of his own and Heidegger's existential analysis. I argued for the common-sense view that in order to know human beings at all it was necessary to "objectify" them, and that this was not to treat them as less than human beings. And we will surely want to argue in a parallel way about God: if we cannot objectify him (have real, potentially propositional knowledge about him), it makes no sense to talk about "encountering" him. That God is merciful to sinners, that he created the world, and so on, are affirmations which can perfectly well be taken as objectively true about God, without turning God into a "neutral" object of research or a non-personal object which we manipulate to our advantage.

Bultmann's denial that God is an object gets all its plausibility (at least to the mind not in the grip of the existence/world dichotomy) from associations of the non-formal sense. But what he wants to deny seems to draw on aspects of the formal sense—for he holds that it is inappropriate to the concept of God to have any enduring ("possessable") knowledge of him, to talk *about* him in an "objective" way, to allow what we know about him to "produce effects within our life." Of course, Bultmann does allow that we can encounter God, and this is obviously to make him an object in the formal sense. The reason that this does not bother him seems to be that at this point he slips back to a reliance on the non-formal sense: to "encounter" God surely avoids treating him as a non-personal object.

His refusal to objectify God can be seen as part of a general tendency of Bultmann's thought. We saw in the last chapter what an important role he implicitly assigns to the technical theologian: the problem of understanding is to be solved by the scholarly and philosophical process of translation, rather than through the individual's nurture and growth in faith. Here we see him playing an equally important role: defending God against impiety. If God can be an object, he runs the risk that men, instead of bowing before him as their creator and giving him the praise and reverence due the almighty Lord, may make him an object of inquiry and instead of worshiping him spend their lives investigating him. But now, instead of warning believers against such impiety, Bultmann feels it his duty to build into the concept of God the impossibility of treating him this way: he simply prohibits *a priori* all talk in which God is referred to as an independent being. But the result of this theological paternalism is that God disappears altogether. He seems to think that a God who is vulnerable to the impiety of men cannot really be God; whereas the truth of the matter seems to be just the opposite: a God who is invulnerable to mistreatment at the hands of men is simply no God at all (or at least not the God of Christian faith).

Bultmann's desire to deny that God is an object in the formal sense is indicated by his denial that God is a being; for the concept of a being is surely unambiguously formal. To say that something is a being is not to indicate what it is, but only that it is something, that is, that it is something determinate, and thus distinguishable from other things. If anything is at all, then it is a being. To be a being is to be something that can become an object in the formal sense; to be something rather than anything or nothing.

When Bultmann says that science's domain is the realm of beings, he might seem to be thinking of physical beings, animate and inanimate. Almost all theologians have denied that God is a physical being, so this would not be a very striking thing for him to say. But he does not so qualify his denial. His denial that God is a "given entity" is usually associated with his denial that we can have a standing (rather than momentary) relation to him, or a "general" (he means propositional) knowledge of him. The denial that God is a being is demanded by his concept of God as transcendent. If there could be general propositions about him (as there can, in principle, about anything which is something determinate—a being), then he would not be transcendent, because we could (in principle, at least) "possess" knowledge of him. And if we could possess knowledge of him, he could, so to speak, become a legitimate party to our inauthenticity. The nature of "existence" requires that God not be a being. That is, his transcendence is precisely equivalent to his being *nothing,* nothing determinate, nothing in any sense which could possibly be grasped by a human being, at least—that is, nothing *to us.* You might say, *pro nobis,* God is and must be nothing.

But what kind of nothing would God then be? Bultmann's denial might be thought of this way: if we took account of all the beings in the universe (everything that was something determinate), God would not be among them. But if he is not among them, is he perhaps the totality of them? This cannot be Bultmann's meaning, for he is opposed to pantheism;[20] God is to be distinguished from his creatures. But if he is not a being in addition to his creatures, even an infinitely higher one, but is nevertheless to be distinguished from them, what can he possibly be? The only answer left seems to be that he is the *negation* of his creatures, in the sense of being the "beyond" corresponding

---

[20] Cf. *FU,* p. 261.

to their finitude (not a being who is beyond, but simply the beyond). God transcends creatures (that is, beings) not by being a greater being, but by being the limit of beings. His transcendence is equivalent to his non-existence; only, we must add, this is a non-existence which *counts,* since it is the limit of man's life. It is not, so to speak, a simple non-existence, for it is the one which we *encounter* as the boundary of our finitude, in the concrete situations of our world.

To attribute existence to something is of a different order from attributing redness or mercifulness. For when we say of a merciful or red thing that it also exists, we have not thereby characterized it any further; we have not said anything more about *what* it is, but only that, whatever it is, there is one. Thus when a philosopher denies that God exists, it is entirely out of order to support the denial by saying that "existence is a category much too inferior to be applied to the greatness of God."[21] Categories too inferior to be applied to God would be such things as pettiness, weakness, or perhaps physical properties. But in this sense of the word, existence is not a category at all. Existence is not on a scale of values or intensities; quite independently of something's description, the thing either exists or it does not. Things can be more or less red, more or less merciful; but not more or less existent. As Kierkegaard says, "A fly, when it is, has as much being as the God."[22] Thus, to say that God exists is not in any way to demean him, to reduce him, as it were, to the status of flies. It is perfectly reasonable to say that God exists and that flies exist; for one has not thereby in any way assimilated the "whatness" of God and flies. On the other hand, to deny that God exists is to say (quite simply) that there is no God. To say that he exists, but only analogically to the way creatures exist, is just verbal confusion; as soon as one introduces the concept of the "way" something exists, one is talking about *what* something is; and the fact remains that as far as existing goes, God either does or he doesn't.

We have seen that it is important for Bultmann that God not be thought of as a "given entity." He often supports his ne-

---

[21] Erich Frank, *Philosophical Understanding and Religious Truth* (Oxford University Press, 1945), p. 44.

[22] *Philosophical Fragments* (Princeton: Princeton University Press, 1962), p. 51, note.

gations in a round-about way, by denying something no theologian would assert: "the belief in the almighty God is not the conviction given in advance that there exists an almighty Being who is able to do all things."[23] Christian belief is certainly not equivalent to the conviction "that there exists an almighty Being." Faith is seeing all the world as God's handiwork, praising him for it, trusting him to provide, to have mercy on one's shortcomings, and to be able to make right even the things that men have made so wrong; it is joy, and hope, and gratitude, peace and confidence and love of neighbor. But belief in God's existence would seem, for the Apostles,[24] to be at least a minimal aspect of faith; for it seems odd, to say the least, to see all the world as the handiwork of a God who does not exist, to trust and rejoice and hope in a God who is not even a being.

In saying that God is an existent being, I certainly do not want to defend the God of the philosophers against Bultmann. Though it is quite out of the realm of the Bible's concern to affirm that God is a being or that he exists, this affirmation can be used to point up some features of the biblical concept. Scripture affirms that he is living, that he created the world, that he loves his creatures, that in the life and death of Jesus of Nazareth he was reconciling the world to himself; it assumes that it makes sense to talk about him and to pass on traditions about him from generation to generation, and that he hears the prayers of his children. That is, it is not correct to say that the logic of *God* is limited to expressions of encounter with our finitude (i.e., with "transcendence"), even happy ones. When I say that the God of Christian faith is an existent being, therefore, I do not mean to ally myself with any metaphysically heavy-handed philosophical tradition, but to make a logical point about the biblical concept of God: it is used referringly; there is no discomfort with the "about" mood; people can be instructed as to God's nature, and so on.

It hardly needs saying that Bultmann's God does not know

---

[23] *JCM*, p. 63.
[24] Let me remind my reader that I am not in any way denying Bultmann's intention to remain faithful to the apostolic faith. My aim throughout is to analyze the logic of Bultmann's theology, which, if my analysis is correct, is sometimes quite distant from an achievement of that intention.

anything, will anything, feel anything, or plan anything, even in the remotest analogical sense. But the question whether God is conscious (which is perhaps identical with the question whether he exists) determines whether there can be any integrity in the activity of prayer. Whereas one might live out of the eventful transcendence which is Bultmann's God, it would surely not make any sense at all to pray to it. Giving thanks, confessing one's sins, interceding to this transcendence would surely be the most ridiculous of activities. It is perhaps this above all which shows that the writers of the New Testament believed God to exist: they prayed. Bultmann does occasionally, in passing, speak of giving "thanks to God"[25] or of speaking "to God."[26] Though he never, to my knowledge, tells us how such an activity is to be positively understood, we can guess what the analysis would amount to: petition and supplication would be the "expression" of our finitude and frail dependence, praise and thanksgiving of our willingness to "receive" the world as a "gift"; prayers of intercession would express our openness and freedom for others; prayers of confession would be reflections on our failure to live out of transcendence. The only prayer I know of in Bultmann's published works is included in the volume of sermons collected from his preaching in Marburg. Surely it is time for us to bring on such "hermeneutical" guidelines as the above, and also to remember clearly the theory of language lying behind Bultmann's work, when we read as part of that prayer,

> Lord, we have indeed tried to carry out tasks as in Your service. But You alone know whether we have done them well or ill; You know too how often our good will failed to become effective, and also how often we were lacking in good will. In this evening hour of worship, allow us to place the past weeks in the light and splendour of Your grace, so that the work we have done may, in spite of everything, turn into blessing for us and bear fruit for the future.[27]

Despite his insistence that God is not a given entity, Bultmann stoutly denies that he has reduced God to a subjective

---

[25] *JCM*, p. 63; *TWAB*, pp. 49f.
[26] *FU*, p. 319.
[27] *TWAB*, p. 57.

experience, as Schleiermacher has been repeatedly accused of doing. In defending himself against this allegation, he says,

> From the statement that to speak of God is to speak of myself, it by no means follows that God is not outside the believer. (This would be the case only if faith is interpreted as a purely psychological event.) When man is understood in the genuine sense as an historical being which has its reality in concrete situations and decisions, in the very encounters of life, it is clear . . . that faith does not mean a psychologically subjective event.[28]

Here we see that Bultmann's defense against the charge that *God* is for him equivalent to *experience of God* is not to say that God is objective, but rather that the structure of man's experience is such that it always includes an objective pole. That is, man's experience of God, like his experience of everything else, is always characterized by "encounter" in "concrete situations." The argument is thus: to be (as a human being) is to encounter and to be encountered; therefore faith as a way of being is not "subjective."[29] But the objectivity of God thus established is, if we may so speak, not objective objectivity, but rather an *a priori* necessary correlate implied by the structure of human existence. In this sense all experience, from the best established fact to the wildest hallucination, escapes the charge of being subjective. On the other hand, the objectivity of God in the sense of his real independence of man is ruled out by Bultmann's notion of human freedom.

The objectivity of God which follows from the intentional structure of consciousness does not make God any more independent of man in the normal sense than Schleiermacherian "psychologism" did. God's independence hangs entirely on the requirements of "faith"; like a slave whose duty it is to criticize his master, God is independent only because faith requires him to be so. And, as we have seen, the reason that God cannot be really independent of man is that he is nothing but the tran-

---

[28] *JCM,* pp. 70f.
[29] Similarly, Bultmann defends the importance of the *fides quae creditur* against those who would reduce theology to an analysis of the *fides qua creditur* by accusing them of misjudging the "intentionality of faith" (*FU,* p. 119).

scendent other side of man's finitude, confronting man's concrete Now in the mode of its intrinsic "promise."

It is the fact that transcendence actually confronts men, calling them to a decision against understanding themselves in terms of the world, that makes it something more than a purely negative conception:

> If God's action must be thought of as hidden, how is it possible to speak of it except in purely negative statements? Is the conception of transcendence an exclusively negative conception? It would be if to speak of God did not also mean to speak of our personal existence. If we speak of God as acting in general, transcendence would indeed be a purely negative conception, since every positive description of transcendence transposes it into this world.[30]

This seems to be what Bultmann has in mind in his cryptic references to "analogy," if we can equate "not exclusively negative" with "real." Speaking of language which expresses what he calls an "act of God," he says, "if such language is to have any meaning at all it must denote an act in a real, objective sense, and not just a symbolical or pictorial expression."[31] Then he goes on to say,

> Such language is therefore neither symbolical nor pictorial, though it is certainly analogical, for it assumes an analogy between the activity of God and that of man and between the fellowship of God and man and that of man with man.[32]

The analogy seems to pivot on the notion of encounter. Just as we encounter men, so we "encounter" transcendence. A fellow

---

[30] *JCM*, p. 66.

[31] *KM*, p. 196. It is clear what he is seeking to protect, but he is confused about the relation of non-literal language to reality. For he thinks that symbolic or pictorial language is not about objective reality. Uncle Sam, thinks he, does not exist; when a person flies down the stairs there is no real flying. But of course the referent of "Uncle Sam" as a symbolic expression is not the man with the white beard, but the federal government, which is real beyond question; and the referent of the flying down stairs is not the image it brings to mind (if it does), but the speedy descent.

[32] *Ibid.*, p. 197.

human being demands something of us (perhaps a decision); transcendence "demands" of us the decision to live "as if not." Persons promise us things and thus bless us; transcendence, when it confronts us (especially, as Bultmann thinks, in the kerygma), holds out the "promise" that in abandoning the world we find our true selves. In our relations with men we may be judged unworthy; when, in confronting our finitude, we turn away and seek to flee, we come under "judgment." By virtue of its being describable in these analogies, our relation to the transcendent (i.e., to our finitude) can be called "personal." In light of these considerations we can understand Bultmann's rather uncharacteristic affirmation that "God is a personal being acting on persons."[33]

In his reference to analogy, Bultmann expresses a concern which is analogous to that of traditional analogy-theorists, but by no means identical with it. Traditionally, God was thought of as a discrete, positively existing being, but one so different from the things our language is designed to refer to that we could not refer to him directly. But since, as we have seen, Bultmann denies that God is a given entity or that one can talk meaningfully about him at all, the concern to establish our language's reference to God is foreign to him. Consequently the question of reality which lies behind his concern with analogy is not the same as that of the traditional theorists. The reality-concern for them was related to God himself (his nature and existence). Bultmann's is related to an event; it is the question whether something happens. People traditionally concerned with analogy were also concerned to state that God really exists; Bultmann is concerned only to state that transcendence is really encountered. But this is a concern shared equally by philosophers such as Jean-Paul Sartre. In respect of it, Bultmann seems to differ from such philosophers only by his vocabulary. He would, of course, like to distinguish himself from them by his attachment to the kerygma; but as my analysis in chapter three has shown, it is very doubtful that he can do so.

The existence/world dichotomy places anything of which we can have standing, statable, possessable knowledge on the side of world. Our relation to every such object must be the "as

---

[33] *JCM,* p. 70.

if not," for authentic existence decisively eschews every security. The dichotomy thus legislates that God shall not be a "given entity," something which could be known and thus depended upon. For it would be odd, thinks Bultmann, if God's true nature allowed an inauthentic relation to him. That is, it would be odd if faith had to treat God "as if not," like other objects of the world.

However, though it seems clear that Bultmann personally does not believe that there is an eternal being who is the *prima causa* of the universe, his position does not require that he deny it. It does not entail denial of the existence of a God who "is *something* wholly different from man, a metaphysical being, a kind of an immaterial world, perhaps of a complex of mysterious forces, a creative source."[34] Only, even if such a being were actually the first cause of the universe, it would not be possible for man to have faith in him, because as existent, as a given entity, he could (in principle) be known, thought about, and perhaps counted on as a source of security; that is to say, he would lack the transcendence which alone corresponds to authenticity. If such a God existed, the man of faith would be compelled to ignore him, to by-pass him for his self-understanding just as he bypasses everything else which is a being, to treat him "as if not."

Thus Schubert Ogden's proposal of a marriage between Bultmannian existentialism and the God of Charles Hartshorne's speculations[35] represents a misunderstanding of Bultmann's thought. Ogden holds that "the major criticism of Bultmann's theological method is that it makes impossible a direct speaking of God,"[36] but attributes Bultmann's failure to the external misfortune that he is entirely dependent on a philosophy (Heidegger's) which happens not to have engaged itself in an analysis of the concept of God. So he proposes that Heidegger's work as a resource for theology be supplemented with Hart-

---

[34] *FU*, p. 57.
[35] *Christ Without Myth* (New York: Harper and Row, 1961), pp. 146-153.
[36] "Bultmann's Demythologizing and Hartshorne's Dipolar Theism" in *Process and Divinity, Philosophical Essays presented to Charles Hartshorne,* ed. W. L. Reese & E. Freeman (LaSalle, Ill.: Open Court, 1964), p. 499.

shorne's. But Bultmann's failure to describe God is not a consequence of a poor education, but of the internal structure of his
thought. As Ogden says, philosophy (that is, Hartshorne's)
objectifies God "as eminent subject or actuality."[37] "For philosophy . . . God is . . . the eminent object of rational understanding. Its focus is the abstract pole in his being, the essential structure or form that individuates him as God and thus is concretely
embodied in all his actual states."[38] Ogden's proposal is the surest sign that he has failed to see to the bottom of Bultmann's
theology. For had he cast his eyes upon that bottom he would
have seen the existence/world dichotomy, and had he understood that basic idea he would have seen that a given, struc-
tured, individuated, describable divine existence conceived as
eminent subject or actuality could never be the object of faith,
but only another temptation of the world. The only God who can
correspond to human authenticity is one who is radically "transcendent"—that is, who is nothing, but is purely potential, who
is constant futurity, who is the void *jenseits* of human finitude,
who by his very nature (if one can call it that) takes away from
man every security.[39]

Our life is characterized by failure, guilt, and death. The
God who is pure transcendence may, if we cast ourselves upon
the bosom of his void, grant us a kind of resigned freedom to
live within these boundaries of our present life. He may teach us
to relax our grip upon this world, and thus to find a happy equilibrium in precisely those aspects of our existence which were
formerly a bitter poison to our souls. Bultmann's God calms our
strivings and demands our heart to coincide with what presently
we are. Courage, hope, trust, forgiveness—these experiences are
in the end all equivalent to a kind of willing resignation.

But the God of Christian faith, the God who is not merely
the non-existence beyond the world, but who, existing incor-
ruptibly from all eternity, made the world, does not leave us at
that. Our finitude is not bounded by a void transcendence, but
rather wrapped in the larger world of God's positive care. We are
not merely resigned to our failure, but promised that failure is

---

[37] Reese and Freeman, *op. cit.*, p. 508.
[38] *Ibid.*, p. 507.
[39] Cf. *Essays*, p. 271.

not our ultimate lot, that however disastrous our life may be, God's success on our behalf is greater than our failure. We are not merely resigned to our guilt, but told the story of how one from God, and indeed identical with God, took our guilt upon his own shoulders so that we would not need to be resigned to it, but could, with positive courage, strive forward to be his children. We are not merely resigned to our death, and therefore really for all the equilibrium of our resignation without hope in the world, but we who believe that God raises the dead have an objective rock to cling to in the face of this life's end. This is what it means for the Christian to believe that God *exists;* this is the difference it makes.

10

Ethics

I. Radical obedience as love of neighbor

Bultmann characterizes Christian ethics as an ethics of obedience. By this he means to keep in the forefront the existentialist conception of man as an encountering being, one whose authentic, as well as inauthentic, life is constituted by his response to the demand (and also the blessings) proffered him in the Now of his concrete situation. Since every concrete Now demands decision concerning his self-understanding, man is always confronted with an absolute either/or: to obey or not.

But this concept enjoys much more than the status of an emphasis in Bultmann's thought. For him it excludes a range of other concepts which have traditionally had a place in reflection, both Christian and pagan, about man's ethical life. Speaking of Jesus, he says,

> His ethic . . . is strictly opposed to every humanistic ethic and value ethic; it is an ethic of obedience. . . . He has no so-called individual or social ethics; the concept of an ideal or end is foreign to him. The concepts of personality and its virtues and of humanity are also foreign to him; he sees only the individual man standing before the will of God.[1]

God's demand . . . aims neither at the formation of "character"
nor at the molding of human society.[2]

Why are concepts like "value," "ideal," "society," "personality,"
"character," and "virtue" ruled out by an ethics of obedience?
The answer is to be found in looking at the distinction which
Bultmann draws between formal and radical obedience; for only
radical obedience is, according to his concept, obedience as such.

In Judaism obedience to God takes the form of obedience
to the law. According to Bultmann the Jew identifies the particular precepts of the law with the will of God, so that to do the
acts prescribed is *eo ipso* to do what God wills. This conception
has two consequences. First, since the written commandments
are the will of God, they become a formal authority: that is, it
does not matter *what* they command; they must be obeyed
simply because, as God's will, they are commanded. They need
not, in the deepest sense, involve the individual who does them,
because they need not be ethically intelligible to him; anything,
if it were God's will, would do as well.[3] Obedience is blind.[4]
Second, since it is written commandments which are the will of
God, and since there is no way for such commandments to en-
compass every aspect of man's life, the claim they make upon
the individual is something less than complete. There is always
an ethically neutral area of life; and this gives the false impression that God's claim upon man is limited to certain aspects of
his life. This in turn leaves room for works of supererogation—
works by which, since he does more than God demands, the individual can indebt God to himself.[5] Thus formal obedience violates God's complete transcendence and precludes man's complete submission.

While formal obedience identifies God's will with the commandment, radical obedience distinguishes between them. The
commandment is not itself God's will, though it does express it.
As Bultmann says (appealing to Philippians 4:11ff. and I Corinthians 9:20–22), "it is evident that the Christian life is not

---

[2] *TNT*, I, p. 19.
[3] *Ibid.*, pp. 11f.
[4] *JW*, p. 70.
[5] *Ibid.*, pp. 77f.

regulated by fixed prescriptions."[6] Radical obedience understands the law as demanding an end to man's self-assertion, to his
attempts to secure his own life. The law calls, as a word of the
transcendent, for man's submission: "Law confronts man as
God's claim, 'Thou shalt (not)!' In other words, law would keep
man from having his own way."[7] But since man can always, simply in virtue of being a man, understand himself as limited, as
not his own master, this essence of the law is always intrinsically
intelligible to him.[8] In fact it is not even possible to follow this
demand blindly; following it implies understanding. It cannot be
obeyed just because it is commanded, but must always, by nature, be obeyed because of *what* is commanded. And, since radical obedience breaks through the specificity of the commandment
to hear the essential demand of the transcendent, it understands
itself as required to submit *entirely;* there can be no aspect, no
moment of life which is justifiably withheld.

But it is not yet clear from our account why obedience to
the specific commandments of the law would have to be mere
formal obedience. It seems neither psychologically plausible nor
historically accurate to believe that the Jews so simply identified
the precepts of the law with God's will that theirs was blind obedience to an unintelligible demand, that the content of the law
was indifferent to them, and that the law's jurisdiction always
left an area of their life untouched by God's will.[9] No doubt one
could always find individuals for whom these consequences held
true. But the question is whether this can be blamed on their adherence to the specific commandments. Could one not understand obedience to the commandments in much the same way
that we understand a growing son's obedience of his father's precepts? Through his father's words the son comes to know his
father, that is, his father's will, the sort of thing his father desires

---

[6] *HE,* p. 46.

[7] *ONM,* p. 44.

[8] *JW,* p. 77.

[9] Bultmann is well aware that "Among the rabbis too the principle is
accepted that one may break the Sabbath in order to save a life." However, he immediately plays down this fact: "But when we read with what
casuistic rules the practical following of this principle is burdened, we see
that the fundamental idea of the Jewish ethic, blind obedience, still
dominates. The will of God is the formal authority of Scripture; ethic is
therefore not distinguishable from law" (*JW,* p. 70).

of him. After a while he is not limited to a blind relation to his father's words, but becomes capable of obeying or disobeying his father. That is, his father's precepts (in their specific content) are intelligible to him precisely as a means of fellowship with his father; they are the didactic basis of a personal relationship. And, on the basis of this personal relationship and knowledge, the son becomes able to make ethical judgments on cases and issues not specifically covered in his father's teaching—indeed, his father's will comes to touch, in principle, every area of his life. And an analogous use of the commandments of God is not only possible, but actual, within historical Judaism. So if we want to know why for Bultmann obedience to the specific commandments of the law implies a failure of radical obedience, we must dig a little deeper.

For a final answer to this question we must refer to Bultmann's understanding of what it is to be an authentic human being. For him man is a potentiality to be, essentially a maker of decisions in the moment, an openness toward the future, and thus a being in radical insecurity, in independence from the world of the actual, the controllable, the possessable and enduring, the secure. Any ethics which lays down possessable guidelines by which man can control the possibilities which confront him and thus secure himself and close himself toward the future will thus be a contravention of his true existence and a temptation to inauthenticity. For this reason Bultmann can say

> every ethic which desires to give *an answer to the question,* What should I do? and thereby to deprive the individual of the answer, must be labelled a misunderstanding of human existence.[10]

Thus in Bultmann's interpretation the commandment to love leaves the individual completely insecure as to what he should do:

> The demand to love . . . appears in a form that is constantly new, and must be fulfilled in a pattern that is constantly new, that is, in the decision of the 'moment' in which man is withdrawn from the world — which means, forsaken by every sup-

---

[10] *GV,* I, p. 234.

port and point of orientation, and faced with his decision in complete isolation.[11]

This interpretation is required by the idea that man is not completely responsible if he has principles or a general view which tells him what is right:

A man cannot control beforehand the possibilities upon which he must act; he cannot in the moment of decision fall back upon principles, upon a general ethical theory which can relieve him of responsibility for the decision; rather, every moment of decision is essentially new. For man does not meet the crisis of decision armed with a definite standard; he stands on no firm base, but rather alone in empty space. This it is which shows the requirement of the good to be actually the demand of God — not the demand of something divine in man, but the demand of God who is beyond man.[12]

Thus he describes for us the meaning of "decision":

The crisis of decision is the situation in which all observation is excluded, for which *Now* alone has meaning, which is absorbed wholly in the present moment. *Now* must man know what to do and leave undone, and no standard whatsoever from the past or from the universal is available. *That* is the meaning of decision.[13]

But of course the commandments of the law come out of the past both in the sense that they are a part of tradition, and in the sense that the individual has learned them and now possesses them as principles; and they are universal in having general applicability to the situations of life. It is because he knows the meaning of decision that Jesus refuses categorically to give ethical advice:

Hence there is naturally no longer reason to formulate general ideas about the highest good, about virtues and values, for every such theory originates from the spectator's point of view. In the view of Jesus there can be no such ethic, and therefore it is fundamentally a mistake to look to him for concrete ethical

---

[11] *Essays,* p. 155.
[12] *JW,* p. 85.
[13] *Ibid.,* p. 88.

requirements or for his attitude toward concrete ethical problems. He always refers the questioner back to his own judgment.[14]

So we have our answer: "Radical obedience" is authenticity. But authenticity is not consistent with any ethic which answers the question "What should I do?" An obedience-ethic consisting of specific commandments answers this question. Therefore radical obedience is not to be gained in Judaism or any tradition which expects adherence to specific commandments.

And we have hereby also provided an answer to the question with which we began—why for Bultmann an "obedience" ethic excludes concepts like "value," "ideal," and "virtue." The answer is that a concern with such concepts is, like Judaism's concern with specific commandments, a concern with guidelines for behavior.

We might be inclined to conclude that Bultmann's view of human authenticity would lead him to reject the law entirely. But he does not do this. On the contrary he insists, as does the apostle Paul, that the law expresses the will of God:

> In fact the teaching that the law as the old way of salvation is abrogated is *not* to be understood to mean that the content of the law is to be rejected![15]

But if it is true that the law as guiding specific behavior is to be eschewed, what can Bultmann mean here by "content"? A couple of pages later he tells us what the essence of sin is:

> The real sin of man is that he himself takes his will and his life into his own hands, makes himself secure and so has his self-confidence, his 'boast'.[16]

But if the essence of sin is man's attempt to secure his own life, and thus not to live in submission to the transcendent, then the essence of the law could be expressed thus: Thou shalt submit to the transcendent—or negatively—Thou shalt not live by thine

---

[14] *JW*, pp. 88f.
[15] *FU*, p. 226.
[16] *Ibid.*, p. 228.

own power. This, rather than acts describable as killing, or stealing, or remembering the sabbath day, or honoring one's parents, will be what Bultmann means by the "content" of the law. Since what would normally be called the content of these commandments is totally indifferent to their real "content," one could not be blamed for calling Bultmann's view of the law, too, a kind of formalism. For any commandment, as long as it expressed the essence above described, would seem to qualify as a commandment of God. And if "Thou shalt not kill" can really mean "Thou shalt submit to the transcendent," then I suppose practically anything at all, which had the form of a commandment, could.

When in the context of ethics Bultmann speaks of authenticity (i.e., radical obedience) he describes it, using biblical vocabulary, as love of neighbor. The I-thou relationship ("Being-with-others") is a primordial feature of man's being. To be related to a Thou is to be "historical," that is, to be a self-transcending kind of being.[17] It is in the encounter with the Thou, and the giving of myself to him in a true act of love, that I so transcend my old actual self as to receive my new self as potentiality.

> *Works* of love are fundamentally easy even when I extort them from myself in certain circumstances with an effort: for in them I remain my old self. The real *act* of love is fundamentally difficult and is not to be extorted by any violence, as I give myself away in it, and attain my being only by losing it in this act.[18]

The "neighbor," in Bultmann's thought, fulfills the same formal conditions as "death" in Heidegger's: that of being a phenomenon that "limits man from the outside and that he himself is not able to give," yet is to be found "as something within his existence, as encountering us in man himself."[19]

> Thus the determination that the man of love acquires from the thou is exactly analogous to the threefold determination of man

[17] *GV*, I, pp. 231ff.
[18] *Essays*, p. 176; See also *ibid.*, p. 13, and *GV*, I, p. 238.
[19] *EF*, p. 109.

by death, which is made visible by existential analysis:

1. "So long as man is, there is a not yet that he will be, a something that is constantly outstanding that belongs to him." Precisely so, however, does the man of faith and love understand himself (cf. Phil. 3.12–14; Rom. 13.8).

2. "The coming to an end of the particular being that has not yet reached its end (or the actual elimination of that which is outstanding) has the character of no longer being-there." Correspondingly, the man of faith understands that he first receives his existence from the thou; if the particular claim of the thou that stands before me were completely eliminated, then I would no longer be I.

3. "The coming to an end involves a mode of being for the concrete man that is absolutely unique to him."[20] Correspondingly, the man who loves knows that the neighbor is uniquely *his* neighbor and that he cannot appoint another to do his loving for him.

Thus, in the same way as in relation to death, the man who has to render love to the thou "stands before himself in his properest possibility of being" and "in thus standing before himself all relations in him" to death "are dissolved."[21]

To put the matter in somewhat more ordinary terms, the three formal features shared by neighbor and death could be called (1) transcendence, (2) possibility, and (3) encounter.

Death is alien to the activities and concerns of everyday life, something different, something outside, a stranger, an intruder. Really to face death in the midst of the activities of our life is to have it disrupted, to be called away from it, to set some distance between oneself and it. Similarly, the neighbor is different from me, outside me. So when his need confronts me as a claim upon me, my response will take the form of forgetting myself, of leaving my own cares and concerns and activities behind, and thus of transcending myself.

Death is something outside my control. Since I cannot say when the moment of my death will be, as long as I live death never becomes something I can fix and dominate, but always has the character of possibility. Thus really to live in the ac-

---

[20] Quotes are from Martin Heidegger, *Being and Time*, tr. John Macquarrie and Edward Robinson (New York: Harper and Row, 1962), p. 224.

[21] *EF*, p. 101; quote is from *Being and Time*, p. 250.

knowledgment of my death is to be reconciled to radical insecurity. Similarly the neighbor may call upon me at any moment. I can never be sure that his need will not demand me completely to change the planned course of my day, or perhaps of my life. Nor can I ever tell ahead of time what action will be called for as the loving thing. Consequently, readiness for the neighbor in love is a radical openness to possibility; it is a life in which the security of plans and patterns of behavior is abandoned.

Death is always my death. It is not just a general notion of something that sometimes happens to people, but it is my death, the death I must face one way or another, the death which no other man can die for me. Similarly the neighbor is really a neighbor to me only insofar as he is mine, as he calls me, by his need, to give myself up for him, as I encounter him as placing a demand upon my existence.

It is because of these three formal features of the neighbor that radical obedience (existential authenticity) can be described as "love."

II. Criticism

Though we cannot here enter into a detailed exegetical debate, there are some observations we must make about the relation between Bultmann's understanding of law and that of Scripture. When St. Paul discusses the law, he typically says two kinds of thing in close juxtaposition, which seem to constitute a paradox. On the one hand, the Christian is justified apart from the law, in such a way that the law even stands in opposition to faith: "man is not justified by works of the law but through faith in Jesus Christ. . . . by works of the law shall no one be justified" (Gal. 2:16; cf. Rom. 7:6, 3:28, 6:14). On the other hand, "the law is holy, and the commandment is holy and just and good" (Rom. 7:12). "Do we then overthrow the law by this faith? By no means! On the contrary, we uphold the law" (Rom. 3:31).

In Paul's thinking this paradox is resolved by the belief that the righteousness of Jesus substitutes for our (lacking) righteousness before God, or alternatively, that in dying upon the cross Jesus took upon himself our sin, thus purifying us. In I Cor. 1:30 he says that no human being can boast before God because God made Jesus "our wisdom, our righteousness and sanctification and redemption." In Rom. 5:18–19 he draws an analogy between Adam, the first sinner, and Christ, the first righteous man: "Then as one man's trespass led to condemnation for all men, so one man's act of righteousness led to acquittal and life for all men. For as by one man's disobedience many were made sinners, so by one man's obedience many will be made righteous." "Christ redeemed us from the curse of the law [namely, sin—our failure to keep it] *having become a curse for us"* (Gal. 3:13). Or, in what is perhaps Paul's most elegant formulation, "For our sake he made him to be sin who knew no sin, so that in him we might become the righteousness of God" (II Cor. 5:21). (See also Rom. 5:6, 9–10; I Cor. 15:3; Col. 1:21–22, 2:13–14; I Thess. 5:9–10.)

Thus Paul can say that the law is holy and just and good because it is God's law, and as such is and remains the standard for righteousness before him; but that it has been superseded by faith because Jesus has stood in our place. We are now righteous before God not by our own "works of the law," but by Jesus' righteousness (that is, his fulfillment of the law) on our behalf, which we grasp by faith in him. The reason, then, that men's attempts to justify themselves by works are so heinous is not that the doing of the law would itself have to be bad (it was, after all, not bad in the case of Jesus, but was his righteousness). The reason is, rather, twofold: before Christ, works of the law failed because, as a matter of fact, all men sinned:[22] *"Since all have sinned and fall short of the glory of God,* they are justified by his grace as a gift, through the redemption which is in Christ Jesus, whom God put forward as an expiation by his blood, to be received by faith" (Rom. 3:23–4). Although Paul does not speculate about it (since it is to him practically unthinkable), if any man prior to Christ had loved God with all his heart, soul, mind and strength, and his neighbor as himself, there seems no reason to think he would not have been perfectly righteous before God; but as a matter of fact, no one did, nor has any done so since Christ, either. And secondly: after Christ, attempts to be justified by works are particularly offensive, because in addition to always failing, they are like throwing in God's face his most loving and precious gift.

---

[22] Bultmann expressly denies this interpretation. See *TNT,* I, pp. 266f.

As we have seen, Bultmann's interpretation of the law is also a way of resolving Paul's paradox. The law is both superseded and retained: superseded in that the specific commandments of the law are no longer binding; retained in that the essence of the law, the call for submission to transcendence, is still to be heard in the commandments.[23] If Bultmann's understanding of the law, thus explicated, seems quite distant from Paul's and a considerable interpretive strain on Paul's teaching, it is because he has denied the propriety of retaining Paul's key to the paradox.[24] According to Bultmann, Paul believes that man was never intended to live by the keeping of commandments.[25] What is wrong with the law is not that men failed to keep it fully and that God offered them righteousness by a man who kept it on their behalf, but rather that the form of a commandment, the specific requiring of some kind of behavior, leads to inauthenticity. The true purpose of the law, which is to call men to authenticity, is subverted by the form of law (its appearing in commandments), which elicits self-assertion and man's closing himself to possibilities. Thus Bultmann interprets Paul:

> The reason why man's situation under the Law is so desperate is not that the Law as an inferior revelation mediates a limited or even false knowledge of God. What makes his situation so desperate is the simple fact that prior to faith there is no true fulfilment of the Law.[26]

It is quite clear from passages like this that for Bultmann faith is the fulfillment of the law. But this differs from the thinking of Paul, for whom *Christ* is the fulfillment of the law. What for Paul makes man's situation under the law so desperate is that prior to Jesus there is no true fulfillment of the law. It is Jesus, the obedient man, the man who as obedient stands in our place before God, the man who is our righteousness and sanctification and redemption—it is Jesus (not faith, except in a secondary and

---

[23] Cf. *TNT*, I, pp. 261f.
[24] "How can the guilt of one man be expiated by the death of another who is sinless—if indeed one may speak of a sinless man at all? What primitive notions of guilt and righteousness does this imply? And what primitive idea of God?" (*KM*, p. 7).
[25] Cf. *TNT*, I, p. 263.
[26] *Ibid.*, p. 262.

derivative way) who changes the situation by bringing into the world a fulfillment of the law.

Beyond this, we can note that Paul is not hesitant to issue ethical and religious directives setting specific limits and projecting specific ideals of behavior. His letters are replete with this kind of discourse. If he were really opposed to the law on the ground that it contravenes radical openness, he would have to be equally opposed to the form of his own exhortations, and either cease giving them or at least accompany them with frequent reminders that they are to be "interpreted." But he is certainly not bashful about giving them, and we have no reason to think that he means them to be taken in any other than the most straightforward way.

Although Bultmann's view of law comes out less clearly in his interpretation of the Sermon on the Mount, it is nevertheless discernible if we keep in mind things he says elsewhere. In the antitheses (Matt. 5:21–48) "Jesus sets the demand of law over against the demand of God."[27]

> It would obviously be a complete misunderstanding to take these 'But I tell you' passages as formal legal precepts of an external authority, which can be fulfilled by outward behavior. . . . All these sayings are meant to make clear by extreme examples that it is not a question of satisfying an outward authority but of being *completely* obedient.[28]

All right. No one will claim that the prohibitions of harbored anger, lust, divorce, oath-taking, revenge, and so on, are legal precepts to be obeyed blindly, or to be fulfilled by mere "outward behavior." But are they to be taken seriously as legal precepts at all—to be obeyed intelligently and by behavior in the everyday sense? Although Bultmann is reluctant, as an exegete, to come out and say it, he seems to be philosophically committed to denying this:

> The demands of the Sermon on the Mount are nothing but the demand for conversion and renewal of will; for they teach that

---

[27] *JW*, p. 91.
[28] *Ibid.*, p. 92.

the will of God is not fulfilled by fulfilling the commandments of law; on the contrary, God demands a good will.[29]

Here we see the same dichotomy between fulfilling a commandment and doing "God's will" (that means, surely, submitting to transcendence) which generally characterizes Bultmann's ethics.

But if this is what his interpretation of the Sermon on the Mount comes to, it is surely as far from the meaning of Jesus (or Matthew) as his reading of Paul is from Paul. It is simply beyond belief that Jesus' sayings are really not about anger, lust, divorce, and so on, but only about conversion and renewal of will. The straightforward reading would be to say that they are about renewal of will *in* being about these other things; it would be to say that God's will concerns these other things, that it has a specific content referred to in these ethical precepts. It would be to say that these commandments, in their specific requirement of behavior (outward and otherwise), are holy and just and good.

Imperatives might be ranged on a scale of specificity—from completely particular commands ("Shut that door now") to rather specified but nevertheless general ones ("Don't boil a lamb in its mother's milk"), to rather unspecified ones ("Do what is right," "Be good"). On the lower end of this scale the imperatives would tend to hem a person in, constrict his options, while on the upper end they would allow him more leeway for individual judgment. The casuistical tradition in ethics attempts thus to hem the individual in by specifying all the demanded and prohibited actions. Traditions like the Kantian, which attempt to reduce all of ethics to a single, very unspecific imperative, or situation ethics, which in its heart would really like to do away with rules altogether, belong to the other extreme. The one tends toward standardization and certainty of ethical judgment at the cost of human spontaneity, the other toward freedom at the price of leaving the individual at sea as to what, concretely, he should do. Bultmann's concept of authenticity as radical openness pushes him far in the direction of the latter theory.

No one will deny it: simply always to do as one is told is to miss being an authentic person. The ethically mature individual

[29] *HE*, p. 98.

makes his *own* decisions. Legalism, at least in part, is acting not on the basis of one's judgment as to what is right, but simply because one is told. And so we might be inclined, as Bultmann is, to think that acting responsibly cannot be the obeying of a commandment, because such obedience contradicts being one's own man.

But it is equally clear that this being responsible and making one's own judgments must have some definite shape if it is to be called ethical. Being ethical is not just anything; it is distinguishable from being unethical or nonethical. And this means that morality, for all its freedom, must be governed by rules; it is of its essence to be patterned behavior and judgment. For example, if a person is refused employment for no other reason than that he belongs to another than the dominant race, we call this refusal an act of injustice, and so it is that the concept has definiteness: it distinguishes one act from another, and the possessor of the concept has the capacity so to distinguish. Further, this definite shape is not a matter of choice; it is external to the person in that he as an individual does not create or constitute the rule. One cannot, by deciding, make an unjust act or person just, or a just one unjust. The judgment one makes regarding a particular act or person is, if correct, governed by the rules of which the concept of justice is constituted. If a person refuses to follow such rules, he simply foregoes making ethical judgments altogether. So whatever it may mean to be ethically free, responsible, and authentic, this cannot exclude his submitting to external standards.

Moreover, having a moral concept implies possessing a kind of knowledge which pre-determines the judgment one will make in encounter with concrete cases. For example, the imperative to love, whose outward form would seem to place it on the upper end of our scale of specificity, can be understood only by someone who has mastered the concept of love. And whoever has mastered this concept will have the ability to recognize particular actions, emotions, and attitudes as loving or unloving. If he cannot give examples, or recognize cases of love, we will be justified in holding that he does not know what love is. Paul not only exercises, but also conveys, this distinction-making capacity when he summarizes some of the criteria of Christian love in I Cor. 13: if a person is loving, he will be patient with others and kind to them; if he finds himself being resentful of others' success, or rejoicing when evil is done, then he will know that he is not being loving; and so on. Within the Christian context, the love commandment does not leave the individual in the dark as to how to comport himself; nor does it leave up to his decision what shape love will have. A whole body of conventional Christian belief and practice undergird that little commandment, to give it firm and definite contours. In that passage Paul succinctly calls attention to some of those contours. And it is in virtue of standing in this tradition and joining in these practices that the individual comes to possess that knowledge by which he will judge and act in the concrete situations of his life.

If it were true that the love commandment left the individual "forsaken by every support and every point of orientation," if it provided no general guidelines as to the specific kind of action required, then we would have no basis for criticizing anybody's action as a failure of love. So if a man claimed that, in the moment of decision, he had loved (i.e., transcended himself in face of another person's claim on him) in committing adultery, or murdering his father for the inheritance, or refusing a kindness to a friend in need, we would on Bultmann's understanding of ethical decision have to accept his action as not immoral. Indeed, in denying the relevance of general ethical standards he seems committed to the view that there can be no such thing as a wrong decision, if only it is a genuine choice of this or that concrete possibility. The only way it can be wrong is to be done with an inauthentic "how": the question is whether the individual, in deciding, chose himself as possibility, or whether he allowed his action (and thus his identity) to be determined by his past. Here we have something like a basis for criticism (though it is very difficult to see how it could be applied, even to oneself); but it is no basis for preferring life-saving to murder, or chastity to adultery, or honesty to lying. And it seems to me clear that a person who has no grounds for such preference can neither make ethical judgments nor be called an ethical person. To deny the relevance of rules governing behavior is surely to abandon ethics altogether.

Part of Bultmann's trouble seems to be a confusion about the status of the concept of obedience. He is inclined to say that there is really only one commandment of God—to obey him. So that all other, specific, commandments of God are but expressions of this essential commandment. But what would it be for God to command obedience and nothing else? Would God have commanded anything at all just by commanding obedience? Would a person have any idea how to respond? The difficulty is that *obedience* does not by itself describe a doing of anything; it is rather a general term for the doing of anything that God (or any authority) demands; if he demands only obedience there is no way to respond (just as, if a person asks what to do and is told to do his duty, he may well ask again, "But what am I to *do*?"). One does not say, "Do this, do that," and then in the same tone of voice say, "Oh, and something else—also obey!" Doing this or that in response to the imperative *is* obeying; and there is no obeying unless there is something specific to do obediently. The imperative "Be obedient to God" should not be thought of as itself a commandment, but rather as a way of recommending his commandments either as commandments or as his. But if, as Bultmann thinks, these commandments are but expressions of the commandment to obey, then there is simply no commandment at all, since there is nothing to do.

His motive for evacuating ethical concepts is of course his fear of legalism.[30] But his view of legalism is very peculiar because he conceives its opposite (authenticity) as radical openness. On this account, if a man's present response to a situation is determined by something from the past or the universal (as of course all ethical principles are), this response is not authentic. The consequence is that legalism is conceived as any following of ethical principles, and so in seeking to avoid legalism Bultmann is driven into a theoretical flight from morality itself.[31]

----

[30] There is a remarkable parallel between the paternalism of casuistry, which attempts to save us from error in ethical judgment by making all the judgments ahead of time for us, and Bultmann's paternalism, which attempts to save us from legalism by removing ahead of time all temptation to it—that is, by doing away with authoritative ethical rules.

[31] Is Bultmann an antinomian? Although he has a strong theoretical stake in evacuating ethical rules of what would ordinarily be called their "content," he is, paradoxically, very careful not to draw the libertinist conclusion. "Who can fail to see that this law code is a real necessity for us and that without it our timid attempts to love God and neighbour could not really begin? For no one will suppose that in order to fulfill the will of God as Jesus understood it, he must become an anarchist" (*FU*, p. 231). Bultmann has three ways of blunting this paradox. First, he constantly re-asserts the importance of the "demand" of the law, though what he really means by this turns out to be a kind of formal essence: Do not

The culprit here is obviously his concept of authenticity. One ought, surely, to be able to conceive authenticity (autonomy, integrity, freedom, individuality) in such a way that it is not the opposite of morality.

The key, it seems to me, is the concept of character. It is not legalism simply to follow a moral rule, but to follow it in a *way* which is less than moral. And the essence of the matter seems to be that the legalist is one who follows the moral rules without having assimilated the moral concepts to his person. That is, while these concepts may succeed in at least partially determining his action, they have not shaped his emotions, his attitudes, his understanding of himself, his perception of the world. Consequently we are inclined to say that his actions are "merely external," for we mean to point out that the rule governing his behavior is alien to his personality in its broader and deeper aspects. Moral understanding is much more than just knowing what action is being required; and so the man who has not appropriated morally the moral rules according to which he acts can be said to lack understanding.

Moral education is not just the transmission of precepts but the inculcation of moral concepts in such a way that not just one's bare actions, but the whole personality is morally qualified. Bultmann seems to think that moral teaching, as something universal and belonging to the individual's past, can be no more than the basis for legalistic adherence to moral precepts. But one can be taught not just that the law must be obeyed and that the law prohibits stealing, but that stealing is an offensive and despicable kind of behavior. And if a person learns well, he will be disposed against stealing, he will find it abhorrent, he

---

be self-assertive. Second, he has a kind of blind and unexplained trust that what, in particular, one ought to do will be evident in the moment of encounter with the neighbor: "If a man really loves, he knows already what he has to do" (*JW*, p. 94). And speaking of the man who has given up self-assertion, he says, "Such a man needs no particular rules for his conduct toward other men; his conduct is determined by renunciation of his own claim" (*ibid.*, p. 109). And third, he seems to fall back on the concept of "dialectic": "Hence formal obedience to the law as such is no radical obedience, though of course true obedience can exist in fulfillment of the law" (*ibid.*, p. 92). That is, though the specific content of the demands of the law is irrelevant to authenticity, one nevertheless follows certain patterns of outward behavior in the mode of the dialectical "as if not."

will be motivated by the spectacle of stealing itself to refrain from committing the deed. The ancients, when discussing authenticity, spoke of the peculiarly moral pleasures and pains to which the mature ethical individual is disposed. The just man, said Aristotle, is one who takes pleasure in just actions. It is this man, the man who does not just refrain from stealing but finds the deed viscerally unsettling, the man who does not merely perform justice but glories in it, for whom morality has become authentic—not because his behavior is unruled, but because the rules have been so deeply appropriated as to govern the whole man.

Moral character, and thus authenticity, is possible because human beings are capable of grasping *concepts*. For part of moral maturity is the ability to judge about what is called for, what is right or wrong, in situations which are new to the individual. *Love* is not the name of a kind of action (as the expression *making love* is), but a concept. A concept differs from a name in the complexity and flexibility of its use, and in the fact that its mastery is more strictly tied to practices. Thus one can teach a child the word *dog* by showing him different dogs, but he will master the concept *three* only by learning the practices of which it is a part: counting, calculating, and the like.[32] Consequently, a person does not grow much beyond childhood in his mastery of *dog,* but he can grow almost without limit in his mastery of numbers, as they become for him more and more powerful tools for the prosecution of tasks. Moral concepts too are mastered only by those who engage in certain practices, namely the practices of the moral life; and through these practices the individual can grow in their use—in the refinement of his attitudes, in the exercise of self-control, in his perception of himself and others, in his desire for the good—almost without limitation. So just as other concepts are practice-dependent, the mastery of a moral concept is as much a moral achievement as an intellectual one. And thus moral judgment is not just the categorizing and labelling of actions and situations (as the casuistical tradition tends to think), but is a complex, flexible, personal capacity given with the mastery of moral concepts.

---

[32] In other connections it is, of course, right to call *dog* a concept: for example, to distinguish it, as a general term, from *Fido* as a proper name.

C. H. Dodd insists that primitive Christianity did not abolish law, but retained a concrete law obedience to which is expected from members of the fellowship, called "the law of Christ." It seems to me that his explanation of this law, and how it differs from a written code, fits well the philosophical remarks I have been making:

> It turns out, then, that the law of Christ works by setting up a process within us which is itself ethical activity. His precepts stir the imagination, arouse the conscience, challenge thought, and give an impetus to the will, issuing in action. In so far as we respond, holding the commandments steadily in view, reflecting upon them, and yet treating them not merely as objects for contemplation, but as spurs to action, there gradually comes to be built up in us a certain outlook on life, a bias of mind, a standard of moral judgment. The precepts cannot be directly transferred from the written page to action. They must become, through reflection and through effort, increasingly a part of our total outlook upon life, of the total bias of our minds. Then they will find expression in action appropriate to the changing situations in which we find ourselves. That is what I take to be the meaning of the "law written on the heart."[33]

I would add that *this* law is imprinted upon the heart not only by training and effort, but first and especially by the gospel of our Lord, which touches the heart by comforting it and speaks to it in such a way that it can begin to hear the law.

All this talk of character, training and disposition is abhorrent to Bultmann because he conceives man as radical potentiality. A man's authenticity does not reside in anything perduring or actual about him, but only in the moment of action in which he affirms himself as a decision-maker. He worries that a preoccupation with the training of one's character will contravene the self-transcendence of authenticity:

> The demands for justice, honesty, fidelity, and purity . . . do not describe an ideal condition, but rather the execution of action. Their original meaning is obviously not: I should have for myself the quality of a just, honest, faithful, etc., man, but rather: I should act toward the other justly, faithfully, honestly, etc.[34]

---

[33] *Gospel and Law: The Relation of Faith and Ethics in Early Christianity*, by C. H. Dodd (Cambridge: Cambridge University Press, 1951), p. 77.

[34] *GV*, I, p. 233.

Now if we disregard for a moment Bultmann's peculiar motives for saying this, as well as the disjunctive form of the proposition, the point is a good one. There is a perversion we might call virtue-egoism, in which the individual so concerns himself with the state of his own virtue that the neighbor becomes an occasion for the exercise of charity, compassion, pity, or self-sacrifice. Then one performs acts describable under these rubrics, but the motive is self-training rather than the neighbor's welfare. This is a subtle perversion, which probably arises most in contexts where there is much preoccupation with virtues and moral education. But there is no reason why the desire to be virtuous must lead to this perversion. Paul, James, and the author of Hebrews give as a reason for rejoicing in tribulation the thought that sufferings have a character-building effect (see Rom. 5:1–5; James 1:2–4; Heb. 12:10–11). The desire for growth in character seems to be one legitimate motive to action; of course, anyone would think it a perversion if it became the only motive. So we might agree that a proneness not to preoccupy oneself too much with one's own virtue, but just to get on with the business of acting virtuously, is appropriate to the truly virtuous man. But it would be quite wrong to make this sort of self-forgetfulness the essence of ethics.

Oddly enough, however, Bultmann's own treatment of the concept of love tends toward this perversion. Heidegger finds in death the phenomenon which can occasion the self-transcendence fundamentally characterizing human existence; Bultmann insists that the "neighbor" is a strictly parallel phenomenon, capable of occasioning the same act of self-transcendence. If ever someone tried to love his neighbor not for his neighbor's sake, but with a view to cultivating a loving disposition in his own heart, his understanding of love would differ from Bultmann's only in that he thought of it as a disposition at the end of a process of education, while Bultmann conceives it as an act which can be performed only in the moment. In both cases it is not the neighbor's benefit which is primarily in view, but the status of the lover himself, whether that is conceived as a virtue or as an act of self-transcendence. The neighbor becomes an occasion for self-improvement.

It seems to me that to make self-transcendence the essence of Christian love is a departure both from the Christian tradition and from good sense. A symptom of the empire of this concept is Bultmann's insistence on dissociating *agape* strictly from *eros*. *Eros* desires the object, and thus does not accomplish self-transcendence (the opposite of self-assertion) in a radical way: "Christian love gives; it does not desire."[35] I know of no Scriptural support for the view that Christian love does not desire God, and fellowship and reciprocation of love from the neighbor. The love of enemies, though commanded, certainly cannot be the ideal; for truly to love your enemy is to want him to cease being your enemy. And heartily to want him to cease enmity would seem to involve wanting him to be your friend; and to want someone to be your friend implies that you want him to love you in return. Far from being the essence of Christian *agape,* the idea of a desireless love (one which does not desire anything for itself) seems to be a piece of conceptual confusion. Love, when it is full and mature, is surely not just a transcendence but an engagement of the self, not an abandonment of desire but a shaping and intensification of it. Christian love is a passion.

We have noted Bultmann's tendency to collapse some of the central concepts of Christian faith into a single idea—that of decisively understanding one's own being as radically different from the world's. Thus *faith* is the name for this act as performed in encounter with what Bultmann calls the "kerygma." "Revelation" and "obedience" are not distinguishable from it, except that the former accents the element of understanding or insight, the latter that of submission to the demand of transcendence. "Belief in creation" is the same act, now with a special eye upon man's difference from the order of nature and his impotence to control his destiny; and "hope," as radical openness to the future, is again the same act, only now viewed with a regard to the temporal aspect: man is not essentially determined by his past, as worldly beings are. And now we see that *love* denotes for Bultmann this same decision, the only difference being that in this connection it is thought of as occurring in encounter with the neighbor.

---

[35] *GV,* I, p. 237.

11

Faith

Bultmann's entire theology is oriented upon the phenomenon which he calls "faith." For him, "theological statements are by nature the explication of believing comprehension."[1] Faith is a new self-understanding constituting a new self, an understanding conceived as an act of decision over against an object which he calls the "act of God" or "Christ Event" or "kerygma." We have already in earlier chapters seen a great deal of the concept of faith. In chapters three and nine I dealt in detail with the concepts of "Christ Event" and "God" as they appear in his thinking—that is, with the objective correlate of the act of faith. In chapter one I expounded the existence/world dichotomy, and consequently also the concept of human authenticity which is formally identical with Bultmann's concept of faith. And in chapter ten we have just seen that, for all practical purposes, he reduces the concept of love to his concept of faith. What remains for us now is the task of reflecting critically upon the remaining elements of this central concept: faith as self-understanding, and faith as act.

I. Faith as an act of self-understanding

Faith is a transformation of the individual. But what kind of a transformation is it? An experience? A new kind of knowledge

---

[1] *TNT*, II, p. 238.

286 PART III: SOME THEOLOGICAL DETAILS

to be learned and possessed? An emotion or set of emotions?
A disposition of the heart? A new world-view? A character
trait? Bultmann would reject all these rubrics. In his view faith
is an act, or what for him amounts to the same thing, a decision.
"It is evident," says he, "that 'faith' has the character of obedience and is an act of decision."[2] In fact this is so evident to
him that though Paul nowhere calls faith an act, Bultmann can
aver that Paul "understands the act of faith as an act of obedience."[3]

> For Paul the acceptance of the message in faith takes the form
> of an act of obedience because of the fact that the message
> which demands acknowledgement of the crucified Jesus as Lord
> demands of man the surrender of his previous understanding of
> himself, the reversal of the direction his will has previously had.[4]

He finds the same thing in the Gospel of John: "And faith is
neither more nor less than the *decision,* achieved in the over-
coming of the offense, *against the world* for God."[5]

> Since faith and unbelief are the answer to the question of the
> divine *love,* they are (notwithstanding the fact that they are not
> achievements or spiritual dispositions) responsible deeds, in
> which it becomes manifest what man is.[6]

Faith in "creation" has the same character: "Christian faith in
creation must constantly be won and realized anew in the decision
of the moment."[7] And since faith is self-understanding, it is not
surprising that even the individual's knowledge of self becomes,
in Bultmann's thought, an act: Collingwood, in his account of
the relation between history and self-knowledge, seems to have
neglected this aspect, and Bultmann would understand the matter "a little more profoundly than Collingwood has done." "Must
we not then say," he asks, that "self-knowledge is consciousness
of responsibility over against the future? And the act of self-
knowledge, is it not at the same time an act of decision?"[8]

---

[2] *TNT,* I, p. 317.
[3] *Ibid.,* p. 314.
[4] *Ibid.,* p. 315.
[5] *Ibid.,* II, p. 76.
[6] *GJC,* p. 156.
[7] *EF,* p. 225.
[8] *HE,* p. 136.

The reason it is so important for Bultmann to describe faith as an act is that it preserves the momentary character of authentic existence, its radical opposition to anything that persists (and can thus be secure) through worldly time. A *Weltanschauung*, as something which can be grasped and held onto through time, is a temptation to "escape from the reality of my existence, which is actually real only in the 'moment', in the question involved in the 'moment' and in the decision called for by the 'moment'."[9] Nor, for the same reason, can faith be a relation to the "transcendent" as something that actually is and thus (at least from our point of view) could be thought of as persisting: "Christian living is always living on the basis of the transcendent as something yet to be—not in the sense of the realization of an idea but on the basis of what can be grasped only momentarily in decision."[10] Similarly, faith must not be thought of as a personal quality which has temporal duration, such as a disposition or trait of character:

> The Christian view of freedom indicates that freedom, as freedom of the individual, is not a quality, but can only be an *event* at any given time. The possibility of freedom is given only in the encounter, which offers freedom in its demand for decision.[11]

Only the moment, which stands in radical contrast to all that is permanent or perduring, is the authentic temporal mode of the human self. Acts, thinks Bultmann, share this kind of temporality. A disposition, or even an "experience," has duration; but an act or decision is unequivocally punctiliar. Therefore faith must be an act.

What happens in this act is that the authentic self of the individual, which has been implied and dimly apprehended but forever frustrated in the other acts of his life, is constituted. "The new self-understanding which is bestowed with 'faith' is that of *freedom,* in which the believer gains life and thereby his own self."[12] As it encounters the event of the kerygma's gracious

---

[9] *Essays,* p. 8.
[10] *Ibid.,* p. 156.
[11] *Ibid.,* p. 310; see also *GV*, III, p. 117.
[12] *TNT,* I, p. 331.

word (which is, of course, also "momentary"), the self performs an act of self-understanding in which it grasps itself as not
belonging to the world of its achievements and possessions (that
is, the actual, anything that the self might be able to control),
but rather as radical potentiality, as utterly open to the "future."
In so understanding itself, it constitutes itself radical potentiality
and thus free.

> In the decision to believe it is not the same as is normally the
> case in other decisions of life (which can, of course, also take
> on the character of decisions to believe from time to time), that
> is, it is not the case that man remains the same in it, and comes
> to his decision on the basis of considerations which remain out-
> side the sphere of his decision — considerations which have
> force for him in all circumstances. Rather are all the considera-
> tions which otherwise have a motivating power for a man up-
> rooted in the decision to believe, and are called in question and
> called to decision, so that man is entirely free—stands, as it
> were, in the open.[13]

Using Pauline-like language to describe this reconstitution of
the self, Bultmann says,

> "Faith" — the radical renunciation of accomplishment, the
> obedient submission to the God-determined way of salvation,
> the taking over of the cross of Christ — is the free deed of
> obedience in which the new self constitutes itself in place of
> the old.[14]

This new self, as radical insecurity, stands outside any essential
relation to the world,[15] and in so doing stands outside any essential relation to the time-continuum. That is how it differs from
the old self, which was "old" precisely in willing itself to be
identified within the time-continuum—for example, in terms of
its past, its concrete future plans, its durable personality and
character traits, and so forth. The momentary act in which the

---

[13] *Essays*, p. 180.
[14] *TNT*, I, p. 316.
[15] Of course, it does not *escape* from the world, and even this act of
self-understanding is always performed in some concrete worldly situation.

self eschews ("dialectically," of course) all such worldly identity constitutes the new self. That is, that act *is* the new self.

But if the authentic self exists only in that act, then of
course the only way for it to stay alive is to be constantly repeating that act. This self disappears as soon as it stops acting
in this way; for it *is* only in its active moment. Thus in interpreting concepts like "steadfastness" in Paul or "abiding" in John,
Bultmann presents us a picture of the believer "constantly" or
"ever anew" achieving this act of detachment:

> Faith is itself desecularization — detachment within the world
> from the world. Or better: faith as the act of believing con-
> stantly brings about this desecularization. It is true faith only
> when it has this constancy; i.e. when it 'abides', when it is
> faithful.[16]

Speaking of John 8:31f., "If you continue in my word, you are
truly my disciples, and you will know the truth, and the truth
will make you free," Bultmann says that since the believer

> makes this freedom his own in faith, his *being* free, in the
> sense of the freedom appropriated by him, is grounded in his
> *becoming* free, conceived in terms of the faith that lays hold
> of it. And in so far as faith can never cease, in so far therefore
> as this becoming free has to continue (as *menein en to logo*)
> and therefore has constantly to be achieved anew, a man experi-
> ences this condition of *being* free only as a perpetual *becoming*
> free.[17]

Behind this "constancy" produced by repetition of the decision to be potentiality, however, is what Bultmann calls the
"identity of the *I* within the flow of decisions." Even if man's
being as potentiality has to be realized by a decision in every
new moment, that decision cannot, as it were, come from nowhere. He is an "I" which is the possibility of this decision, a
being whose nature it is to be confronted in every moment with
this choice. Or, to put it another way, even where a man lives
in an inauthentic failure to understand himself as radical potentiality, and thus does not perform this act in which he realizes

---

[16] *TNT*, II, p. 86.
[17] *GJC*, p. 437; see also *EF*, p. 57; *TNT*, I, p. 322; *TNT*, II, p. 79.

his being, he nevertheless, through all this, remains potentiality. It is only on the condition that he *is* potentiality that his refusal so to *understand* himself can be the contradiction which we call "inauthenticity"— a not being what he is.

> *The human person* is not completely recognised so long as it is not explicitly taken into account that in the decisions of the individual there is a personal subject, an *I*, which decides and which has its own vitality. This does not mean that the *I* is a mysterious substance beyond or beside the historical life. Life is always within the historical movement; its genuineness stands always before it in the future. But the subject of the ever-new decisions is the same, namely, the *I*, as an ever-growing and becoming, an ever-increasing, improving or degenerating *I*. Signs of this identity of the *I* within the flow of decisions are memory and consciousness and the phenomenon of repentance.[18]

But the constancy of this "I" is nothing *actual* such as what we normally call personality, which by its constant features allows us to predict how an individual will behave or feel in typical circumstances. "For it must be stressed that what we call *personality* is also temporal-historical and is constant only as a possibility which is ever to be realised."[19]

Also it is worth noting that when Bultmann speaks of the "I" as "growing and becoming," "improving or degenerating," these dynamic terms can only be taken to express what happens in the "moment," viewed from one or both of two points of view. On the one hand, "becoming" may be taken to refer to the act of desecularization in which the self "becomes" what it is. From the perspective of worldly time this "becoming" obviously has no duration. Correspondingly, "degenerating" could only refer to moments in which this act was not performed. On the other hand, "becoming" might refer to the inner dynamic of existential time, as I described it in chapter one. Here a peculiarly human kind of time is constituted by the individual's act in which he eschews his past as constituting his real self and plunges into the open of the future (or the transcendent). Thus the becoming would be this metaphorical plunge. To this sense

---

[18] *HE,* p. 145.
[19] *Ibid.,* p. 146.

of "becoming," however, there would be no corresponding dynamic sense of "degenerating," for to degenerate would be equivalent to not constituting existential time at all, not plunging into the future. Or, if inauthenticity is to be thought of as an act too, then one might think of this failure to constitute existential time as a backward movement in which the individual understands himself in terms of his past.

Since the authentic self exists only in the moment, it cannot improve or degenerate across a stretch of the time-continuum. An obvious consequence is that faith is rendered unsusceptible of quantitative increase or decrease; there is no such thing as maturation or growth in faith:

> And the believer does not educate and develop himself into a more and more perfect believer, but is what he is as a believer, either entirely or not at all. The 'moments' of decision through which he passes may well be understood from the human point of view in the context of a development of character; but from the standpoint of faith they are not in the context of a development-process, or of some kind of progress; for they demand that the believer should always hazard his own self in them, to win or lose himself entirely. The encounter of the 'moment' seeks always to make him new, and to free him from himself, just as he comes into the situation of the 'now'.[20]

"From the human point of view" it may look as if old Uncle Hezekiah gets saintlier as the years go by. He grows kinder and more forbearing, more serene in the face of death, more joyful at the thought of Christ's love, more forgetful of himself and eager to help others. But all that is, according to Bultmann, not Uncle Hezekiah's real self. That is only the inauthentic self, the self insofar as it can be objectified and observed by others—insofar as it belongs to the time-continuum. The real self does not progress through time, like the body which grows stronger and then weaker with years, or the personality or character which develops in various ways; the real self is always entirely what it is at any given moment, and as such is always faced with the alternatives of understanding itself as belonging only to the moment, or falling into the inauthenticity of understanding itself

---

[20] *Essays,* p. 158.

in the terms of the time-continuum. This is why, as we saw in chapter eight, there is no such thing as Christian education.

But though Bultmann removes the authentic self from the time-continuum (while of course "dialectically" leaving it in), he can still assert that

> The decision of faith is not an experience which is confined to a single moment! *I am not,* in fact, the person that I am as the object of an isolating, psychological observation at an isolatable moment; and my existence is not constituted by the sum of single moments. For the world it appears like that because the world knows no real future and consequently also no real present. But life is just this: the world's sham life (in which the moments have always fallen into the past, into death) has ceased; and man can now live in the future.[21]

The authentic moment constituted by the act of faith, in which man actively takes responsibility[22] for his past by eschewing it (as opposed to passively identifying himself in its terms) and actively plunges into his authentic future by opening himself to possibility as such (as opposed to closing himself to possibilities by identifying himself in the terms of actual plans and hopes), is precisely the opposite of an "isolatable moment" in the sense of a very short snippet of worldly time. It is, rather, the whole of existential time as that dynamic plunge from one's own past into the radical openness of the future. It is true that, seen from the perspective of worldly time, it is a vanishing snippet. But to see it as no more than that is to miss man's true temporality entirely. Thus Bultmann can hold, in effect, that the reason Realism (Flaubert, Zola) was unable to see man as a "stable and constant person" was that it did not understand man as belonging to the moment:

> Man was understood as coming out of a past on which the present depends. But the past is not *his* past, strictly speaking, qualifying him in his genuine self, which he can appropriate as his past and from which he can distance himself. His present goes into a future which, strictly speaking, is not his future, for which he can make himself open, or against which he can

---

21 *FU*, pp. 181ff.
22 Cf. *ibid.,* pp. 315ff.

close himself and for which he is responsible. Therefore it must be said: a genuine self seems not to exist at all.[23]

Just as a stable person in the ordinary sense is one for whom there is a certain constancy and consistency across a duration of time, so the Bultmannian man of faith is stable in an analogous sense relating to existential time: for in the act of the moment his past and his future are welded into a unitary whole.

But for our purpose the essential thing to see is that Bultmann's removal of the authentic self from worldly time into the moment is a denial that Christian faith is in any way constituted of dispositions or traits of character. Thus he opposes belief with personal qualities: the believer "is new simply because he believes, not because he has been given newly existent qualities."[24] Spiritual dispositions, as susceptible of development, are to be classed among "works": "If faith and unbelief are not the works of man, neither are they spiritual dispositions (*diatheseis*) which can be developed."[25] "The Christian view of freedom indicates that freedom, as freedom of the individual, is not a *quality,* but can only be an *event* at any given time."[26] "As free deed of decision, the obedience of faith is also insured against another misconception. 'Faith' is not an 'experience,' not the 'truly religious in religion,' not a state of soul, not a *diathesis* (propensity, disposition) or an *arete* (virtue, excellence)."[27] "Theologically expressed, faith is not a new quality that inheres in the believer, but rather a possibility of man that must constantly be laid hold of anew because man only exists by constantly laying hold of his possibilities."[28]

And I hardly need to reiterate here that for Bultmann faith does not involve believing anything, in the ordinary sense of the word. That is, it does not involve believing this or that about what is the case. For him it is not a *Weltanschauung,* a set of beliefs about the ultimate nature of the universe. Nor does it involve the believing of propositions about God and Jesus Christ. Faith is the act of self-understanding in which the be-

---

[23] *HE,* pp. 108f.
[24] *FU,* p. 316.
[25] *GJC,* p. 156.
[26] *Essays,* p. 310.
[27] *TNT,* I, p. 316.
[28] *EF,* p. 96.

liever understands himself precisely in independence from all
knowledge which, expressible in propositions, could be possessed through time.

II. The concept of self-understanding

For several reasons, self-understanding is a useful focus
for an attempt to describe Christian faith.

First, to think of faith as a way each believer understands
himself is to guard against the error of conceiving belief as
simply assenting to doctrines. It is to affirm that to believe *these*
doctrines entails a transformation of the individual.

Second, to conceive faith as a new self-understanding is to
acknowledge the way that understanding determines being this
or that kind of person. For example, being a courageous person
means to be the kind of person prone to do courageous deeds.
But doing something courageous logically entails understanding
of various sorts: an understanding of dangers, of the complexi-
ties of the situation in which a deed is to be performed, of the
extent of one's capacities, of how one would and ought to respond to failure, and so forth. Similarly Christian faith, as a
qualification of the human person, is logically dependent on
the understanding of certain things about oneself and the world.

Thus, third, understanding functions criteriologically with
respect to faith, in a way that concepts like action or behavior do
not. To describe how a Christian understands himself, though
difficult, is much less likely to be ambiguous than to describe
how a Christian acts. For there is no action which is Christian
action in the way that there is an understanding which is the
Christian understanding. For example, advocating the cause of
the oppressed is a kind of action which is typically Christian,
and yet in adjudicating the question whether any particular
advocacy of the oppressed was a Christian action, we are forced
back to the question how the acting individual understood himself and his situation; for without the right understanding, we
have warrant for denying the adjective *Christian* to any action.
How a man sees himself and the world implies kinds of behavior,
whereas kinds of behavior do not always imply that a man
perceives the world in a certain way.

A fourth reason for approving self-understanding as a
rubric for description of faith is the universality of human in-

terest in the question "Who am I?" The question which, in one way or another, every reflective person asks concerning his own identity, is one which Christian teaching answers: "How am I to understand myself?" The concept of self-understanding casts us into the arena of questions to which no person can long remain insensitive, questions about his happiness and the meaning of his life.

What I shall now do is make a few remarks about features of our everyday concept of self-understanding. I shall be asking, "What is it for a person to know who he is?" This inquiry should help us to get some perspective on the concept of self-understanding which Bultmann proposes.

There is, first, that range of things which to know is to know oneself in a shallow or minimal sense. This range of things becomes apparent when we consider the case of amnesia. What does Socrates no longer know when he has ceased, in this sense, to know who he is? He will have ceased to know such things as that his name is *Socrates*, that he lives in such and such a house and has a pug nose, that he sometimes receives instructions from a good daemon, that he fought at Potidaea and Amphipolis and Delium, that he is Xanthippe's husband and the teacher of Plato and Glaucon, and so forth. A person who knows things of these types can be said to know who he is, in a shallow sense. A person who does not know them would have to be sick or in some way impaired. For such self-knowledge is minimal to being a person at all. Even people who in another sense have very little understanding of themselves will know who they are in this sense. Furthermore, there is little room for deepening of this kind of self-knowledge; one either knows these things or one does not. One does not grow in a knowledge of where one lives, or of what one's name is.

But there is a range of things which to know is to know oneself in a deeper sense. Here one can be quite healthy and yet not be very clear about who one is; and the possibilities of growth in this kind of knowledge of self are practically unlimited. Unlike the knowledge described above, this knowledge can appropriately be called "understanding."

A kind of self-knowledge which we might call prudence is an understanding of one's capabilities and limitations. The mature business man is one who knows when he has reached the boundary of his own competence to make, for example, an investment decision—when he is in a sphere where outside advice is needed. Also, he knows when he *is* competent to make judgments, and so he has a certain judicious confidence in himself, even when others doubt his judgments. Such knowledge of himself, and such firmness of confidence in it, are only the product of many years of acting and reflecting and self-testing in a wide variety of situations. Similarly, an athlete needs the kind of self-knowledge which will allow him neither to underestimate his abilities (so as not to fail to push himself "all the way") nor to overestimate them (so as not to poop out in the middle of the game). And those who have tarried for some time in the Academy will attest to how many years of testing and trying it sometimes takes for a student to learn where his own talents lie.

There is an analogous knowledge of one's moral capacities and limitations. Some people should, perhaps, not marry, since they lack the firmness of character so to limit and concentrate themselves, to suffer through the difficulties and overcome the temptations. Unfortunately, it is those who in reflecting upon themselves find some cause for hesitation who are by this very seriousness best suited to such a moral commitment; and it is just those lacking in the requisite character who also lack reflectiveness about themselves, and who consequently enter recklessly upon this venture. The depth and difficulty of this kind of self-understanding is shown by the fact that when such an unreflective person is told by someone else about this weakness, he may still not see the truth about himself, or grasp its full weight.

To prospective disciples Jesus makes it clear that one may be called upon to give up one's family and one's own life (Luke 14:25ff.). "Whoever of you does not renounce all that he has cannot be my disciple" (v. 33). Then in two little parables he invites his hearers to reflect on their own capacity to see this renunciation through: "For which of you, desiring to build a tower, does not first sit down and count the cost, whether he has enough to complete it? Otherwise, when he has laid a foundation, and is not able to finish. . . " (vv. 28–29). The hesitation about discipleship which Jesus here commends is a kind of morally serious reflection about oneself in the light of a proposed commitment demanding enormous resources of personal strength and steadfastness. How little Jesus' original disciples understood themselves in this regard is evident from a look at the story of Peter's discipleship, or the thoughtless "We are able" of the sons of Zebedee in response to Jesus' question, "Are you able to drink of the cup that I drink, or to be baptized with the baptism with which I am baptized?" (Mark 10:35-40).

There is also a kind of self-understanding that relates to one's desires. When we say that someone "knows his own mind" we mean that he is clear about what he wants. If we are talking about the central and orienting wants of a man's life, rather than the incidental ones, we mean hereby that he is not the sort of person who wants one thing one day and something quite different a month later, or one who is easily swayed to set off in a different direction from one in which he has started. The indecisive person, the one who does not know his own mind, is the one who cannot predict from week to week, or year to year, what he will want. His life is not characterized by wanting anything definite. On the other hand, by desiring some definite orienting end rather than either whatever happens to strike one's fancy at a given moment or something very general (desiring too general an end can be the same as indecisiveness and lack of orientation), he comes also to *know* what he wants and thus to know himself.

Another way of failing to understand oneself is self-deception about what one wants. The professor who tells himself that his primary desire is to help students gain knowledge, but produces sloppy lectures and spends his time writing esoteric but prestige-producing books, is one who in failing to acknowledge what he really wants also fails to understand himself. Here the barrier to self-understanding is not a failure to want something definite, but a lack of honesty.

The situation in which a person finds himself determines his identity, and the way he knows himself as having such an identity is through the concepts with which the situation is described. A man cannot grow in his knowledge that he is a father, but he can grow indefinitely in his understanding of what it is to be a father, and thus of himself as father. The concepts 'father', 'mother,' 'husband,' 'wife,' 'son,' 'daughter' are, as descriptive of a person in his connection with others, also *moral* concepts. To understand oneself more profoundly as husband or father is to grow morally; it is for an identity to become a trait of character. To call someone a father may be to say no more than that he stands in a certain causal-biological connection with one or more other people. But to understand oneself as father may also be to have a range of emotional susceptibilities, behavior dispositions, and capacities for judgment appropriate to being a father in a fuller and moral sense. Understanding oneself as father may thus constitute a total determination of one's self-awareness, touching and transforming practically everything else of importance in life.

To see that men were created as brothers is to understand myself in a very different way than if I think the world a place where natural enemies, engaged in a struggle of acquisition and self-preservation against one another, employ the concord of ruled fellowship merely as a means to save them from the mutual destruction naturally consequent upon their being men. For if all men are brothers, then I am the brother of all men, and my understanding that entails a susceptibility to be hurt when they are hurt, to rejoice when they are happy, to be guilty when I transgress or fail the bonds of brotherhood. It entails a certain kind of character, a certain shape of soul, one to which it is natural that I should gladly share my goods with those who need them, and be willing to receive from others when I am in need. If all men are brothers then my identity consists in being a brother to all men, whether I understand that or not; and the task of deepening the moral life is simply that I should come to understand it. Here, to understand myself is to come to understand the situation into which I have been set: the situation in which all men are brothers.

To understand oneself is also to be clear about one's emotions. It is a notorious observation of psychiatry how capable men are of deceiving themselves or otherwise remaining ignorant of even the most dominating emotions of their life. We all want to think ourselves loving and happy, and the power of this desire to distort our image of ourselves is so great that we can almost say that the only person who would ever be totally clear about himself would have to be the man who simply *was* loving and happy, for failure here almost entails some self-deception. There are, of course, degrees of clarity with which I can grasp that I am a vain, hateful, or jealous person; and it would clearly be absurd to hold that only a loving and happy person can perceive that he is hateful and jealous. If there were not degrees of clarity about our emotions, we could not experience remorse about ourselves; and remorse, when healthy and strong, is an affective symptom of and motive to the growing purer of the soul. To understand myself as jealous, vain, or hateful, in such a way that I feel the moral weight of such a judgment, is therefore to be on the way to vanquishing the jealousy, vanity and hatred of my heart. The dark emotions cannot withstand self-understanding as the happy ones can. The happy emotions, since they do not require any covering up, are the ones which make us transparent to ourselves. There is, perhaps, no completely happy person on this earth, though there are many who come close to complete unhappiness. Most of us are a mixture of darkness and happiness; but what we, speaking relatively, call the happy person, is the one who knows himself and has some distance on this or that dark emotion. That is why the Christian gospel, with its promise of forgiveness and hope, can break into our darkness and foster honesty and transparency about ourselves.

In the foregoing sketchy descriptions of self-understanding, what is common is that the knowledge of self always has reference to some specifiable *identity* of the self. These remarks make it apparent that the ways an individual is identified are quite various: there is that enormous range of physical, spatial, institutional, interpersonal and historical things which to forget is to suffer amnesia; a person's capabilities and limitations, moral and otherwise, also individuate a person and give him his identity; the specificity of one's identity can depend on the firmness and definiteness of one's desires; the situation, wider or narrower, especially as established by an individual's relation to other people, determines his identity; and finally his emotions, thought of not as episodic feelings but as long-range personal traits, distinguish him as a person. To put it somewhat glibly, the analysis seems to indicate that self-understanding depends on having a self (though it also indicates that having a self depends on self-understanding), and that having a self is a complex matter involving physical characteristics and relations to the physical world, definite relations to other people, and personal traits such as abilities, goals, and emotions.

All these things which give the self identity fall on the worldly side of the Bultmannian dichotomy. The authentic self is not constituted by its past; nor by qualities of the soul; nor by its situation in the physical world; nor by its situation in the universe (as might be described in a *Weltanschauung*); nor by its ruled connections with other people; nor is it constituted by its relation to any specific future, but only to *constant* futurity, radical openness and transcendence. It is true, of course, that Bultmann allows all these things "dialectically"; that is, whenever an individual decides to understand himself as radical potentiality and thus in independence of all these worldly determinations, he nevertheless makes this decision as a physical being with character-traits, a specific past, concrete plans for the future, and so on. But the point to see is that although all these worldly elements may be present as the decision is made, the decision is to understand oneself, and thus to be oneself, in independence of these elements. The self *as authentic* is none of these things, but rather potentiality, radical openness only.

What Bultmann is proposing, in effect, is that the most authentic self-understanding is an understanding of a self to which all identity is denied. For if we try to imagine what it would be to identify Socrates independently of his name, his spatial location and bodily peculiarities, his roles in life among men, his relations to other people, his membership in institutions, his past deeds, his abilities and limitations, his concrete projects, his emotional makeup, and so forth, it becomes obvious that in losing the world in Bultmann's sense we have completely lost Socrates. And surely Socrates' identity is as lost for himself as it is for us. In becoming radical potentiality, he has become exactly nobody at all. To understand oneself "authentically" in this sense is precisely equivalent to not understanding one's *self* at all—for there is no longer any self to understand.

It may be replied that Bultmann is not thinking of such ordinary cases, but of the extraordinary religious moment of salvation. But then we must note that we are dealing with a very different "self" from what human beings can actually understand when they talk about understanding themselves and others. This is a "self" absolutely bereft of identifying marks, totally without definiteness. It is ironical that Bultmann, known for his concern with the concreteness and individuality of the individual, is precisely the one who, by denying the essentiality of the world in constituting and identifying the true self, makes every true self indistinguishable from every other. Every self is exactly like every other, for they are all equally unrecognizable, unknowable, and unsusceptible of understanding.

III. Act, disposition, and context

Act is a word used to refer to almost any discriminable thing a person or persons might do. Taking a bath, smoking a cigar, eating a meal, attending a seminar, hanging out the laundry, writing a letter, making a decision, hitting a baseball—these are all human acts. There are also acts of bodies such as Congress or the Council of Bishops. And there are acts which are shared by more than one individual: begetting a child, sailing a boat across the Sound, playing a game of tennis.

Although very few acts are really punctiliar as Bultmann would have us believe (even hitting a baseball can be thought of as including waiting for a good pitch, watching the ball), they do seem to be distinguished by having a definite and relatively short duration. Assembling an automobile is an act, but a career at the Ford assembly plant is not; begetting a child is an act, but rearing him is not.

There are usually many ways of describing what an individual is doing at any given time; thus what his act is will depend on what the describer or the doer is interested in. A person who is taking a bath may also be getting ready to go out, wasting water, warming himself, defying his wife, scrubbing his toenails, disobeying a house rule. A person who is writing a letter may be doing a duty, clarifying his thoughts, insulting somebody, ordering a chicken coop from Sears-Roebuck. To do more than one thing at a time in this sense does not at all require an expertise like the juggler's who can spin a pie on his nose while singing "Yankee Doodle," but is a function of the richness of the concepts with which we can describe human doings and thus cast light from various angles and upon the specific details and contextual peculiarities of those doings. It shows the extent to which what an act is depends upon concepts expressive of human interests and needs.

One of our ways of describing and discriminating acts is by the expression "act of_____," where the blank is filled by the name of a virtue or vice (roughly speaking). Thus we have acts of love, spite, courage, hatred, compassion, kindness, generosity, defiance. Christians speak of acts of faith in a similar way, and Bultmann uses an expression at least superficially akin when he talks about *the* "act of faith." So perhaps we will get some perspective on these phenomena if we reflect upon one of the related expressions above.

When we attribute to someone an act of courage, we lay ourselves open, in defense of this attribution, to a range of questions about the *person* to whom we attribute it, and the *context* in which he did the claimed deed. Consider the following case.

A middle eastern city is under siege from Palestinian guerrillas, and a downtown street is cordoned off to exclude traffic. But somehow there appears on it a single car driven by a young woman looking frightened and confused. Her fright is multiplied when a teenage soldier, brandishing a sub-machinegun, stops her and then, seemingly without cause, begins to smash the windows from her car with the butt of his gun. Only a little knowledge of the human heart is required to explain why, with the hundreds of eyes peering from the surrounding buildings upon that scene in the street below, this woman, perhaps in mortal danger, is left for some moments to her own devices against the crazed soldier. But then from one of the buildings there appears on the street a third figure, a large man who confronts the armed and angry soldier on behalf of the lady. The boy melts into sobs and relinquishes his weapon, and seems glad to accept the comforting embrace of the older man, who then gets in the car and drives the woman and her baby to a safer part of town.

We would certainly call what this man did an act of courage. But what makes it an act of courage can be clarified by reflecting on the kinds of considerations which might bring us to doubt this description of it. If it emerges that the man knew the soldier's mental condition and was thus completely certain that he would acquiesce without resistance when confronted by a show of authority, then we become less inclined to think this an act of courage. Similarly if he knew the gun to be empty. If in addition to there being no danger we also find that this man was motivated only by the belief that he would be offered a reward for rescuing the woman, we may be even further inclined away from our original description of the act. (Sometimes we are willing to call an act courageous even when it is otherwise morally dubious; we may, speaking somewhat loosely, say that a thief who steals something in a particularly daring way is "courageous." But generally we prefer simply to call him daring or brazen, and to reserve "courageous" for virtuous acts.) And if we further find that in the past he had always been a cringing coward, and that subsequently he continued to be such for the rest of his life, we will surely have to withdraw our original judgment altogether. Even in the absence of a redescription of situation and motive, an act thus thoroughly out of character would be so suspect as to force us to look for possible redescriptions of these other elements. When a confirmed coward does what looks like a courageous act, the act requires explanation, and this can take the form either of showing that the act is not courageous (by giving an alternative account of its motives and circumstances), or of showing that the man is not cowardly. This latter might be accomplished by showing that we had misjudged him in the past (that there is a better way to describe some acts which we thought cowardly), or by showing that he has changed; and to show that he has changed will require looking to see what follows in his life—whether the patterns of pusillanimity are actually replaced with patterns of courage.

Notice that when we redescribe in certain ways the *situation* in which the act is performed (that is, the agent's apprehension of that situation) the possibility ceases of its being an act of courage. Roughly speaking, if we eliminate the danger from our description of the situation, an act of courage is rendered impossible. The same thing happens (though perhaps not as tightly) when we redescribe the individual's *motives;* certain kinds of motives seem to be inconsistent with acts of courage, at least in the strongly commendable sense. And this is connected with the question of the individual's *character,* for not just anybody can be moved by just any motive; one has to be susceptible to motives for them to be motivating and that is a function of what kind of person one is. (Only kind people can be motivated by opportunities for kindness.) And it would be extremely odd, if not impossible, for a person to perform a single deed of courage when all the rest of his life, both before and after, was characterized by cowardice; as I have noted, such a claim would force us to look for an explanation of the act.

There is no such thing as an act of courage outside a certain describable type of situation, or apart from an agent with a certain type of character. And this is not to say only that the act has to be performed "in" a situation, but rather that the description of the situation is *logically* tied with the description of the act. Similarly, the description of the person (his character) is logically tied with the description of the act.

And since the act is logically situational in this sense, we can say that courage is not itself an act. It is not, for example, some single inward act of the will, which then gets expressed in various situations with outward behavior. Courage is not an act, but a *way* of doing an indefinite variety of acts. We speak of fighting, working, speaking, thinking, driving, climbing, resisting, and the like courageously.

Bultmann would tell us that we are truly persons only in our acts. But if our analysis so far is correct, it has shown that there could not even be acts of courage if there were not situations of particular types and persons with particular types of dispositions. Now Bultmann is obviously not asserting that there could actually be acts apart from other kinds of conditions. He does, however, seem to be denying that these other kinds of conditions go to constitute the essentially or authentically personal life. But why, if the other elements are logically necessary to acts of courage, should they be excluded from what is essential to personal life? The only answer seems to be that they fall on the wrong side of the existence/world dichotomy. Bultmann's policy of making acts the fundamental characteristic of human life seems to be the consequence of a philosophical compulsion to find a single essence, a single authentic core or aspect of the human being. But if we can somehow free ourselves from this compulsion, and avoid that dichotomy which dictates Bultmann's particular results, we will see that personal life is characterized by an enormous variety of things—that indeed there need be no single essence to it at all, and that personal life is in fact quite worldly.

If the authentic self really consisted solely of its acts, who would it be who was acting? We do in fact distinguish a person from his acts, and this distinction would seem to be necessary to the retention of both the concept of an act and the concept of a person. A systematic identification of the self with its acts would render the self so episodic that there would be no criterion of self-identity; if the self were the self only in the moments of its acts, there would be nothing to hold the various acts together as acts of a single self. But having an identifiable self seems to be a logical condition for *doing* this or that. If I were successful in understanding myself so as to deny all soul-accretions of my true self, and became simply the radical act of denying these (and all other worldly determinations) to be the real me, that is, if I became a pure act of decision (albeit, of course, always in a concrete situation), it is hard to see what warrant I would have for saying that *I* am acting, and thus that I am *acting,* at all. For who, in that case, am I? Does not my doing this strip me entirely of the identity which is the condition for my doing anything at all?

Is Bultmann correct in describing understanding as an act? This way of thinking is, at any rate, extremely odd when we juxtapose it with instances of what we usually call understanding. If I say that I understand Schleiermacher, I certainly do not imply that I am presently performing any kind of act; indeed, I may have understood him for years, at any point during which I could truly have answered Yes to the question "Do you understand Schleiermacher?" and at many of which points I would have been totally preoccupied with other matters. What I do imply by the claim to understand him is that I can repeat his theories and arguments upon request, can catch others when they misrepresent him in cardinal points, can see connections between this and that thing he said when they are pointed out to me, and so forth. Here it would seem more correct to say that understanding is a *capacity* to do this variety of things, rather than an actual *doing* of anything.

Understanding of ourselves is like this too. Think of the man about whom we say "He knows his own mind." We do not hereby imply that he is constantly renewing some act of observing himself, or always reaffirming a decision to see himself in a certain way. Indeed, he may never have actually *decided* to understand himself this way. He manifests his understanding of himself by the fact that he is decisive in making his choices, that his activities betray symptoms of the definite goals which orient them, that he is not easily led off into non-characteristic kinds of behavior. His self-understanding is his capacity to decide between alternative courses of action, to predict what he would do in given circumstances, to make judgments about whether he is the man for such and such a job.

We can imagine a modification of Bultmann's picture of faith, in which living out of transcendence is conceived not as an act, but as a disposition. Here understanding oneself as not of the world would be something like a trait of character. It might mean that when one made money one would not be inclined to hoard it or to be disturbed were it stolen or lost. Or that when one wrote a book, it would be completely indifferent whether one got credit for having written it by having one's name printed on it; or that when conviction of one's own approaching death became particularly vivid, one would not seek in terror to turn away from that thought, but welcome it with a kind of willing resignation. In this altered view one would not be performing a single act on each of these various occasions; one's acts would be such things as making the money, blessing the thief, refusing to print one's name upon the book, reflecting about death. Self-understanding here would be a disposition to perform these acts in characteristic *ways*. But the concept of world here would not be the same as Bultmann's, nor as radical. For the self could be identified as something persisting through sequential time, something which develops and can be educated and "controlled." It is against these possibilities, and thus in relation to a much more radical concept of world, that Bultmann insists on conceiving authentic understanding solely as an act. The difficulty is that this idea has ceased to be like anything which human beings usually call understanding.

Or is it so? Is Bultmann's concept of understanding perhaps more like those moments of flash insight at which we suddenly exclaim "I understand!"? Try an example: I am reading Schleiermacher and have been puzzling over some little paradox for a week. Suddenly everything seems to fit together, and I jump up and cry "I see!" Was that understanding? Well, it may have been, or it may not. There are criteria. We would not, for example, be warranted in calling it understanding if I were not subsequently able to do certain kinds of things which before the "insight" I was unable to do: to explain how the paradox is not a real one, to point out connections which I had not seen before, to correct misconceptions I had had before, and many other things. If abilities of this sort do not follow the moment of insight, then what happened in that moment will never be enough to constitute understanding. Sometimes one may feel like saying, "I understood, but now it has slipped me." But how can we (or the individual himself) in this case tell the difference between understanding and only having the impression of understanding? Where understanding is identified with the momentary insight, there is no practical difference between real understanding and merely having an impression of it. Criteria have been denied us, and *understanding* has become the name of an experience, nay, not even *an* experience, but just *any* experience which an individual at some moment might feel like dubbing with the name.

The same thing can be said for self-understanding. If the concept of self-understanding is to have any shape, if the claim that someone understands himself is to be a definite claim about him, then understanding cannot be momentary. The momentary episode of insight (even here it is mostly incorrect to call it an "act," for it is more like a suffering than a doing of anything) cannot rightly be called understanding unless it is connected with gaining a capacity. Rather than conceive understanding as the episode of a moment, it is better to think of it as a relatively perduring personal trait.

Bultmann seems to think that the essence of every true act is that it is a decision. It is clear enough what kind of thinking leads him to this view: an act, thinks he, if it is truly a human act, must be responsible. It must not be something that I do to-day simply because I did it yesterday, like a robot that is so programmed. But the way the act becomes my act, the way it comes under my responsibility, must be that I decide on it each time anew. It is as though if the core of the act is not a decision, then it must be mere hollow outward movement, having nothing to do with the essential me.

But in thinking this way Bultmann seems to have narrowed in on one aspect of the responsible life, and unjustifiably exalted it to the status of an essence. Much of the responsible life, however, consists in sticking to a course upon which one has set out, letting one's present actions track into the pattern of the old ones. Responsible marriage, for example, is not deciding again and again whom to sleep with (even if one makes the right decision); it is behaving as though that is no longer a matter of decision at all. And the fact that this decision is not repeated does not mean that the acts which form the course of a faithful marriage are any less one's own, that one is any less firmly aware of one's commitment. Again, to be responsible in business is not to decide on each new occasion how one will treat those with whom one has contracts; to be responsible to a contract is to treat its performance as though that is no longer a matter of decision. For the decision was made when it was signed; being responsible now takes the form of leaving that past decision unquestioned. This is why the "decision" to be radically open would in some respects be the *opposite* of the decisive and responsible life. Really to decide is to narrow the options, and to be willing to live with that narrowing.

But if responsible life cannot be everywhere a matter of decision, it is equally clear that there is no such life which does not involve making decisions. If one marries without deciding in the appropriate way, attempting to keep the options open and taking comfort in the thought that we can always get a divorce if it doesn't work, then one does not marry as a responsible person. He who has so much difficulty making political decisions that he never votes is not a responsible citizen. Bultmann seems to be confused by the fact that there is no responsible *life* which does not involve making decisions, into thinking that there is no responsible *act* which is not a decision, or that the personal essence of every true act is a decision.

Furthermore, it is significant to note that not every person has the same capacity for decision. There are, of course, decisions which are not personally demanding; even a child can decide whether he wants raspberry or chocolate ice cream. But to decide to marry, or to become a monk, or to venture without environmental support upon some arduous career, requires considerable maturity of character—especially self-knowledge and perseverance. The reason that not everyone is capable of personally demanding decisions like these is that the criteria for a decision's having been made are not limited to questions about what happened in the moment of decision, but include questions about what followed in the individual's life. Abram decided to leave Haran and to journey into the country where the Lord directed him. What if the next morning he had thought better of it? Would we still say that he had made a *decision?* And if he turned back after three days' journey? (Personally demanding decisions are characterized by gradations of firmness, manifest in what follows the moment; but somewhere toward the lower end of the spectrum we simply say "He didn't really decide at all.")

The existence/world dichotomy legislates that faith shall not be in any respect a disposition, character trait, or quality of the personality. For if it were, the self itself would become a potential source of security (one could, for example, possess knowledge of it, or control it through education), and thus of inauthenticity. How free the New Testament writers are of this dichotomy is indicated by the fact that, in describing the life of faith, they liberally employ disposition-concepts. Joy, hope, peace, kindness, love, hatred of evil, steadfastness, trust, zeal, patience, gentleness, self-control, forbearance, are perhaps the main ones. In all these cases there are episodes—usually behavioral or emotional—which can be described by the words. That is, of course, what it is to have a disposition; they are all dispositions *to* something. But since for the biblical writers all these things go to constitute the life of faith, Bultmann, it seems, has a stake in denying that the words work the same there as in everyday discourse. No theologian would doubt that there is a difference between, say, Christian joy and other kinds of joy. But for Bultmann the difference cannot be just that these are different dispositions; rather, it must consist in the Christian ones' not being dispositions at all. His position commits him to the view that joy, hope, love, gentleness, are either themselves acts or (more likely) aspects of a single act. Understandably, he never makes a case for denying that the biblical writers are using these disposition-words in the dispositional sense. For the case, if it were explicitly made, would have to be so outlandish that it would do more to discredit his position than has the silence for which he opted. Instead, he skirts the issue when doing exegesis, and when doing theology simply asserts without support that faith is a momentary act.

A concept such as love applies, in ordinary human affairs, in two different but mutually dependent ways. We speak of *acts* of love, and thus distinguish them from acts which are not loving; but we also speak of loving *persons,* and thus distinguish them from persons who are not loving. The mutual dependence of these facets of the concept is shown by our expectation that loving persons will do loving acts, and that they will seldom be found acting hatefully or indifferently toward people; and that unloving persons will seldom if ever be found to act in a loving way, and will often do acts of hatred or indifference.

The difference between a person's being disposed to acts of love (in the appropriate situation), and a window pane's being disposed to shatter (when struck by a hard enough object with sufficient force), is that in the former case a variety of other person-concepts are determinative. We do not say that the window pane acts, because concepts like responsibility, motive, and intention are not appropriate. Window panes do not make judgments, or deliberate; people do. But a similarity between the cases is instructive. In speaking with disdain about "qualities of the soul," Bultmann would have us think that such a conception excludes the human being's openness for new situations, the undecided character of our ever-new meetings with what comes to us in the world. It is as though if love or faith is a disposition, then everything has already been decided; all the holes which make the human susceptible to the future have been plugged up; his soul is congested with actuality, and he can't get an existential breath. But this is a gross misunderstanding of dispositions. To say that the window pane is fragile is not to say that (perhaps in the misty mode of potentiality) it is already shattered; but it is to say that it has properties such that *if* certain conditions hold, it will shatter. The "ifness" and the properties are irrevocably married. A sponge cannot have the same "ifness" (be open to the future in the same way) as the window pane, because it is a different sort of thing. True, to have a disposition is not to be *radically* open to the future, but by now we have come far enough to see that that is an impossible idea anyway, inconsistent with being a person. Love, as a disposition, is a mode of openness; for it means that given a situation under a certain range of description, the person will judge, feel, and act in ways which we call loving. And judging, feeling, and acting are çertainly personal ways of being, if anything is. Although the disposition to love is a more or less perduring quality of the person, the freedom of which it seems a contravention is really only an impossible philosophical abstraction. For radical openness, far from being true human life, would be the demise of the self altogether. If we believe that loving judgments, feelings, and behavior are more appropriate to the human breast than their opposites, then it is precisely in this disposition, in this constriction of a man's openness, that his true freedom is to be found.

Unlike Bultmann, the New Testament never calls faith an act, or speaks of *"the act* of faith." It does, however, describe many acts which we could reasonably call acts of faith.

The Gospels recount numerous stories of people coming to Jesus trusting that he will be able to help them. They come sometimes on their own behalf, as did the woman with the hemorrhage (Matt. 9:20–22) or on behalf of somebody else, like the centurion with the paralyzed servant (Matt. 8:5–13). This coming to Jesus with a request or a hope could be called an act of faith, though probably not of Christian faith. Such faith does, however, involve at least the belief that Jesus can help. It also presupposes a situation of need, usually a disease or disability of some kind or demon possession. The motive for coming need not be an especially noble one; the desire to be cured will do. We are not told very much about the persons in these stories, so we cannot say how confirmed they were, say, in Jewish belief in God. Jesus often compliments them for their faith, but the primary sign of it usually seems to be no more than the fact that they (often with some importunity) sought him out. Here we are of course not talking about anything that Bultmann would be willing to call the act of faith, for what is sought is a quite worldly end. But it is worth noting that, temporally speaking, this kind of act is closer to Bultmann's description of faith than any other kind we will find. For we can imagine faith of this sort being momentary. Coming trustfully to Jesus for help on a given occasion does not seem to presuppose very much in the way of character; nor would it require redescription if the person's subsequent life were debauched or impious.

One could also use the expression "act of faith" for the act of obedient submission or assent to the gospel message at conversion. Although Paul's letters, as directed to Christian congregations, are not concerned directly with conversion but rather with nurture, he does obviously assume a conversion as lying between the pagan (or Jewish?) and the Christian life. The same thing could be said for the Johannine writings; and the book of Acts recounts several such conversions. Whether in subsequent generations, where children are nurtured from the beginning in the faith, an act of conversion would always have to stand at the beginning of life in Christ, is certainly not self-evident. And even where a person comes to Christ from paganism, one could imagine a gradual growth of susceptibility and of conviction such that the convert could not pinpoint a moment in which he "acted" in assent. But be that as it may, we can see why someone would be inclined to call this act *the* act of faith; for it stands at the beginning of the Christian life, and seems to be the moment from which everything else in that life pro-

ceeds. Ideally, it would seem that this act should not be performed more than once in a person's life; for a subsequent need
for it would imply that he had fallen away from faith. Bultmann
in effect exalts the moment of conversion to the status of an essence of the whole of Christian faith. Thus for him the whole
communicatory function of the church is contained in a proclaiming which presents the hearer Sunday after Sunday with
a choice, the same choice, essentially, as is presented to pagans
in evangelistic preaching; and he has nothing to say about Christian nurture, a nurture which would presuppose that the basic
choice has already been made. But he differs from some pietists
whose emphasis on conversion induces them to recur again and
again and nostalgically to that moment when they first came to
the Lord, in that for him that moment is not just the all-important beginning, but the whole of the life of faith, and thus must
be reduplicated in each new moment, rather than remembered.

Paul does, however, constantly exhort his congregations to
a life conformable to the gospel of Jesus Christ, reminding them
of this gospel and explaining what it implies about behavior and
emotion. It is clear from his exhortations that the faithful do not
always or in every respect behave as faithful men. Romans 12 is
typical:

> I appeal to you therefore, brethren, by the mercies of God, to
> present your bodies as a living sacrifice, holy and acceptable to
> God, which is your spiritual worship. Do not be conformed to
> this world but be transformed by the renewal of your mind, that
> you may prove what is the will of God, what is good and ac-
> ceptable and perfect. . . . Let love be genuine; hate what is evil,
> hold fast to what is good; love one another with brotherly af-
> fection; outdo one another in showing honor. Never flag in zeal,
> be aglow with the Spirit, serve the Lord. Rejoice in your hope,
> be patient in tribulation, be constant in prayer. Contribute to
> the needs of the saints, practice hospitality. (vv. 1–2; 9–13)

Thus the acts of the Christian life (such as praying, doing loving deeds to one's neighbor and enemy, reflecting upon the grace
of God), when done by someone who is presently falling short
of his calling, can be thought of as acts of turning or returning
to the Lord. Setting one's mind on the Spirit rather than on the
flesh (Rom. 8:6)—that is, turning one's attention to, reflecting
upon, the grace of God in Jesus Christ—can be such an act.

One could understand Paul as summarizing the exhortations to such acts of turning when he tells the Romans, "present your bodies as a living sacrifice," or "yield your members to righteousness for sanctification" (6:19), or "yield yourselves to God as men who have been brought from death to life" (6:13). Here yielding would not be any one act, but it could be thought of as a class of acts, namely the acts which peculiarly characterize the Christian life, only now in the particular context of somebody's having fallen short. Yielding would be the name for that wide range of acts which compose the struggle to remain, or to become more deeply, a Christian.

Fourthly, then, we can call "acts of faith" all those acts which belong to the life of faith. Healing, prophesying, speaking in tongues, contributing money for those in need, rejoicing with those who rejoice and weeping with those who weep, giving a cup of water in Christ's name, blessing those who persecute you, preaching the gospel, associating with the lowly, taking thought for what is noble in the sight of all, defying the authorities when the situation demands it (Acts 4), speaking before the council as Stephen did (Acts 9), paying taxes to whom taxes are due, praying, writing letters as Paul did, and so on and on—as acts constituting the life of faith, these could be called the acts of faith. Of course, many of these things could also be done by a man without faith, and in that case would not be acts of faith. What makes them so is that they are part of a whole way of life, including the particular beliefs, expectations, motives, attitudes, and emotions which go to make up Christian faith.

Let us now examine a case of an act of faith in a little more detail. At the age of about 55, a Christian man of my acquaintance sold the business which he had built up with long years of labor and which was his sole means of income in order to give himself full-time to the preaching of the Word and the care of souls. At the time of this transaction, because of his advanced age, he was not assured of a church position, but he trusted that the Lord would provide work and income. The termination of his income also necessitated the sale of his house, which was quite adequate by English standards. For some years now he and his wife have subsisted in cramped temporary housing arrangements and on the meager income which the English Methodists pay their part-time clergy. To this day he has not yet found a stable position, and yet his confidence and enthusiasm remain undaunted. This man's venture is what we call an act of faith. What alteration in this account would warrant us in doubting it to be such?

If the man did not believe certain things about the way the universe is constituted, selling his business could not be an act of faith. If he did not believe that God wills his children to hear the gospel, and that he will care for those who proclaim it and nurture people in its way, then selling his business could not have the purpose it has, nor could his expectation of being provided for have the ground it has. If asked, "Why did you give up all that security?" he may answer, "Because God desires that I give my time to preaching and pastoring." Or if asked where his sustenance will come from, he may answer that God will provide. In the absence of such possible explanations of his action (beliefs), it could not be called an act of faith.

And so the question of the act's motives is relevant too. The answer to the first question above expresses the motive of obedience, the desire to do God's will. It might also be expressed in other ways, as the love of men, or an appreciation of the love of Jesus Christ and the desire to share his blessings with others. But if it turned out that this was only a rationalization, and the real motive for selling the business was spite against his heirs, we would have reason to deny that it was an act of faith. And, as in our analysis of courage, we see here that since an act of faith is determined by its motives, it is also determined by the character of the agent. Not just anyone can perform an act of faith, but only one whose character makes him susceptible to the motives appropriate to such an act.

The situation of this act makes it eminently an act of faith, distinguishable from the other acts of the faithful life. The situation in which it was done made possible the act of faith in this eminent sense because it was a situation of risk and demanded sacrifice. The individual I have described, because of his age and situation in life, risked unemployment, poverty, and the discomforts and dangers which those entail, for the sake of a higher purpose. For the average seminarian, going into the ministry involves only relatively minor risks and usually little sacrifice, and so in this respect is less a candidate for description as an act of faith. (Though acts are always situational in one sense or another, this does not mean that one can have faith only in certain situations; that would be true only if faith were identical with acts of faith.)

Related to motives and beliefs is the question of *emotions*. An act of faith is one which is done gladly, confidently, expectantly. If a person ran however great a risk, but did so with resentment, pessimism, and bitterness, his act would not be an act of faith. And again, here we are necessarily speaking of character; for risking something important with gladness, confidence, and expectation requires a particular sort of person. But in the case of faith these emotions are grounded in the individual's beliefs; if asked how he can be so confident and expectant in a situation which looks perhaps quite desperate, the believer may respond, "It is God's will; he will provide." Here the beliefs about God's nature and existence and power have become a deep part of the dispositional life of the individual. Although they can be thought of as propositions to which he assents, they are not merely that, but have become motives for some of the most important actions of his life, and grounds for the emotional dispositions which go a long way toward constituting the happy person.

Also, how the act fits together with the individual's subsequent behavior determines whether it was an act of faith. Even if the situation, motives, beliefs, and emotions all seem to indicate an act of faith at the time of the transaction, what follows can throw doubt on the propriety of the description. If after a few weeks our man became bitter and in disgust gave up looking for a place to exercise Christian ministry, we would be warranted in doubting whether the sale of his business was an act of faith. For it seems now that he did not really know what he was doing; he did not rightly appraise the situation's risk, or he did not know himself adequately to know how much suffering he could bear or that his confidence and expectation were not founded on his belief but on something else. Of course, there are gradations here; it is certainly not impossible that a man perform a true act of faith, and then later fall away. And the clarity with which someone appraises the situation and knows himself is susceptible of a large range of degree.

So it is perfectly proper and scriptural to speak of acts of faith, just as we speak of acts of courage, hatred, compassion, love. But it is not proper to say that faith is an act, if one means thereby that there is some one act which is the act of faith; nor is it proper to say that faith is act, if one means thereby that faith exists only in the act, only in the moment when the acts of faith are performed. Faith, courage, love, are determinants of personality, that is, of character, of a shapely dispositional life. We would have no warrant for calling a person faithful who never acted faithfully; however, faith is not an act, but a class of acts: those acts which are proper and peculiar to the faithful man. As such, with respect to any given act, faith has an adjectival or adverbial character: the act is faithful, an act of faith, something done faithfully or out of faith.

But as a class of acts, faith is also a class of emotions, virtues, and capacities of judgment: it is hope, love, joy, peace; it is patience and humility and kindness; it is having the mind of Christ. Faith is a whole bunch of dispositions clustering around and determined by believing the church's teachings about God, man, the world, and Jesus Christ. Since faith has so many facets, we can find that in various parts of the New Testament it is contrasted with different things: for example, Paul often contrasts faith with works; in the Sermon on the Mount, Jesus sets faith in antithesis to anxiety; the book of James presents it as contrary to moral and religious sloth; and John's Gospel strongly emphasizes that faith is the opposite of unbelief that Jesus is the Christ. But the fact that different parts of Scripture emphasize different aspects of the concept does not mean that they have different concepts of faith. All would think that it includes humility before the grace of God, that it involves peace of heart, that it is active and aggressive and passionate rather than indifferent and slothful, that it entails believing some things to be true.

Bultmann's insistence that faith is a decision is a way of insuring that preaching be rousing, and that faith be characterized as something crucial and momentous. But if faith can become a trait of a man's character, then he certainly does not always have to decide for it. Paul seems to think it possible for men to be in bondage not only to sin, but also to righteousness. He says to the Romans,

> But thanks be to God, that you who were once slaves of sin have become obedient from the heart to the standard of teaching to which you were committed, and, having been set free from sin, have become slaves of righteousness. (6:17–18)

The slave yields himself in obedience to his master, and there-after does not decide whether to obey, but obeys simply because this is his master. Luther, commenting on an earlier passage in that same chapter of Romans, assumes a growth of Christian character such that a choice for or against faith is no longer possible:

> In time, the spiritual life is gradually so strengthened that a turning away from it will be utterly impossible, for no one endowed with the unshakable strength of the perfection of an eternal will would want to turn away from it.[29]

I have noted that where somebody grows up from childhood in Christian faith, he may never have made a decision for or against faith; certainly the life of faith (like any kind of human life) involves making decisions, but for some people faith itself may not be a decision. So there is no conceptual necessity that faith be a decision, as there is, for example, that it be trust and belief; and very mature faith would seem to contravene even the possibility of such a decision.

Another motive for Bultmann's reducing faith to act is probably a philosophical predisposition to think that, essentially, faith must be some one thing. In every moment of true faith some one thing must be happening, and for him that thing is "the act" of faith. But if in disputing him I say that faith is disposi-tional, I am not claiming that it is some one other thing (perhaps a pigmentation of the catechized soul). Rather, I am trying to let it be all the things it is: beliefs, acts, emotions, feelings, de-sires, attitudes, capacities of perception and judgment.

Bultmann seems sometimes to argue that faith cannot be a disposition because if it were, one would be trusting in faith rather than in God. This argument, along with its correlate no-tion that faith is radical insecurity, seems to be founded on think-ing that *trust* must have a univocal meaning. The cure for this confusion is to see a little of the complexity of the concept of trust. We do, of course, trust our dispositions; and as a disposi-tion, we also trust our faith. For example, if a man lives a faith-ful life, he makes plans taking into account (mostly quite im-plicitly) that he will be tomorrow more or less what he is today.

---

[29] Lectures on Romans, tr. Wilhelm Pauck (Philadelphia: The West-minster Press, 1961), p. 185.

A mature man who loves Jesus Christ can reasonably assume that tomorrow he will still love him; and on that basis he perhaps pledges money, for some time ahead, to the church. But the fact that his love for Jesus, as a disposition, makes him somebody who can be counted on (and thus makes him able to trust himself for certain things) does not mean he counts on his disposition for his *salvation*. Indeed, his disposition precisely excludes his counting for that on anything but Jesus. No doubt trust is often confused and perverted, and sermons are even preached on having faith in faith. But we *can* trust all sorts of things, among them our dispositions, without entrusting to them our eternal welfare.

When one first reads in Bultmann that faith is an act, one may be inclined to think this a mere infelicity of speech, an awkward expression inherited from German philosophy, which has tended to use the word for about everything human under the sun. This, I would guess, is the case with Karl Barth, who also calls faith an act.[30] But when we see the empire of the existence/world dichotomy in Bultmann's thought about faith, we see that it is no accident, but a necessary consequence of the logic of his thought: faith must be an act (thought of as something which happens only in the moment) because if it could perdure through time, then as self-understanding it would necessarily be a worldly self-understanding, and thus inauthenticity. Faith must be an act for the same reason that Jesus Christ must be an event occurring in the Now: it must be radically noncontrollable. For Barth, a thinker than whom one farther from the existence/world dichotomy cannot be conceived, calling faith an act need be no more than a terminological infelicity or conceptual peccadillo.

We have seen that for Bultmann faith is the act of self-understanding in which a man grasps himself as radical potentiality to be, and thus as distinct from everything that is worldly. In so understanding himself he gains his true self and becomes free; he continues to live in the world, but in this act his relationship to it becomes "dialectical"—though in the world, he has become discontinuous with it. Bultmann's favorite text, in

---

[30] Cf. *Church Dogmatics,* IV, 1, tr. G. W. Bromiley (Edinburgh: T. & T. Clark, 1956), pp. 757f.

which he finds support for this understanding of faith, is I Cor. 7:29–31:

> I mean, brethren, the appointed time has grown very short; from now on, let those who have wives live as though they had none, and those who mourn as though they were not mourning, and those who rejoice as though they were not rejoicing, and those who buy as though they had no goods, and those who deal with the world as though they had no dealings with it. For the form of this world is passing away.

Now what we have to say, I think, is that this passage expresses *one* element of Christian faith which bears a formal resemblance to Bultmann's concept of authenticity. Faith is a new self-understanding in which the individual lets go of his old worldly self, abandons certain kinds of security, and gains a larger view of himself than that expressed in everyday relations with his wife, in worldly sorrows and joys and transactions. For Paul, the Christian does stand in a dialectical relation to the world; he is in it, yet not of it. But this dialectical is only formally similar to Bultmann's because for Paul it is not based on any ontological distinction between worldly being and existence. Paul does not think that a man is truly human only in his acts of decision; and consequently faith for him is not a living out of transcendence in the sense of living (dialectically, to be sure) as if one belonged to no world at all. It is, rather, living (through expectation and belief) on the basis of another world, which may, ontologically, be quite similar to the present one. *Contra* the existence/world dichotomy, the New Testament never doubts that man is, ontologically, a cosmic being. Consequently, the New Testament's dialectic does not consist in the fact that essential or *eigentlich* existence is always played out in a context which is ontologically inessential—namely, the context of the worldly —but rather in the fact that one lives in *this* world in hope of *another,* and that such hope transforms one's whole apprehension of self and situation. Thus what is peculiar to the Christian self-understanding is not the ontology upon which it is based, but the *beliefs* which form it.

IV. Belief

We have seen that if our thought is governed by the existence/world dichotomy, the idea of self-understanding is not coherent. The reason is that as soon as we have authenticity on this conception, we cease to have anything resembling a self to understand; and also that if authentic life is as radically in the moment as that dichotomy dictates, it cannot include understanding, since temporal continuity is necessary to understanding. If faith is to be thought of as self-understanding, it must be in some sense dispositional (and thus non-dialectically worldly) as a condition for there being either a self or any understanding of it. An examination of the New Testament on this question shows that it is as opposed to the existence/world dichotomy as any other form of good sense is.

What is peculiar about the New Testament, and what gives particular shape to the self-understanding of faith, is Christian belief. All four Gospels tell the story of the ministry, death, and resurrection of Jesus of Nazareth. This is the story of God's atonement, his reconciliation of the world to himself, which manifests Jesus as the Son, the Messiah, the Lord who is also servant, the Lamb of God which takes away the sin of the world, every man's brother who is at the same time the first fruits of the resurrection of the dead. As the story of the atonement, Jesus' story is in a certain sense the story of the world, and thus a story which includes every man. John sums it up thus: "For God so loved the world that he gave his only Son, that whoever believes in him should not perish but have eternal life" (3:16). Or Paul: "God was in Christ reconciling the world to himself, not counting their trespasses against them. . . . For our sake he made him to be sin who knew no sin, so that in him we might become the righteousness of God" (II Cor. 5:19, 21).

What the gospel story does, then, is to depict the world in a new light, to redescribe it in such a way that because of Jesus' identity, every person in the world has a new identity. To the question, "Who am I?" the gospel answers, "You are a child of God, one for whom he gave his only Son; because of his having come into the world, you are a forgiven man, indeed, you have become the righteousness of God." This, according to Christian belief, is the identity which each man has, whether he knows it or not, by virtue of living in a world which God has reconciled to himself in Jesus Christ.[31] Just as a person is the son of a

---

[31] The doctrine called limited atonement is not biblical, if it amounts to saying that there are some for whom Christ did not die. One cannot

given father whether or not he knows that (his identity being determined by this situation), every man is a person for whom Christ died, even if he is ignorant of the fact and denies it. If the gospel story is true, then that is his identity.

Belief is the way the identity constituted by the situation depicted in the gospel story comes to determine the dispositional life of the individual. As belief deepens, a man's personality comes to reflect the identity which is his by virtue of his having a part in the story of the world which God has loved. Joy, hope, trust, peace in the Lord, humility, love of neighbor and of God— these are the dispositions entailed by belief in the story of Jesus. In a certain sense, then, a man gains an identity as he comes to faith. His character is transformed, he gains a new self and thus also a new self-understanding. But in another sense he comes to have this identity only because, through the situation in which he stands, he already has his identity as a child of God and brother of Jesus Christ. Here, as in contrast with Bultmann's understanding of the matter, the individual really does have a concrete, particular self—constituted by his situation and the dispositions of his heart.

Bultmann's assertion that faith always has an object is a constant theme. Yet the existence/world dichotomy has so thoroughly disabled him to allow any propositional description of that object (e.g., in the form of narrative), that it has lost not only its own shape, but also the corresponding power to shape the life of faith. He is worried about the evil effects of possession which may come from allowing something as graspable as a proposition to be determinative for faith. Possessiveness is no doubt a vice and inconsistent with the Christian heart. But in the sense of *possess* in which a person might possess knowledge of God and Jesus Christ, he possesses it also when asleep; and certainly there possessing does not entail possessiveness. But in another sense, it is part of the graciousness of God's grace that in

---

imagine Paul or John or Luke saying that. They do, however, seem to leave open the possibility that some will not believe the good news. But in the very passage where Paul attributes this evil to God's action in hardening hearts (Rom. 9:18), he ends by making that disbelief provisional and directed to God's ultimate purpose that all should receive mercy (Rom. 11:30–32). And the form of Christian preaching is never: If you will believe, then Christ died for you; but rather simply: Christ died for you.

Jesus Christ he gives himself to us as a truly possessable worldly object, stable and describable—to us whose passions are fickle and momentary enough already, and whose real need is a rock of salvation, a steadfast and abiding source of grace from which to nurse our shifty souls into life.

Conclusion

I began this essay by remarking about the impression of profundity which Bultmann's writings give us. By now we are in a better position to understand this impression. Jean Daniélou, speaking of the theological system of Origen, notes that "Origen reduces the whole of his teaching to two propositions." Daniélou calls this "an indication of the profundity of his system."[1] For someone who combines esthetic sensibility with a love for ideas, this is a natural thing to feel: the pleasure of being able to see, on every page of Origen, the operation of two simple but all-important ideas, begins to look, via a confusion of esthetic with Christian ideals, like an appreciation of the profundity of the theologian.

Bultmann's theology is, I think, seductive for a similar reason. After some reading we begin to sense a kind of esthetic beauty in the whole because, through all the intellectual struggling and all the supposed rigorous and disinterested scholarship, there runs a single informing and governing idea. Indeed, the effect of his work is to *reduce* the content of Christian theology to a single idea: that of the act or decision in which man draws his self-understanding and thus his self into conformity with his authentic being as potentiality to be. If now we have seen that even that one idea is but an impossible vacuity suspended in a web of idle words, there is a sense in which we can still say, "Never mind; it has been beautiful."

And if Bultmann were not a theologian, that is, one pur-

---

[1] *Origen,* tr. Walter Mitchell (New York: Sheed & Ward, 1955), p. 206.

porting to teach the Christian faith and aid the faithful in their relation to God, then we could just leave it at that. If he were writing symphonies or novels or poems, then it would be perfectly appropriate for his profundity to consist in the ingenious way he has made everything reducible to a single idea. But the profundity proper to Christian faith is of a different kind than this resourceful rendering of diversity into systematic wholes, even when the whole in question happens to be the body of Christian teaching. And this for two reasons.

First, it seems that Christian teachings as beliefs and their attendant concepts just do not lend themselves to reduction to a single principle (or perhaps even a small set of principles), so that attempts to do so end up doing them violence. The result of the present study is surely to show what a disaster has resulted from Bultmann's attempt, and we can guess that parallel projects will have similar issue.

Second (and this goes also for non-reductive systematic theology), such esthetic theology strongly seduces us into misplacing our effort and joy at the unification of Christian ideas. Christian concepts do require unification, but not the kind they get in a theology which lays out (usually over several hundred or thousand pages) their interconnections. The only unification the Christian concepts require is the one they gain as they come to integrate the passions, emotions, behavior, perceptions and attitudes of the individual Christian, and the communal life of the Christian church. The Christian concepts do their work as they govern the Christian *life*, and they regain in each generation a kind of *ad hoc* unification as the exigencies of that life bring them together in the course of its prosecution, conceived both as the life of the individual and as the life of the Christian fellowship. Such unification is simply identical with the integration of the Christian life. It goes without saying that in each generation and for each individual a fundamental constituent of the integrating process will be *reflection,* for we are not born Christian, and becoming Christian certainly does not come naturally. But that kind of reflection is very different from the kind which goes to produce tomes of systematic theology. The tomes may titillate a certain odd esthetic sense, if the seminary has so perversified our taste; but the profundity proper to Christian thought conduces to another kind of pleasure: the foretaste of that life of praise to which we have been appointed according to the purpose of Him who accomplishes all things according to the counsel of His will.

A List of Works Cited

Aquinas, St. Thomas. *Summa Theologiae*, Blackfriars Edition. New York: McGraw-Hill, 1964–.

Barth, Karl. *Church Dogmatics,* IV, I, tr. G. W. Bromiley. Edinburgh: T. & T. Clark, 1956.

——————. *The Epistle to the Romans*, tr. E. C. Hoskyns. London: Oxford University Press, 1933.

Bauer, Walter. *A Greek-English Lexicon of the New Testament,* tr. and ed. William F. Arndt and F. Wilbur Gingrich. Chicago: The University of Chicago Press, 1957.

Braaten, Carl, and Roy Harrisville, eds. *Kerygma and History.* Nashville: Abingdon Press, 1962.

Bultmann, Rudolf. *Essays Philosophical and Theological,* tr. James C. G. Greig, SCM Press, 1955. This is a translation of *Glauben und Verstehen,* vol. II.

——————. *Existence and Faith: Shorter Writings of Rudolf Bultmann,* ed. and tr. by Schubert Ogden. New York: The World Publishing Company, 1961.

——————. *Form Criticism: Two Essays on New Testament Research*, tr. Frederick C. Grant. New York: Harper and Row, 1962.

——————. *Faith and Understanding,* ed. Robert Funk and tr. Louise Pettibone Smith. New York: Harper and Row, 1969. This is a translation of most of the articles contained in *Glauben und Verstehen,* vol. I.

——————. *The Gospel of John: A Commentary,* tr. G. R. Beasley-Murray, R.W.N. Hoare, and J. K. Riches. Philadelphia: The Westminster Press, 1971.

——————. *Glauben and Verstehen,* I, II, III, IV. Tübingen: J. C. B. Mohr (Paul Siebeck), 1933, 1952, 1960, 1965.

——————. *History and Eschatology: The Presence of Eternity.* New York: Harper and Row, 1962.

——————. *History of the Synoptic Tradition,* tr. John Marsh. New York: Harper and Row, 1963.

——————. "Humanism and Christianity." *The Journal of Religion,* 1952.

——————. *Jesus Christ and Mythology.* New York: Charles Scribner's Sons, 1958.

——————. *Jesus and the Word,* tr. Louise Pettibone Smith and Erminie Huntress Lantero. New York: Charles Scribner's Sons, 1958.

——————. *Kerygma and Myth: A Theological Debate,* rev. tr. R. H. Fuller. New York: Harper and Row, 1961.

——————. *Myth and Christianity: An Inquiry into the Possibility of Religion Without Myth,* with Karl Jaspers, tr. Norbert Guterman. New York: The Noonday Press, 1958.

——————. *The Old and New Man in the Letters of Paul,* tr. Keith R. Crim. Richmond: John Knox Press, 1967.

——————. *Primitive Christianity in its Contemporary Setting,* tr. R. H. Fuller. New York: The World Publishing Company, 1956.

——————. "Protestant Theology and Atheism." *The Journal of Religion,* 1972.

——————. *Theology of the New Testament,* I, II, tr. Kendrick Grobel. New York: Charles Scribner's Sons, 1951 and 1955.

——————. *This World and the Beyond,* tr. Harold Knight. New York: Charles Scribner's Sons, 1960.

Dahl, Nils A. *The Crucified Messiah.* Minneapolis: Augsburg Publishing House, 1974.

Daniélou, Jean. *Origen,* tr. Walter Mitchell. New York: Sheed and Ward, 1955.

Dodd, C. H. *Gospel and Law: The Relation of Faith and Ethics in Early Christianity.* Cambridge: Cambridge University Press, 1951.

Frank, Erich. *Philosophical Understanding and Religious Truth.* Oxford University Press, 1945.

Funk, Robert, ed. *Journal for Theology and Church,* 2. New York: Harper and Row, 1965.

Heidegger, Martin. *Being and Time,* tr. John Macquarrie and Edward Robinson. New York: Harper and Row, 1962.

James, William. *The Will to Believe.* New York: Dover Publications, Inc., 1956.

Kegley, Charles, ed. *The Theology of Rudolf Bultmann*. New York: Harper and Row, 1966.

Kierkegaard, Søren. *Philosophical Fragments,* tr. David Swenson. Princeton: Princeton University Press, 1962.

Leibrecht, Walter, ed. *Religion and Culture: Essays in Honor of Paul Tillich.* New York: Harper and Row, 1959.

Luther, Martin. *Lectures on Romans,* tr. Wilhelm Pauck. Philadelphia: The Westminster Press, 1961.

Malet, André. *The Thought of Rudolf Bultmann,* tr. Richard Strachan. Garden City: Doubleday and Company, 1971.

Oden, Thomas. *Radical Obedience: The Ethics of Rudolf Bultmann.* Philadelphia: The Westminster Press, 1964.

Ogden, Schubert. *Christ Without Myth.* New York: Harper and Row, 1961.

Reese, W. L., ed. *Process and Divinity: Philosophical Essays Presented to Charles Hartshorne.* Lasalle: Open Court, 1964.

Robinson, J. M., ed. *The Beginnings of Dialectical Theology.* Richmond: John Knox Press, 1968.

Schmithals, Walter. *An Introduction to the Theology of Rudolf Bultmann,* tr. John Bowden. Minneapolis: Ausburg Publishing House, 1968.

Strong, Augustus Hopkins. *Systematic Theology.* Westwood, N. J.: Fleming H. Revell Company, 1907.

Wittgenstein, Ludwig. *On Certainty,* tr. Denis Paul and G.E.M. Anscombe. Oxford: Basil Blackwell, 1969.

——————. *Philosophical Investigations,* tr. G.E.M. Anscombe. New York: The Macmillan Company, 1953.

Young, Norman. *History and Existential Theology.* Philadelphia: Westminster Press, 1969.

Index

332   INDEX